THE ANCIENT GREEK HISTORIANS

• THE BARNES & NOBLE LIBRARY OF ESSENTIAL READING •

THE ANCIENT GREEK HISTORIANS

J. B. Bury

Introduction by Sarah Bolmarcich

BARNES & NOBLE

NEW YORK

THE BARNES & NOBLE
LIBRARY OF ESSENTIAL READING

Originally published in 1909

This edition published by Barnes & Noble Publishing, Inc.

Cover Design by Stacey May

2006 Barnes & Noble Publishing, Inc.

ISBN 13: 978-0-7607-7635-3
ISBN 0-7607-7635-0

Printed and bound in the United States of America

1 3 5 7 9 10 8 6 4 2

CONTENTS

INTRODUCTION   VII

I. THE RISE OF GREEK HISTORY IN IONIA   1

II. HERODOTUS   23

III. THUCYDIDES   47

IV. THUCYDIDES (CONTINUED)   67

V. THE DEVELOPMENT OF GREEK HISTORIOGRAPHY
   AFTER THUCYDIDES   95

VI. POLYBIUS   121

VII. THE INFLUENCE OF GREEK ON ROMAN
    HISTORIOGRAPHY   142

VIII. VIEWS OF THE ANCIENTS CONCERNING
     THE USE OF HISTORY   154

APPENDIX   167

ENDNOTES   173

INDEX   189

SUGGESTED READING   199

INTRODUCTION

In the spring of 1908, the eminent British scholar John Bagnell Bury delivered the prestigious Lane Lectures at Harvard University. Bury's lectures dealt with the development of Greek historiography and the men who created and refined it as a literary genre, men as diverse in time and interests as Herodotus, Thucydides, and Polybius. When published the following year, Bury's lectures were well received by his peers, and since its publication the book has remained a standard in the field, much like other great works penned or initiated by Bury, such as *A History of Greece to the Death of Alexander the Great* (still used in Greek history classrooms today), *The Cambridge Ancient History*, and *The Cambridge Medieval History*. Bury is widely regarded as one of the fathers of Byzantine history, and his skills in the field of ancient Greek history were no less.

John Bagnell Bury was born in County Monaghan, Ireland, in 1861, to highly educated parents who encouraged his early aptitude for learning. His father, the Reverend Edward John Bury, taught his young son Greek and Latin from the age of four, and found his student so adept that at the age of ten Bury was able to pass college entrance examinations in Greek and Latin without a single mistake. Bury entered Trinity College, Dublin, in 1878, after he had placed first in the examination for the Classical Scholarship, and eventually became Fellow of Trinity College in 1885. That same year, he embarked seriously upon the career of scholarly publication that he had begun as an undergraduate with an edition of Euripides' *Hippolytus*. In all, Bury published

369 books, articles, notes, or reviews in a wide variety of journals and other publications before his death in 1927 in Rome. These publications ranged in topic and interest from classical Greek history to Byzantine history to the first modern English-language biography of St. Patrick. Bury's diverse interests won him the honor of being both Regius Professor of Greek at Trinity as well as Professor of Modern History, and he later became Regius Professor of Modern History at Cambridge, where his inaugural lecture was standing-room only. Bury closed that inaugural lecture with the observation, "History is a science, no less and no more," and that statement is key to the understanding of much of his historical work and in particular *The Ancient Greek Historians*.

The aim of *The Ancient Greek Historians* is, as Bury put it on the very first page, "to trace the genesis and the development of the historical literature of the Greeks. I will attempt to bring into a connected view the principles, the governing ideas, and the methods of the Greek historians, and to relate them to the general movements of Greek thought and Greek history." To that end, the work is arranged chronologically, with several chapters offering the pre-history of Greek historiography before Herodotus, and a bridge between major figures like Thucydides and Polybius. Bury's belief in history as a science informs his criticism of all these historians, and those whom he most favors, Thucydides and Polybius, are those whom he regards as the most scientific. *The Ancient Greek Historians* also concludes with a chapter on another interest of Bury's work in his later career, an interest in history as progress as opposed to cyclical, best expressed in his last book, *The Idea of Progress*. Bury's aim in *The Ancient Greek Historians*, then, was both to explore Greek historiography and its practitioners on their own merits and within their own culture, and also to offer a criticism of that culture and its idea of history.

Accordingly, Bury began his lectures with one reflecting on the early "historiography" of Greece. In his review of the book, E. M. Walker criticized Bury for ignoring the odd fact that the Greeks were quite slow to develop historiography, compared to other cultures like the Hebrew culture. But Bury does in fact consider this question, albeit not in the terms of comparison with other cultures that Walker desired. Arguing that the early lack of Greek political acumen (i.e., their inability to conceive of themselves as a unified people) makes their lack of an early historical record no surprise, he points to what the early Greeks did consider "history": the Homeric poems, local epic poetry, geographical studies, and mythological genealogies and chronologies. These served the early Greek desire to be connected to the heroic past by relating individuals or their communities to a Homeric hero, as opposed to a desire to know the facts of their own history. In this same vein did the historian Herodotus, the subject of the second lecture, write. Herodotus was an Ionian Greek from the town of Halicarnassus on the coast of Asia Minor, whose history told of the relationship between Greece and Persia from the sixth century to 479 BC. Herodotus' contribution to Greek history, according to Bury, was that he combined so many different histories into a connected narrative with a single point of focus, the Persian Wars. And as a historian Herodotus created a literary masterpiece, establishing historiography as an independent genre: he was "a collector of historical material, and an accomplished artist in arranging and presenting it" into a unified and symmetrical whole. Herodotus established by example three maxims of historical criticism: first, suspect anything extraordinary; second, keep an open mind to the facts (although bias is inevitable); and, third, the best evidence is that of first-hand information and autopsy. Under Herodotus Greek history became a true craft. In so arguing, Bury reclaimed Herodotus from his prior reputation as the "father of lies" and strengthened his claim to the title "father of history."

Herodotus' successor, Thucydides, occupies two lectures, for of all the authors Bury discussed in the book, Thucydides was in his view the greatest practitioner of Greek historiography. He was born an Athenian, but was descended from a Thracian noble family, and during the second half of the fifth century BC he witnessed the great Peloponnesian Wars between Athens and Sparta (461–446, 431–421, 413–403 BC), even at one point serving as a general for the Athenians in Thrace. Under the influence of the fifth-century Sophistic movement, he showed a far more stringent intellect than Herodotus, and so great was the Sophistic influence on Thucydides that Bury believed that "if he had belonged to an earlier generation, he could not have been Thucydides." Like Herodotus, Thucydides brought much that was new to the newborn genre of historiography: specifically, he "sets up a new standard of truth . . . and a new ideal of historical research." Thucydides did not much care whether his work was popular or not, so long as it was permanent because it was true, and taught men lessons from history so that they would not repeat the mistakes of the past. He accurately relates the facts and takes care to ascertain them, entirely eliminates the mythical element of earlier historiography, and he does not offer the reader a detailed account of all his sources if they were contradictory, as Herodotus did. In chronological matters he was especially strict, and unlike Herodotus and his predecessors he believed that a strict chronology was necessary for history to be accurate. Where Bury compared Herodotus' artistic methods to those of Homeric poetry, he links Thucydides' artistic methods to those of the drama, an argument that had also been made in 1907 by a fellow Cambridge don, Francis Cornford; Bury thus contributed to a scholarly movement away from seeing Thucydides as a purely cold and rational historian. Like the dramatist, Thucydides seeks to reveal the truth, although his interest is in political history, and so he examines the external and internal politics of a state from an exclusively political, albeit dramatic, point of view.

Thucydides' historical method unfortunately was not followed by fourth-century Greek historiographers, the subject of Bury's fifth lecture. Fourth-century Greece was a land of small city-states engaged in constant petty warfare with one another, occasionally rising to brief prominence on the shoulders of a great leader; accordingly, fourth-century historical writers were more interested in political science, local history, and biography in their histories than in following the methods of Thucydidean historiography. Xenophon, an Athenian military man who resumed Thucydides' history at the point where it ended in

411 BC, was not worthy of the responsibility in Bury's eyes. The works of others who might have been more talented, like Cratippus, or Philistus of Syracuse, possibly the most Thucydidean of fourth-century historiographers, survive in fragments alone. One bright light in the fourth century was Ephorus of Cyme, whose work is also preserved in fragments, but who penned a quasi-national history, unlike his contemporaries, who confined themselves to telling, poorly, of local affairs and what passed in the fourth century for great men. The attention that Bury pays to these lost historians in a history of Greek historiography is especially welcome because too often these fragmentary authors are passed over in silence, their contribution to Greek history ignored.

It was not until Polybius, the subject of Bury's sixth lecture, that Greek historiography returned to the principles of Thucydides. Polybius, who lived in the third century BC, wrote Roman history in Greek. In Bury's view, he combined the better qualities of Herodotus and Thucydides: like Herodotus, his arrangement of his history was masterful, while, like Thucydides, his philosophy of history was political, pragmatic, and universal. Like both his predecessors, he traces the causes of the events he described, which led in his case to a conversion from a belief in luck and divine providence as significant factors in history at the beginning of his work to a rejection of those elements by the end of his history in favor of a pragmatic and realistic view. Because so few historians had espoused the philosophy of Thucydides in the intervening centuries, Polybius, like Thucydides, is a reactionary in his conviction that the first duty of the historian is not to entertain, but to discover and relate the facts. But also like Thucydides, Polybius believes history to be cyclical, a view Bury would reject in his final lecture. Polybius, although Greek, is usually considered a Roman historian, and Bury's inclusion of him here enables him to argue for a hitherto unexplored link between Thucydides and Polybius.

Bury's seventh lecture is the last to deal with historiography. Here he traces the adaptation of Greek historiography by the Romans. Bury believes that Roman historiography "in its methods and principles is Greek." Like Greek historiography, Roman historiography began with poetry before developing into prose. Unlike the Greeks, however, Roman historians like Sallust or Tacitus put an original stamp on their works not by their methodology or literary methods, but by sheer force of their personality, by the very strong opinions they held. Roman historiography also allowed for the development of sub-genres; for instance, the writings of Julius Caesar were in effect political pamphlets. Roman historiography might be Greek in spirit, but it took into account much more the personal attributes of the historian, be it the personal goals he wished to further (Caesar) or simply his personal view of historical events (Sallust and Tacitus).

Throughout *The Ancient Greek Historians*, Bury sought to put each historian in context, and to link him with his contemporaries and his predecessors. His final lecture draws together the contributions of the Greek historians and also offers a criticism of their work and worldview. The ancient historians wrote in order to enable men to judge the present and the future by the past; history therefore had a practical use. Historians of the ilk of Thucydides and Polybius tended to assume that similar situations would recur, hence the writing of history. By contrast, modern historians—like Bury himself—tend to think that history is worth it for its own sake, and the advance of over two thousand years since the times of Thucydides and Polybius has led to the realization "that the assumptions on which the ancients grounded the claim of history to practical utility are untenable." For modern men have realized that history is not cyclical, but rather, it advances, an idea that Bury explores further in his previously mentioned work *The Idea of Progress*. The Greeks and Romans knew there would be a future, but they speculated little on it, nor did they conceive of a more advanced civilization than their own developing; both attitudes are very unlike those of twentieth-century men who speculated on what extraordinary advances man might have made by the year 2000. The conception of the future in contemporary thought has led to "a new ethical principle, namely, duty towards the future heirs of the ages." All this is not to say that ancient historiography was wrong, or nothing like history today, for the belief of history as education held by Thucydides is right, in Bury's view, and so too are the scientific methods he used, which themselves are educational. Thus Bury can truly conclude that "[t]he Hellenic conception of history as humanistic is truer than ever."

The Ancient Greek Historians was well received by contemporary critics. They especially praised Bury's treatment of Thucydides and his solution to the problem of the speeches in Thucydides. Thucydides himself says that at times the speeches he records are not what was actually said, and Bury solves this dilemma by arguing that when the speeches, all of which are very difficult to read (and were so even for the ancient Greeks), are written in such an unnatural style, they represent, essentially, Thucydides' opinion and points he wishes to make. There were many other interesting suggestions as well, e.g., Bury's identification of the mysterious Oxyrhynchus Historian, whose fourth-century work is known only in fragments found on papyri scraps in Egypt, as Cratippus, the Athenian who may have continued Thucydides' work. Bury's final lecture on the use of and attitudes toward history, ancient and modern, also drew praise. Even R. G. Collingwood praised his realization that "there were philosophical problems connected with historical research," although Collingwood does criticize the organization of *The Cambridge Ancient History* and *The Cambridge Medieval History*, both of which Bury was an early editor of, because they were the work of a committee, each chapter by an individual hand, with no overarching intellect to guide the work. This criticism does not apply to *The Ancient Greek Historians*, however, and it remains perhaps Bury's greatest historical monograph.

Sarah Bolmarcich received her doctorate in Classics from the University of Virginia. She currently teaches at the University of Michigan.

LECTURE I

THE RISE OF GREEK HISTORY IN IONIA

IN these lectures I propose to trace the genesis and the development of the historical literature of the Greeks. I will attempt to
bring into a connected view the principles, the governing ideas,
and the methods of the Greek historians, and to relate them to
the general movements of Greek thought and Greek history. I
need hardly apologize for devoting much of our time to
Herodotus and Thucydides, who, however familiar to us from
childhood, have the secret of engaging an interest that is never
exhausted and never grows stale. As a Hellenist, I shall be happy
if I succeed in illustrating the fact that, as in poetry and letters
generally, as in art, as in philosophy, and in mathematics, so too
in history, our debt to the Greeks transcends calculation. They
were not the first to chronicle human events, but they were the
first to apply criticism. And that means, they originated history.

§ 1. *The historical aspect of the Epics*

Long before history, in the proper sense of the word, came to
be written, the early Greeks possessed a literature which was
equivalent to history for them and was accepted with unreserved
credence — their epic poems. The Homeric lays not only entertained the imagination, but also satisfied what we may call the historical interest, of the audiences who heard them recited. This
interest in history was practical, not antiquarian; the story of the

1

past made a direct appeal to their pride, while it was associated with their religious piety towards their ancestors. Every self-respecting city sought to connect itself, through its ancient clans, with the Homeric heroes, and this constituted the highest title to prestige in the Greek world. The poems which could confer such a title were looked up to as authoritative historical documents. In disputes about territory the *Iliad* was appealed to as a valid witness. The enormous authority of Homer, the deep hold which the Trojan epics had won on the minds and hearts of the Greeks, may partly explain the puzzle, why it was so long before it occurred to them to record recent or contemporary events. For when we consider the early growth of their political intelligence, the paucity of their historical records must strike us with surprise. In the seventh century they were far advanced in political experience. Sparta, for instance, had a complicated constitution; yearly magistrates had been introduced at Athens. The number of the small independent states which had to live together, some of which had special relations to one another, tended to develop the political sense. Intensity of political life had been the outcome of the institution of the *polis,* and the Hellenic world was the scene of numerous and various experiments in government. In these conditions, political literature originated. Archilochus, Tyrtaeus, Solon, and Theognis were the most eminent of the ancient publicists who dealt with current politics in metrical pamphlets. But the Greeks of this period felt no impulse to record their experiences in historical records; the only history they cared for was still furnished by the epics. Long before this, Egypt and Assyria had abundant contemporary records, narratives of conquests and achievements, inscribed for the glorification of some powerful monarch. But the early Greeks, even despots, were free from the kind of self-consciousness which prompted an Assur-bani-pal to draw up a narrative of his deeds; Periander and Peisistratus did not think of securing posthumous fame by such appeals to posterity. Had Peisistratus been an oriental ruler, he would have invited his literary friends to celebrate his own career; being a Greek of his time, he appointed a committee of men of letters to edit the Homeric poems. There were indeed some records kept in the seventh century, and perhaps sooner, which at a later time were to prove useful; but they were bare enumerations of names, such as lists of magistrates or priests.

Now it is important to realise that the historical interest of the Greeks of those days, concentrated as it was on the epic traditions, was active and productive. The epics were still growing in the seventh century, though the period of growth was soon to be over. It is almost certain that the *Iliad* and *Odyssey* did not reach the fulness of their present compass much before 600 B.C. I need only ask you to recall the lectures which Mr. Gilbert Murray delivered at this University last year; some things he said happen to prepare the way for the consideration of the origins of historiography. He insisted, rightly as I think, on the fact that the groundwork and principal motives of the Homeric epics were historical; and he showed, with admirable insight, how the development of the poems, in its successive stages, responded to, and reflected, the ideas, manners, and tastes of successive periods. But besides this moral and social criticism which Mr. Murray traced, there was another kind of criticism which betrayed the spirit of historical inquiry. The epics relating to the Trojan war, which existed, let us say, about 800 B.C. in order to fix our ideas, would raise in an inquiring mind many questions as to the course of the war, its final conclusion, the fortunes of many heroes who took part in it, —questions to which Homer gave no answer. To quench the thirst for such information was the office of later poets, who related events which the older bards did not know or assumed as known. They had to fill up interstices and to explain inconsistencies, and this process necessarily entailed a definite consideration of chronological sequence, an element which the original creators of myth do not take into serious account. It is impossible to say how far these later poets of the Homeric school drew upon local legends, how far upon their own invention, but in their hands the traditions of the Trojan expedition and its heroes were wrought into a corpus of Trojan epics, chronologically connected, in which the *Iliad* and the *Odyssey* had their places.

The new instinct for systematizing tradition gave rise at the same time to the school of genealogical poets, of which Hesiod was the most distinguished and perhaps the first. Their aim was to work into a consistent system the relationships of the gods and heroes, deriving them from the primeval beings who generated the world, and tracing thereby to the origin of things the pedigrees of the royal families which ruled in the states of Hellas.[1] The interest in genealogies linking actual families with legendary heroes[2] was closely allied to the interest in "origins" connecting the foundations of cities with the heroic age. This interest gave rise to a group of what we may call local epics, approximating in style and character to the Hesiodic school, recording the mythical origins (κτίσεις) and the pedigrees of the founders. We know, for instance, of the *Corinthiaca,* ascribed to Eumelus, which may have been the source of certain later sections of the *Iliad;*[3] of the Naupactian poem; of the *Phoronis* which took its name from Phoroneus, reputed the first King of Argos.

In all this intellectual activity, we can recognise in a crude form the instinct of historical inquiry, guided by the ideas of consistency and chronological order. The genealogies inevitably brought chronology into the foreground. We can also see that the poets possessed a certain kind of historical sense. They were conscious up to a certain point of the differences between their own civilisation and that of the heroic age, and this consciousness expressed itself in the archaism which we can observe in the *Iliad* and *Odyssey.* The poets always retained, for instance, the obsolete bronze armour of antiquity.

One epic poem, belonging to the seventh or perhaps the sixth century, claims a special mention here, the *Arimaspea* ascribed to Aristeas of Proconnesus. The subject of this work was Scythia, which the author seems to have visited, and its importance for our present purpose is that it anticipated the interest in geography and ethnography which, as we shall see, accompanied the rise of history proper. It seems too to have contained a reference to an event of what for Aristeas was modern history, the movement of the Cimmerians in the seventh century, a movement which he very properly explained by the pressure of neighbouring peoples.[4] The *Arimaspea* however is not altogether isolated. A geographical interest is distinctly present in the *Odyssey*; M. Bérard has illustrated its significance and the historical background. But perhaps it is rather in the ancient Argonautic poems, ranging into the same regions which Aristeas visited, that we may seek the inspiration of the *Arimaspea*.

Up to the middle or end of the sixth century, then, their epic poetry satisfied the historical interest of the Greeks. For us it is mythical, for them it was historical. And further, during the later centuries of the epic period, it was becoming quasi-historical in form. The body of traditions was being submitted to crude and rudimentary processes of what we may call historical inquiry. The later poets of the Homeric school, and the poets of the Hesiodic school, worked in obedience to the need of systematic arrangement and chronological order. There was no absolute chronology, no dates; but time-sequence determined the completion of the Trojan cycle, and the relation of the Trojan to other cycles (such as the Theban), and, in the very nature of the subject, it controlled the genealogical poems. Scattered and contradictory traditions were harmonized more or less into a superficially consistent picture of the past by the activity of these poets. Their work must have counted for a great deal in both satisfying and stimulating the self-consciousness of the Greeks.

§ 2. *The foundation of history by Hecataeus*

It might be expected that such an examination of the ancient literature and traditions, though carried out with no under-thought of questioning their truth as a whole, would have sown the germs of criticism and prepared the way for incredulity. This is a difficult question, as our knowledge of this literature is so fragmentary. We can point at least to the notorious scepticism of Stesichorus about the story of Helen. But we can do more. The truth seems to be that towards the end of the epic period there arose in Ionia a spirit which it would be going too far to describe as incredulous, but which was certainly flippant and sceptical and might at any moment break out into positive incredulity. This spirit is revealed, as Mr. Murray has well shown, in some late parts of the *Iliad*, especially in the episode of the Beguiling of Zeus; it appears in the *Odyssey* in the lay of Demodocus, which tells of the punishment of Ares and Aphrodite by the injured husband Hephaestus.

Such tendencies to scepticism, evolved by the Ionian temper, were reinforced by the rise of Ionian science and philosophy. Science and philosophy meant criticism, and it would not be long before criticism which the early thinkers applied to the material world would be systematically applied to human tradition also, and the result would be, in some form or other, the distinction of history from myth.

At the same time the mythopoeic instinct of the Greeks was still potent and still felicitous in its operation. But myth assumed a new shape. Supernatural beings no longer appeared upon the stage; and, with the exception of oracles, omens, and visions, the supernatural *mise en scène* was discarded. Fictions gathered round historical persons, contemporary or recent, but all these stories, such as the saving of Cypselus, the wooers of Agarista, the ring of Polycrates, kept well within the fence of the possibilities of human experience. They are not in the crude sense incredible, ἄπιστα τῷ καθ᾽ ἡμᾶς βίῳ. This new order of myths corresponds to a new interest, which we might call the philosophy of life; it is reflected in the gnomic poetry of the period. Sages have taken the place of heroes; the Septemvirate of Wise Men was one of the mythical creations. The authority of Delphi is established beside the authority of Homer, and Delphi seems to have been a centre for fiction of this order.

Now let us suppose that before the end of the sixth century a thoughtful man began to reflect upon the past fortunes of the Greeks. He would be struck by the fact that the character of their history had completely changed. The age of the heroes, as described in the epics, was marked by divine interventions, frequent intercourse between gods and men, startling meta-morphoses, and all kinds of miracles. How was it that the character of human experience had changed and that such marvels had ceased to happen? It was inevitable that the question should be asked: can we believe the epic poets and take all they tell us for literal fact? And we find that before 500 B.C. a philosopher of Ionia, Xenophanes, had arraigned the credibility of Homer and Hesiod.[5] He rejected the anthropomorphisms of popular theology, and branded the Greek myths as ancient fictions (πλάσματα τῶν προτέρων). His rationalism was in the interest of cosmic law. He was applying, whether explicitly or not, the principle formulated by later rationalists that what was possible once is possible still, and what is incredible now is incredible always. And he was also concerned, in the cause of ethics, to denounce the attribution to the gods of conduct condemned by the contemporary moral standards of Greece.[6]

Besides the efforts of Ionian men of science to explain nature by reason,—besides the dawn of philosophy,—there was another fact which contributed, in the second part of the sixth century, to widen the horizon of intelligent minds in Ionia. The power of Persia had been extended to the Aegean, and the Asiatic Greeks had been incorporated in the Persian empire. A natural consequence was the stimulation of interest and curiosity among those Greeks about the other lands of the great realm to which they were now attached; and their new position provided facilities for gratifying this curiosity. Oriental geography and history presented to the Greeks a new field of study, and this exercised, as we shall see, an important influence in bringing history to the birth.

Its birth is associated with the name of Hecataeus of Miletus. He was, first and foremost, a geographer. I do not dispute the title of Anaximander to be called the "father of geography," but Hecataeus may be considered one of the founders of geographical science; his chief contributions to knowledge were in that field. Born perhaps near the middle of the sixth century, he not only travelled in Greek lands and on the shores of the Black

Sea, but explored the interior parts of the Persian empire, and Egypt, which had been annexed by Cambyses. Perhaps his travels extended to southern Spain. Everywhere he collected facts for a geographical work which was published under the title of a *Map of the World*. But this work ranged beyond the sphere of pure geography. There is no doubt that it contained, besides descriptions of countries and places, a great deal of ethnography and history, and especially it introduced the Greeks to oriental history and sketched for the first time the successive monarchies of Assyria, Media, and Persia. The writer almost certainly touched upon the Ionian history of his own day, in which he himself played a part. Herodotus, you may remember, mentions advice tendered by Hecataeus to the Ionians on more than one occasion, advice which they did not follow. The most likely person to record advice which has not been followed is the adviser; and we may pretty confidently assume that the source of Herodotus was Hecataeus himself.

Hecataeus thus initiated the composition of "modern" history, though only in a work which was geographical in its title and main argument. He also wrote a work on the ancient history of Greece. It was a prose compilation from the genealogical epics. But, though its title, *Genealogies*, shows how potent the influence of the epics was, it was a critical investigation. The opening words are striking and might have stirred a reader to expectancy of a thoroughgoing and drastic revision of what currently passed for the ancient history of Hellas. "What I write here," says Hecataeus, "is the account which I considered to be true. For the stories of the Greeks are numerous, and in my opinion ridiculous." The actual fragments of the work would not enable us to judge to what lengths his scepticism ventured. The few instances of rationalistic interpretation which we can note are of a sufficiently innocent kind, but show us that, while he did not adopt the doctrine of Xenophanes that the myths are fictions, he applied a canon of inner probability. For instance, he explained the hound of Hades which Heracles was related to have dragged up from the under-world, as the name of a terrible serpent which haunted Taenarum. Again, he transported the home of Geryones and his cattle from distant Spain to the more accessible pastures of Epirus.[7]

But a clearer view of the attitude of Hecataeus may be derived from certain passages in Herodotus to which I shall have to draw attention in the next lecture. We shall then see that his scepticism in regard to the ancient history of the Greeks had been stimulated by the acquaintance he made in Egypt with the historical traditions of the Egyptians. There he made the discovery that in days when gods were supposed to be walking abroad on the hills and in the vales of Hellas, Egypt at the distance of a few days' voyage was managed exclusively by mere human beings. It was an obvious inference that the age of the gods in Greece must be relegated to as remote a date as the age of the gods in Egypt, and that the heroic age of the not very distant ancestors of the existing Greeks must be divested of the supernatural atmosphere with which poetical fable had encompassed it. We may conclude that the prefatory announcement of Hecataeus was not excessive, and that his rationalism was more complete than the few meagre fragments of the work might lead us to suppose.

Hecataeus, as I have said, wrote in prose. His choice of prose was a proof of his competence and a condition of his achievement. But prose had, in all probability, been used already at Miletus for the treatment of a historical subject. The very existence of Cadmus the Milesian has been called in question by some modern critics, and he is certainly a misty figure. The evidence seems to me — though I speak with diffidence — to point to the conclusion that he existed, and was one of the earliest prose writers of Ionia.[8] My idea of Cadmus is that he lived in the early part of the sixth century, contemporary with Anaximander and Pherecydes of Syros, and wrote a book on the Origins of Miletus and other Ionian cities, a work which was notable only because it was written in prose, and not differing in treatment or character from epics like the *Corinthiaca* and *Phoronis*. This is perhaps the best we can do for the reputation of Cadmus; he was a very early prose writer or *logographer,* but there is no reason to suppose that he was more of a historian than Eumelus or Eugammon. The claim of Hecataeus to be the founder of history cannot be disputed in his favour.

A logographer, as you know, means a writer of prose, not specially a historian.

The early historical literature of the Greeks had no distinctive name. It formed part of the general prose literature which was then springing up in Ionia and which included philosophical and scientific works, and, for instance, the fables of Aesop. In their nomenclature, the Greeks regarded only the difference of form. The *epopoioi* had now to be distinguished from the *logopoioi*, the epic poets who composed verse from the logo-poets who composed prose. The *logopoioi* were also called *logographoi*, which means exactly the same thing, only emphasizing the fact that they used the pen. Heracleitus and Sophron were as much logographers as Hecataeus.

History had at first no distinctive name. The term ἱστορίη did not then mean what it came to mean later. Yet, as it was used by the Ionians, we may say that it suggested the new element which discriminated the *logoi* of Hecataeus from the epics (and, as I suggest, from Cadmus). You remember how in Homer a legal dispute is brought before a ἵστωρ, a man of skill who inquires into the alleged facts and decides what the true facts are, ἱστορίη meant an inquisition of this kind. We saw that the later epic poets did a certain amount of inquiring and comparing, and, in so far as they did this, they were leading up to history. But in the preface to the *Genealogies* of Hecataeus the conception of a historical inquiry stands revealed. He endeavoured to deal with his data more or less like a ἵστωρ, and to elicit the truth, applying canons of common sense. Of course his methods were unsound; but in his aim and effort he was a pioneer, and prose, as he saw, was the right vehicle for moving along the new paths which he opened up.

The rise of prose was probably a condition of the rise of history; it is almost inconceivable that history could have emerged from its shell if the new vehicle of critical thought had not been there to carry it. It was not indeed a foregone conclusion that Hecataeus should choose prose. Verse and prose were still rivals, they had not yet clearly differentiated their spheres. If Cadmus had recorded the foundation of Miletus in prose, Xenophanes related the foundation of Colophon in metre. Parmenides was writing verse, while Heracleitus was expressing his deeper thoughts in prose; it is not insignificant that Heracleitus was incomparably the greater thinker. In the choice of prose the founder of history displayed his insight.[9]

Both sides of the activity of Hecataeus, the genealogical in which he is a mythographer, the geographical in which he is also a historian, had a far-reaching influence on the development of Greek historiography; and announce on the very threshold its weakness and its strength. In treating their "ancient" history the Greeks were always to remain under the influence of the epics: the sceptre was never to fall from the hands of Homer and Hesiod; and the historical investigation of early Greece was never to be anything but at best a more or less clarified and arbitrarily rationalised mythography. On the other hand, it was the treatment of Persia and the East in the Geography of Hecataeus that inaugurated "modern" and "contemporary" history in which the Greeks achieved such high excellence.

§ 3. *Early Mythographers*

I may take "ancient" history first. The *Genealogies* of Hecataeus soon led to new works on the same subject. In the next generation Pherecydes of Leros, who settled at Athens, and Acusilaus of Argos —they seem to have flourished before the middle of the fifth century—again served up the epic legends in prose. These writers have no claim to the title of historians; they were simply mythographers and it would be well always to describe them as such.

The work of Pherecydes was distinguished by its comprehensiveness. He modified the traditions for various reasons, but not on any systematic principle. For instance, on chronological grounds he makes Philammon, instead of Orpheus, accompany the Argonauts. In order to connect the poet Homer with the poet Orpheus, he invents genealogical intermediaries. The interpolation of links in pedigrees is a feature of his method; and here he is working simply on the lines, and in the spirit, of the later epic poets themselves. If he modifies a legend, it is not to rationalise, but rather in the interests of popular superstition. The old legend made Apollo slay the Cyclôpes because they furnished Zeus with the thunderbolts which destroyed Asclepius. Pherecydes makes him slay not the Cyclôpes but the sons of the Cyclôpes, evidently to indulge the popular belief that the Cyclôpes are still busy with the manufacture of thunder.[10] We may say then that Pherecydes was a systematizer of the epic traditions on conservative lines, contrasting not only with the revolutionary method of Hecataeus, but with the freer treatment of the legends by the Attic tragedians.

In Acusilaus we can detect the influence of Hecataeus. He cannot resist the temptation to rationalise up to a certain point. He will not admit, for instance, that Zeus could change himself into a bull, and so he holds the animal which carried off Europa to have been a mere common bull sent by Zeus, not the metamorphosed god. He describes the fleece of Colchis as not golden but purple, and explains that it was empurpled by sea-water. More interesting than these halting concessions to improbable probability is his reconstruction of the causes of the Trojan war. He asked himself why the goddess Aphrodite should have united herself to the Trojan Anchises. Such an occurrence as the union of a goddess with a mortal required a motive. He found it in an oracle that the descendants of Anchises should reign when the kingdom of Priam had fallen. When her son Aeneas grew to manhood, the object of Aphrodite was to bring about the fall of Priam's dynasty, and for this purpose she caused Paris to fall in love with Helen. Then when Helen had been carried off, she helped the Trojans in order that they might not, in despair at defeat, surrender Helen and save the throne of Priam. The story of the judgment of Paris, which, according to the *Cypria*, was the original cause of the war, is thus rejected, and the war is attributed to the ambitious schemes and Machiavellian policy of

Aphrodite. This is rationalism of a sort. The accepted view ascribed the cause of a great movement to the vanity of a goddess; Acusilaus, retaining the action of the goddess, explained her motive as political ambition, and so, raising the transaction to a higher level, fancied that he made it more credible.

A later writer, Herodorus of Heraclea, carried the method of Hecataeus much further than Acusilaus. It will be enough to illustrate the character of his mythography by one instance. The legend told that Apollo and Poseidon built the walls of Troy for King Laomedon. According to Herodorus, what really happened was this. Laomedon built the walls in the ordinary way, but he defrayed the expenses by the sacred treasures which had been accumulated in the shrines of Poseidon and Apollo. This is an example of the method of interpretation by which Herodorus sought to explain away the miraculous.[11]

The work of Pherecydes then represents a conservative reaction against the rationalism of Hecataeus. The compilations of Acusilaus represent a compromise between rationalism and conservatism, but leaning heavily to the conservative side. Herodorus took up the rationalistic method of Hecataeus, and developed it further. Reason was a gainer by the work of Hecataeus; it is a landmark in the progress of criticism; but the Hecataean method could not advance positive knowledge. It led, beyond Herodorus, to Palaephatus and Euemerus; it led ultimately nowhere, and I will not follow it. It was not the mythographers, but the Attic tragedians, whose criticism of mythology was interesting and illuminating, Aeschylus by moralising and Euripides by discrediting it.

§ 4. *Early Historians*

Hecataeus, the historian, as distinguished from the mythographer, had two immediate successors who took up the subject of oriental history in which he had shown the way. Charon of Lampsacus[12] composed a history of Persia coming down at least as far as the destruction of the fleet of Mardonius by a storm off

Mount Athos in 492 B.C., but probably including the invasion of Xerxes, of which he was in the fullest sense a contemporary.[13] His narrative was probably brief, but as one of the first historical works which descended to the writer's own age it possessed considerable importance for the growth of historical composition. There was another writer of the same period who was perhaps equally important and treated the same subject as Charon. Dionysius of Miletus likewise wrote a history of Persia which came down to the death of Darius and included the defeat at Marathon. But he followed this up by a continuation which had still greater interest, entitled *The Sequel to the Reign of Darius*; which narrated the events of the Persian war.[14]

Now while these works of Charon and Dionysius included very important episodes in the history of Greece, they were properly and formally histories of Persia. The first Greek writers who wrote modern history wrote of Greece only incidentally. Their theme was the great empire which had subjugated a part of Greece and attempted to subjugate it all. The circumstance that the writers, who undertook to record the relations of Greece with Persia, conceived those relations as part of the history of the Persian state, had an advantage for the unity of the subject. To write the history of Greece at almost any period without dissipating the interest is a task of immense difficulty, as any one knows who has tried, because there is no constant unity or fixed centre to which the actions and aims of the numerous states can be subordinated or related. Even in the case of the Persian invasion, one of the few occasions on which most of the Greek cities were affected by a common interest, though acting in various ways and from various motives, it facilitated the task of the narrator to polarise the events of the campaigns by following the camp of the invader and describing them as part of Persian history, though with Hellenic sympathy. But this method of treatment was a heritage from Hecataeus. The impulse which led to the "Persian" books of Charon and Dionysius came from the geographical work of Hecataeus, and in all probability he was one of their chief guides for oriental history up to the Ionic revolt.

There is one other observation I would make about the lost history of Dionysius. He was an Ionian, writing after Ionia had been delivered from the Persian yoke and had entered the confederacy of Delos, with the prospect of becoming dependent on Athens. The history of Ionia had not been brilliant, politically, during the past hundred years. It had been subdued first by Lydia and then by Persia; it had revolted from Persia and ignominiously failed; it had been compelled to aid its master in attempting to enslave the free Hellenes. It held a somewhat undignified position between Persia and free Greece. The Ionian point of view was therefore different, necessarily, from the Spartan or the Athenian; and the Ionians had some reason to feel that their actions were open to misconstruction, and that a rôle, not too heroic, would gain in their own telling. In any case the story of the Great Invasion told at Miletus would have a considerably different colouring from the same story related at Susa or at Athens. We may reasonably suspect that the history of the war by Dionysius had a value for Ionian self-love; that it may have done less than justice to the victorious Greeks; but that it probably did more justice to Persia than the enemy would have received from an Athenian writer. This Ionian logos of the Persian war was, we may conjecture, a challenge to unreserved admirers of Athens; we shall see in the next lecture how such a challenge was taken up.

There is another writer of this early school of historians whose name I cannot pass over, the Carian Greek, Scylax of Caryanda. He was employed by Darius to survey the course of the river Indus, and he published an account of his exploration. But he also wrote a work of contemporary history which centred round the figure of his fellow-countryman, Heracleides, Prince of Mylasae, who deserted the Persian cause and helped the Greeks in the invasion of Xerxes. A chance ray of light has recently been shed on Heracleides by an Egyptian papyrus, which contains a fragment of the work of the historian Sosylus on the Second Punic war.[15] This fragment relates to a naval action, probably the battle fought at the mouth of the Ebro in 217 B.C. The author illustrates a point in the naval tactics by comparing a certain action of Heracleides which thwarted a Phoenician manœuvre at the battle of Artemisium. The episode is not mentioned by Herodotus (though he refers to Heracleides elsewhere) and it probably comes from the work of Scylax.[16] How far that work was what could be called biographical we cannot tell, but it is at least noteworthy as the earliest Greek book we know of that made an individual the centre of a historical narrative.

We shall not wrong these early historians if we describe them as credulous and uncritical. The able literary critic, Dionysius of Halicarnassus, in whose days many of their works were still in existence, says that their aim was simply to compile and publish traditions and records, "without adding or subtracting anything"; and he appreciates their style as clear, concise, appropriate to the subject, bare of any artificial technique, though not careless or ungraceful.[17]

The historical impulse initiated by Hecataeus extended after a time beyond Ionia into the neighbouring land of Lydia, which had been permeated by Greek culture under the last Lydian kings. The Lydian Xanthus composed in Greek a history of his country for which he used local traditions and perhaps consulted inscriptions in the palace of Sardis.[18] But in the development of historiography he is less important than two other writers who, like him, wrote during the latter half of the fifth century, Antiochus of Syracuse and Hellanicus of Lesbos. Antiochus composed a work on the history of the western Greeks. He investigated the early history of Sicily and Italy and the plantation of the Greek colonies in those lands. So far he was dealing with the subject of origins, in which the early historians inherited an interest from their epic predecessors, whose legends they supplemented and modified by local traditions. (The epic itself had here a late offshoot in the poem which Panyassis of Halicarnassus produced towards the middle of the fifth century on the colonisation of the Ionian towns.) But the great significance of Antiochus is that he wrote the modern and contemporary history of an important section of the Greek world. A comprehensive history of western Hellas was a step towards a comprehensive history of Hellas as a whole.

His contemporary, Hellanicus of Lesbos, indicated, and prepared the way for, a further advance; and it is important to grasp his significance in our development. It has been usual to classify him with the elder successors of Hecataeus, because he wrote in Ionic Greek and covered practically all the fields which they had covered. But he broke new ground and became, as has been said, "the corner-stone" of the historical tradition of the Greeks. The range of his literary activity was wide. He wrote on the history of Persia; on the customs of the barbarians; on the mythical period of Greece; on the origins of the Greek cities in Asia; on the later history of Greece and especially the history of Athens. His principal achievement was the construction of a systematic chronology which laid the foundations for subsequent research.

The subject of chronology must have been pressed on the attention of Hecataeus, not only by his research into Greek genealogies, but by his study of Egyptian and oriental history. The Greeks had not yet invented any method of chronicling events. They had, as we saw, no chronological records, except lists of names, like those of the priestesses of Hera at Argos, of the archons at Athens, of the priests of Poseidon at Halicarnassus. It was only rarely that a name in these lists would yield the precise date of an event, such as the archonship of Solon which supplied at once the date of his reforms. Beyond these very barren records the only data were the genealogies. These furnished a very rough method of reckoning periods of time by generations. But there must have been considerable perplexity how the generation-unit should be calculated in terms of years. Ultimately it became usual to reckon three generations as equivalent to a hundred years, so that the unit was roughly 33 years. But there are early traces of another system which equated the generation with 23 years,[19] a principle which would yield widely different results. There was another system based on 40 years. It is probable that Hecataeus reckoned generally with generations, and not years, as his units, for the more distant past. But for "modern" history he had valuable auxiliary data of a precise kind. The oriental monarchies had an exact method of reckoning by means of the regnal years of the kings, and records of events dated in this way were preserved. These dates at once supplied synchronisms with events in Greek history and fixed a number of chronological landmarks, such as the capture of Sardis. But it is not likely that chronology was treated by Hecataeus more carefully or methodically than by Herodotus; its fundamental importance was not realised till later.

The problem which Hellanicus undertook was to reconstruct a complete chronicle of Greek history, with the help of the genealogies, lists such as that of the Athenian archons, and the oriental dates. It is possible that attempts had been made to work out this highly speculative problem already. Charon had compiled a book called the *Hôroi* of Lampsacus. It is generally assumed to have been a local history or chronicle of his native city. But the fragments suggest that it had a wider range than the affairs of Lampsacus. Perhaps the work consisted of annals, dated by yearly magistrates of Lampsacus, but recording, as well as local events, other events also of general historical interest. We have a parallel in a vast number of medieval chronicles which possess at once a local and a general side. Annals of Paderborn, for instance, take special account of Paderborn affairs, but also record the general history of the Western Empire. This is only a conjecture,[20] and in any case it was reserved for Hellanicus, even if he had the help of previous attempts, to achieve the construction of a chronicle which in its main lines found general acceptance, and influenced the course of subsequent chronological study. He made the list of the Argive priestesses of Hera the framework of his general chronicle of Greece.[21] He also compiled a special chronicle of Attic history, in which events were naturally arranged under the archon years from the year 683–2 onward. In its first form, this work came down to the year

411. After the termination of the Peloponnesian war the author continued it to 404 B.C.[22] The notices of events were brief, but it was not without a certain political colouring, evincing sympathy with Athenian democratic patriotism.

Without entering upon a minute criticism of the method of Hellanicus, it is enough to say that, mistaking the character of mythical traditions, he erected an ingenious edifice on foundations which had no solidity. The most perfect genealogies could not even approximately determine absolute dates; and the genealogies were full of inconsistencies which had to be overcome by arbitrary interpolations and manipulations. Moreover, quite recent events, which had not been recorded at the time, might present almost insuperable difficulties to a chronographer. One case, which we can control, will illustrate how dangerous the procedure of Hellanicus was. If he had consulted a certain inscription, which we are fortunate enough to have recovered, he could have found that several military events which he chronicled occurred in the same archonship, corresponding to the latter half of 459 B.C. and the former half of 458 B.C. Ignorant of this authentic evidence, he distributed these events over three archonships.[23] Yet these events must have happened within his own lifetime. His whole chronology of the thirty-five years after the Persian war was arbitrary; and it illustrates how in the absence of records precise chronology is hopeless. The instance of error which I have given suggests another observation. There were numerous stones at Athens, officially inscribed and precisely dated, from which, if they were all preserved, a modern student would probably construct without difficulty and with absolute certainty an exact chronicle of Athenian history in the fifth century. But it never occurred to Hellanicus to look for them, and in this he was only like most other Greek historians. The Greeks used such records when they came across them, but as a rule they did not seek them out systematically. Was the labour of deciphering them too laborious? It is remarkable that Thucydides describes a sixth-century inscription, which he quotes, as written "in faint characters"; yet a portion of that same inscription which has survived seems to a modern epigrapher quite clear, after more than two thousand years.

When we realise the nature of the data and the methods of the first chronologists whose ingenious constructions determined the received tradition, we shall hardly be prepared to dispute the conclusion at which Mahaffy arrived more than twenty-five years ago, that there are no well-established exact dates in Greek history before the seventh century.[24] For the seventh and even for the sixth there are only a few. Nay, we can hardly say that a clear and definite chronicle begins before 445 B.C., the year of the Thirty Years' Peace.

It is to be deplored that the early historians failed to realise how desirable it was to reckon time by a fixed chronological era. The practical Romans dated historical events from the Foundation of the City. The Greeks might have adopted, for instance, the year of the invasion of Xerxes. They could have dated Before and After, πρὸ τῶν Μηδικῶν and μετὰ τὰ Μηδικά, as we do with our era. But the most natural, and perhaps the best, chronological starting-point would have been the Trojan war. It did not matter in the least that the actual date of that event could not be known with certainty, so long as a definite year was fixed upon. Our era is not the true date of the Nativity; the true date cannot be ascertained; but this does not affect the utility of the conventional era. Now as a matter of fact the Trojan war was occasionally used, as a sort of reference date, by fifth-century historians,[25] and it is much to be regretted that Hellanicus did not systematically adopt this method of reckoning. The years of magistrates or priests are not only clumsy, but convey no chronological idea. For it is to be observed that when dates are expressed by cardinal numbers proceeding from a fixed year, not only is calculation simplified, but the numbers present to the mental vision a clear historical perspective.

But recognising the defects both in the mechanism and in the methods of Hellanicus, who attempted the impossible, we must give him credit for having framed the ideal of a chronological system which should embrace all the known facts of history; and if he established many erroneous dates, it is probable that he also rescued some that were correct.

§ 5. *Summary*

To sum up. (1) The historical study of their past by the Greeks arose out of the epic tradition and was a continuation of the work of the later epic poets. The tradition of the Homeric and Hesiodic poets maintained its control to the end. What we would designate as the post-mythical or historical period over-lapped by means of genealogies with the mythical period; the existing families of Greece were connected in line of blood with the heroes and thereby with the gods. The genealogical princi-ple, lying at the base of their historical reconstruction, hindered the Greeks from drawing a hard and fast line between the myth-ical and the historical age. The historians who approached the subject never got beyond criticism of details and rationalistic interpretation of miracles. But (2) at the very time when the study of mythological tradition began to assume a more critical character, the interest of the Greeks expanded to the "modern" history and institutions of non-Greek states, and here they were in a region not mythical, but historical. This intellectual move-ment originated in Ionia; its main cause was the Persian con-quest, and the resulting contact of Ionian thinkers with oriental history. The rise of Ionian science not only promoted the spirit of criticism, but also created an interest in geography, for the study of which the new political status of Ionia furnished oppor-tunities; but it was principally the new vision of oriental history that brought to birth Greek historiography. It was from the "modern" history of the East that the Greeks went on to study the "modern" history of Hellas. And the struggle with Persia in the first twenty years of the fifth century impelled them to begin to write histories of their own time. Further, as I will attempt to show more fully in the next lecture, their contact with the tradi-tions of non-Greek lands within the Persian empire suggested to the Greeks a new kind of criticism of their own mythical traditions. In all three fields of ancient, modern, and contemporary history, as well as in the allied sphere of geography, Hecataeus was a pioneer; his originality lay in responding to the stimulus from the non-Greek world.

The work of Hellanicus, who conceived the idea of a general history of Greece and laid the slippery foundations of its chronology, has brought us to a date from which we shall have to retrace our steps to examine the work of a greater writer than any of those who have claimed our attention to-day. We have only considered those points of light, obscured by time, which form the Ionian constellation; we have yet to examine a star of the first magnitude which is still as luminous as ever. Herodotus (we must not call him an Ionian) will be the subject of the next lecture.

LECTURE II

HERODOTUS

In the last lecture the necessities of our subject obliged us to consider works of which only scraps have survived, and of which we can form only dim ideas by groping methods, although we may feel tolerably confident as to the general character and value of the literature to which they belong. The names of their authors are forgotten by the world, and their chief function now is to tantalise the special student of literature or history. To-day we come to a work which time has not been allowed to destroy or diminish.

Of the life of Herodotus, son of Lyxes, of Halicarnassus, we know hardly anything except what may be gleaned from his own statements. Born early in the fifth century, he left his birthplace before 454 B.C., banished by Lygdamis the tyrant, who put his cousin Panyassis, the epic poet, to death. He stayed apparently for some time in Samos, and then went to Athens, whence he proceeded to Italy as one of the first citizens of the new colony of Thurii (443 B.C.). He survived the first years of the Peloponnesian war (431–0 B.C.[1]). Into this framework we have to fit his travels, which included the coasts of the Euxine, Babylon, Phoenicia, Egypt, and probably Cyrene. It is not necessary to discuss the disputed subject of the chronology of his journeys. I need only say that his most important journeys, those to Babylonia and Egypt, were probably undertaken in the later period of his life, while he was a citizen of Thurii. The years which elapsed between his banishment from his native city and his departure for his new home seem to have been spent in Greece, perhaps chiefly at Athens, and to have been devoted, as we shall see, to investigating and composing the story of the invasion of Xerxes. Though he may naturally have visited Athens again, on his way to or from the East, there is no evidence to entitle us to presume, as some have thought, that he deserted Thurii permanently and dwelled at Athens during the last years of his life.[2]

The argument of his history is a narrative of the relations between the Greeks and the oriental powers from the accession of Croesus to the capture of Sestos in 478 B.C. — a "modern" history in the fullest sense of the term. The division into nine Books is not due to the author himself, for in his day such divisions had not yet come into fashion. But the Alexandrine editor who was responsible for it was a man of extraordinary insight. His distribution perfectly exhibits the construction of the book and could not be improved by any change. But it can be rendered more perspicuous by observing that each of the nine Books is truly a sub-division and that the primary partition is a threefold one.[3] The work falls naturally into three sections, each consisting of three parts. The first section, or triad of Books, comprises the reigns of Cyrus and Cambyses, and the accession of Darius; the second deals with the reign of Darius; the third with that of Xerxes. The first is mainly concerned with Asia including Egypt; the second with Europe; the third with Hellas. The first displays the rise and the triumphs of the power of Persia; the last relates the defeat of Persia by Greece; while the middle triad represents a chequered picture, Persian failure in Scythia and at Marathon, Greek failure in Ionia. And each of the nine subdivisions has a leading theme which constitutes a minor unity. Cyrus is the theme of the first Book, Egypt of the second, Scythia of the fourth, the Ionian rebellion of the fifth, Marathon of the sixth. The seventh describes the invasion of Xerxes up to his success at Thermopylae; the eighth relates the reversal of fortune at Salamis; the final triumphs of Greece at Plataea and Mycale occupy the ninth. In the third alone the unity is less marked; yet there is a central interest in the dynastic revolution which set Darius on the throne. Thus the unity of the whole composition sharply displays itself in three parts, of which each again is three-fold.[4] The simplicity with which this architectural symmetry has been managed, without any apparent violence, constraint, or formality, was an achievement of consummate craft. The writer's management of the digressions, for which he is notorious, is hardly less striking, exhibiting a rare skill in the choice of the best and perhaps the only fitting places to stow away loose material he wished to make use of.

But, perfect as is the architectural unity of the work of Herodotus, it would seem that the plan as it was finally carried out was not conceived when he commenced to write, and that the unity was achieved not in conformity to a design thought out from the beginning, but by a process of expansion due to an after-thought. There is a variety of internal evidence which points convincingly to the conclusion that the last three Books were composed before the first six, and there are indications that he wrote this portion between 456 and 445 B.C., before he began his travels.[5] The natural inference is that he originally contemplated no more than a history of the invasion of Xerxes; and that it was in the course of his travels that he conceived the idea of a larger work, of which the "Invasion of Xerxes" should form the finale. The idea doubtless shaped itself gradually; and the first six Books were not composed in the order in which they stand. But the author has worked with such skill that only a searching analysis has detected the series of facts which demonstrate the priority of the last three Books[6] and make it clear that the Persian war was his original inspiration.

At whatever moment the idea of expanding his original history to its fuller compass presented itself, whether it was suggested by his journeys or prompted him to become a traveller, it was certainly connected closely with his travels, and the occurrence of long geographical excursus is one of the most striking features of the expansion.

So strongly marked indeed is the geographical element, so long are the geographical sections, in the work of Herodotus, that some critics have been led to think that considerable parts of it were originally intended to form part of a geography, and were afterwards incorporated in his history. There is nothing that compels us to adopt a hypothesis of this kind. Association with geography was a characteristic of the early historical literature of the Greeks, and these excursus in Herodotus attest the influence of the Hecataean school, and were natural in the work of a historian who was himself a traveller. And it is worth observing that when he was writing, both Egypt and Scythia, the subjects of his longest historico-geographical digressions, had a particular practical interest for the Athenians; and of the Greek public it was unquestionably the Athenians to whom the historian designed his work pre-eminently to appeal. I need only remind you of the Athenian adventure in Egypt in the middle of the fifth century and of the voyage of Pericles in the Euxine Sea. It has even been conjectured that this Periclean expedition (444 B.C.) was the occasion of the historian's visit to the Pontic regions. However this may be, it is not insignificant, in judging these digressions, that Egypt and Scythia possessed, at the time Herodotus wrote, an interest of a political kind, subordinate indeed to that of Persia, but distinctly actual.

It is also to be noted that the digressions in general had an artistic justification. They are an epic feature, deliberately designed;[7] one of the epic notes of the work. Homer was the literary master of Herodotus; without imitating him in any obvious way, the first great master of prose studied and caught the secrets of his effects. By means of digressions he achieved epic variety. We cannot do better than read the observations of the accomplished literary critic Dionysius.[8] "Herodotus knew that every narrative of great length wearies the ears of the hearer, if it dwell without a break on the same subject; but, if pauses are introduced at intervals, it affects the mind agreeably. And so he desired to lend variety to his work and imitated Homer. If we take up his book, we admire it to the last syllable, and always want more."

Besides diversifying his work with digressions and episodes, Herodotus adopted another epic feature, not less characteristic. Like Homer, the historian makes his characters speak. He introduces not only short and pointed conversations, but dialogues and orations of considerable length. For instance, Xerxes, Mardonius, and Artabanus make each a speech in Council before it is decided to invade Greece. I may recall the conversations of Solon with Croesus, of Xerxes with Artabanus and with Demaratus; and the speech made by the Corinthian envoy when the Spartans were considering the policy of forcing Athens to restore the Peisistratids. If the historian were charged with abusing this artifice by introducing in the Corinthian envoy's speech a long episode from Corinthian history, which is really quite irrelevant, he could appeal to the discourses of Phoenix and Nestor in Homer; and this case illustrates the fact that in introducing speeches he was influenced by the Ionian epic and not by the Athenian drama. It is impossible to say whether any of the older prose writers had adopted this practice, which makes the scenes vivid and the work alive. The bits of Hecataeus we possess are too brief to judge; but I may note that in one case at least he put words into the mouth of an actor.[9]

The Homeric qualities of Herodotus, which communicate to his history an epic flavour, accord with the object to produce a work which like Homer should fascinate the minds of men. It was his aim to hold his audience or readers entertained; to do for his own world in prose what Homer had done for the ancient world in numbers. We cannot tell how far any of his prose predecessors had sought to make their works attractive or entertaining,[10] or whether the influence of epic poetry affected their method of presentation. But we may confidently say that Herodotus was the first who discerned in "modern" history the possibilities of a treatment which was epic, and not Hesiodic but Homeric, in spirit and style.

His theme, the struggle of Greece with the Orient, possessed for him a deeper meaning than the political result of the Persian war. It was the contact and collision of two different types of civilisation, of peoples of two different characters and different political institutions. In the last division of his work, where the final struggle of Persia and Greece is related, this contrast between the slavery of the barbarian and the liberty of the Greek, between oriental autocracy and Hellenic constitutionalism, is ever present and is forcibly brought out. But the contrast of Hellenic with oriental culture pervades the whole work; it informs the unity of the external theme with the deeper unity of an inner meaning. It is the keynote of the history of Herodotus. The digressions and stories which delay the action, besides their intrinsic interest, and besides their epic use as pleasant pauses, have also the value of sounding that note, and of contributing distinctly, but without emphasis or iteration, towards impressing that contrast on the reader's mind. The interview, for example, of Croesus with Solon, the self-confident Eastern potentate with the thoughtful, self-controlled Greek, strikes this chord loudly; and most of the oriental and Hellenic stories are calculated to suggest the antithesis which finds its supreme expression, and is more elaborately wrought out, in the final collision of the Persian wars.

In the execution of this conception the Herodotean work has assumed the character of a study in the history of civilisation. Just as the Homeric poems present a large and living picture of the culture of ancient Greece, so the history of Herodotus gives us panoramic views of the Hellenic civilisation of the sixth century, and describes the cultures of all the Eastern peoples who directly or indirectly come within range.

And if it is a study in the history of civilisation, we may also say that it has certain features of a universal history. It is not universal either in space or in time. Not in time; it does not attempt to go back far in Greek history, and only touches upon the ancient period incidentally. Not in space, for it hardly touches upon the Western Greeks at all, and does not include what Hecataeus would have supplied about the peoples of the Western Mediterranean. But it has the higher quality of what we mean by universal history or *Weltgeschichte,* in focussing under one point of view, and fitting into a connected narrative, the histories of the various peoples who came into relations with one another, within a given range; so that they are drawn out of their isolation and recognised to have a meaning, greater or less, in the common history of man. Within that range, which is determined by his theme, Herodotus is irreproachably comprehensive; and his book, though he never formulates the idea, is a lesson in the unity of history.

Although Herodotus does not enter upon the history of the heroic period, he has frequently occasion to refer to mythical tradition, and here he shows himself distinctly a sceptic. Not that he was a rationalist in regard to theology generally, or had any clear and consistent philosophical view. He looked upon human life as under the control of superhuman powers, who in exercising their incalculable government were prompted by motives of envy and nemesis or righteous anger, who acted to some extent on principles of justice and retribution, and who might communicate knowledge to men by means of oracles, portents, or dreams. But any further converse of gods with men, any divine appearances alleged to have happened in recent times, Herodotus is not prepared to accept, though he is never dogmatic. His philosophy was not strong enough to deny that the gods had ever carried on the sort of intercourse with men that is described in the epics, or generated human progeny; for his ultimate line between the divine and the human was not fast. But it was a great comfort for common sense and everyday experience, to push the age in which such things could happen as far back as possible. Herodotus reveals unmistakably his incredulity about all the mythical wonders in which, according to tradition, ancestors of living people, some fifteen or twenty generations back, played bright or shady parts. He accepted the genealogies, but when he got to Perseus or Heracles, he did not regard them as sons of a god. Heracles is the son of Amphitryon, Helen is the daughter of Tyndareus. Sometimes he relates legends or tells tales involving superhuman agency, but he never takes any responsibility for them, and occasionally treats them with delicate irony. He mentions a legend of the Thessalians that the ravine through

which the Peneius makes its way to the sea was wrought by
Poseidon. "Their tale is plausible; and any one who thinks that
Poseidon shakes the earth and that clefts produced by earth-
quakes are the works of that god, would on seeing this mountain-
ravine ascribe it to Poseidon. For it appeared to me to be the
result of an earthquake." Gibbon might have taken lessons in the
art of irony from Herodotus as well as from Pascal. Consider
again the admirable caution with which he speaks of the divine
snake said to live on the Athenian Acropolis. "The Athenians say
that a great snake lives in the Sanctuary as guardian of the citadel;
and they present a honey-cake every month as to a creature
existing" (ὡς ἐόντι). This commits him to nothing.

But though disposed to accept only what experience led
him to regard as possible, in any given case, Herodotus, as I
have said, did not draw theoretically a hard and fast line
between the human and the divine; and he did not reject as
ridiculous the notion that at one time gods moved visibly on
the earth and consorted with men. Why then did he reject the
divine parentage of heroes like Heracles and Perseus? It is
important to comprehend the reason for this scepticism
which he derived from Hecataeus. I touched on this point in
the first lecture. It was not due to the canons of Ionian science
or to the influence of Ionian philosophy. It was due to the study
of comparative mythology which had opened for Hecataeus a
new perspective of the world's history. The Egyptian studies
which Herodotus pursued in the footsteps of the Milesian traveller taught him that human history in that country went back
for thousands of years before the age of the gods was reached.
The Egyptians, for instance, had a god corresponding to
Heracles, and they reckoned that 17,000 years had elapsed
since he had appeared in Egypt. Hence the conclusion which
Herodotus accepts that there was an ancient god Heracles, but
that he must be sharply distinguished from the human son of
Amphitryon, ancestor of the Heracleidae.[11] The Greek tradition that the age in which gods walked the earth was still current some eight or nine hundred years ago could not be true.

For even apart from the suggestions of comparative mythology, it was inadmissible to suppose that while Egypt was in a prosaic age of mere men, Greece was trodden by deities and the scene of miracles; and the Egyptian tradition was vouched for by records. The argument demolished the received mythology of the heroic age so far as it was superhuman.

Herodotus deserves credit for having accepted the argument, to which contemporary writers like Pherecydes were deaf; and if he asks pardon from the gods and heroes for his boldness, this does not mean that he felt hesitation or reluctance; it was merely an insincere and graceful genuflexion. He was doing what a Christian preacher sometimes does, when having delivered an extremely heterodox sermon he winds up with a formal homage to orthodox dogma. Herodotus is extremely courteous, perhaps ironically courteous, to both parties. He says, as it were, to the gods and heroes, "Please, do not be angry with me,—supposing you to exist. But at this time of day, you know, one must really draw the line somewhere." On the other hand he says to the infidels who disbelieve in oracular prophecy, "I know you will think me credulous. But still in this case the evidence is so remarkably clear that I do not see my way to resisting it."[12] The mythological argument, however, of which I am speaking was not due to Herodotus himself. He may have put it in his own way, and added some points, but he owed it, as I have said, to Hecataeus. It has long been recognised that his description of Egypt is not an original work, put together exclusively from his own observations and inquiries, but largely reproduces the account which Hecataeus had given in his *Map of the World*. When Herodotus visited Egypt, he doubtless had the book of Hecataeus with him, and used it like a barrister's brief for cross-examining the temple-servants and guiding him in his investigations. He added corrections and new information, but the great Ionian supplied the groundwork. He does not say so; he does not acknowledge his debt to Hecataeus; for, as you know, the ancients had very different views from the moderns about literary obligations. It was not the fashion or etiquette to name your authorities except for some special reason,—

for instance, to criticize them, or to display your own learning; and you were not considered a plagiarist if you plundered somebody else's work without mentioning his name, Hecataeus brought out the importance of the Nile by the striking phrase that Egypt was the gift of the river; Herodotus adopts the phrase as if it were his own. One of the most convincing tests by which suspected plagiarism can be established is the occurrence of the same mistakes. Now Herodotus reproduces the errors which Hecataeus had committed about the hippopotamus. But there are a whole series of points in which we can trace the contact between the two writers in regard to Egypt. As for the mythology, we are left in no doubt because Herodotus names Hecataeus in this connexion. "When Hecataeus was in Thebes he told his pedigree to the priests and connected himself with a god in the sixteenth generation. And the priests did to him what they did to me, though *I* did not relate *my* pedigree. They took him into the hall of the temple and showed him wooden statues of the high priests. The high priesthood descends from father to son, and each high priest sets up his own statue in his lifetime. They counted 345 statues, and they set this genealogy against that of Hecataeus, but *they* did not derive their pedigree from a god or a hero."[13]

The author's motive in naming his predecessor here is, obviously, to rally him for having "given himself away" by stating his own genealogy and divine ancestry to the priests. "*I* was not so incautious" is the implication. But we have no right to infer that Hecataeus had not already drawn the sceptical conclusions which Herodotus explains. The sceptical words with which Hecataeus introduced his *Genealogies* show that he was not deaf to the lessons in history which he learned in Egyptian temples. His very expression, when he says that "the *logoi* of the Hellenes are absurd," not "the stories of the poets," suggests the contrast of non-Hellenes whose *logoi* he had compared. The distinction of what the Greeks say from what the Persians, Phoenicians, or Egyptians say often recurs in Herodotus, and is an echo, I believe, from Hecataeus.[14] But we have another proof. Herodotus cites the Egyptian priests as dating the age of the gods in relation to the reign of Amasis. As the visit of Hecataeus to Egypt would have fallen not long after the death of Amasis, the dating indicates that Herodotus was copying the statement of Hecataeus.

The note of scepticism, perhaps we may say the characteristic note of Ionian scepticism, is struck in the first paragraphs of the Herodotean work. It opens with the statement of a theory that the wars of the Greeks and Persians were the manifestation of a secular antagonism between Asia and Europe—what our English historian, Freeman, was fond of calling the Eternal Question. This at least is the abstract way we should formulate the tenor of the statement which I may abbreviate as follows:— "The quarrel began thus: Phoenician traders carried off from Argos Io the king's daughter. Subsequently Greek adventurers from Crete carried off the princess Europa from Tyre. The next aggression came from the Greek side, when the Argonauts ravished Medea from Colchis. The Asiatic reply to this outrage was the rape of Helen by Paris. The Trojan war which followed generated in Asia a feeling of hostility to the Greeks, and the Persian war was the ultimate issue of this feeling." But the theory was not originated by Herodotus. He disavows all responsibility. It was a theory of the Persians, he tells us, and he states it only to set it aside in his ironical way.

The whole passage reads as if it might be the condensation of a friendly discussion between a Greek and a Persian as to the responsibility for the Persian war. It was undeniable that the Persians and not the Greeks had been the aggressors; the conquest of Ionia by Cyrus had been the beginning. The Persian advocate could only remove the blame from Asia by going farther back. The summary I gave of the argument does not reproduce its flavour, and I will take the liberty of throwing it into the form of a dialogue.

Persian. The Greeks had no business in Asia. They belong to Europe, and they should have stayed there. Their expedition against Troy was the first trespass; it began their encroachments on a continent which belongs to Asiatic peoples of whom the Persians are the heirs.

Greek. Oh, but you are forgetting that on that occasion the Trojans were the offenders; Paris carried off Helen.

Persian. That was no sufficient reason; but even if it were, the act of Paris was only a reprisal for the Greek crimes of carrying off Medea and Europa. And the Asiatics were far too sensible to make a *causa belli* of such foolish elopements.

Greek. Well, if you go back so far, you must go back farther still. What about the rape of Io from Argos?

Persian. Well, yes, I admit it. That was a Phoenician business, and we Persians must allow that the Phoenicians began the mischief, though we hold you really responsible, through your folly in taking such an affair seriously. Only fools would make war on account of such escapades. Men of the world know that, if these women were carried off, they were not more reluctant than they should be.[15]

Evidently we have here an invention of Ionian *esprit*. The nature of the argument, dealing as it does entirely with Greek legend, shows that the Persian was a fictitious disputant; and the attribution of the theory to a Persian is an effect of literary subtlety quite in the manner of Voltaire. Though Herodotus thought little of this speculation about ancient wrongs, he seems to have taken it as seriously meant. "Whatever we think about all this," he says, "I will begin with the first Eastern monarch who undoubtedly committed injustice against Greece, Croesus, who subdued Ionia without provocation." But it is highly significant that he should place in the portals of his work a speculation which set mythical tradition in a ridiculous light.

The passage I have discussed is one of several that evince those acute tendencies in the Hellenic mind which culminated in the movement of the Sophists. For instance, the story of the wife of Intaphernes. She chose to save her brother rather than her husband or children, on the ground that husband and children might be replaced but she could never have another brother. That is a clever Ionian subtlety; there is no reason to suppose that it was invented in the period of the Sophists. Or take the demonstration of the power of custom by Darius. He dismayed some Greeks by the question what they would take to eat their dead fathers, and then equally horrified some Indians of a tribe who ate dead parents, by asking them how much they would take to cremate theirs. The immense power of custom was an observation redolent of the age of the Wise Men; Pindar, whom Herodotus quotes, designated Custom as king of the world; and the idea afterwards became the basis of sophistic theories. The story quoted by Herodotus is a drastic Ionian illustration.

Again, the famous discussion of the comparative merits of democracy, aristocracy, and monarchy by the seven Persian conspirators who overthrew the false Smerdis, belongs also to presophistic speculation. It is obviously a fiction; for the discussion was appropriate in the Greek world, but was quite out of place in Persia. But it was not a fiction of Herodotus, for he states expressly (careful though he generally is not to commit himself) that these opinions were really uttered by the Persian noblemen, although some of the Greeks consider this incredible. The historian was taken in, just as he was taken in by the persiflage about the rapes of the fair women of legend. There can hardly be much doubt that some publicist threw his reflexions on the comparative merits of constitutions into the shape of this historical deliberation. The distinction of three fundamental types of constitution is older than the period of the Sophists; it is recognised in an ode of Pindar not later than 473 B.C., and it was then probably a commonplace.[16] We may suspect that we have to do with some publication of the first half of the fifth century.

Now there is one feature common to these passages. Greek ideas and reflexions are transferred to an Eastern setting or connected with Persian history. Their origin was assuredly Ionian.[17] They betray the naïve interest of the Ionians in their masters, and show the Greek mind projecting its own reflexions into a world of which it had only a half-knowledge, with the instinct of making that world more interesting and sympathetic.[18]

But I must return to the scepticism of Herodotus. I have already observed that in the historical post-Homeric period the mythopoeic faculty of the Greeks did not slumber, but myth now took the form of the historical anecdote, or, as the Germans call it, "historische Novelle." Here they showed consummate felicity in constructing stories with historical background, historical actors, historical motives, and possessing, many of them, a perpetual value because they are seasoned with worldly wisdom and enshrine some criticism of life. These tales differ from the old myths not only in the tendency to point a moral, but also in the circumstance that for the most part they do not involve physical impossibilities, though they may imply highly improbable coincidences, or what we may call psychical or political impossibilities. The work of Herodotus is richly furnished with these tales; he had a wonderful *flair* for a good story; and the gracious garrulity with which he tells historical anecdotes is one of the charms which will secure him readers till the world's end. Gibbon happily observed that Herodotus "sometimes writes for children and sometimes for philosophers"; the anecdotes he relates often appeal to both. He accepts them generally at their face value, and most of them have been taken as more or less literally true till very recent times. The story of the intercourse between Croesus and Solon was rejected as fiction only because it seemed impossible to reconcile it with chronology.[19] But we are now more sceptical about good stories of this type, and we have come to see how often they are wrought upon, or woven into, some ancient *motif,* which is adapted to a historical setting. The tale of the funeral pyre of Croesus sprang from the burning of the Assyrian god Sandan; it was an up-to-date version of the legend of Sardanapalus. The story of the ring of Polycrates turns on an old motive, the finding of something lost in a fish's belly, but its point in connexion with Polycrates has been explained only the other day. The casting of the ring into the sea was symbolic of thalassocracy; it was the same mythical ring as that of Minos, which in the poem of Bacchylides Theseus sought in the halls of Amphitrite; its recovery was fatal to the ruler of the seas.[20]

Herodotus is the Homer of this later form of historical myths, in which the supernatural machinery consisted of oracles or significant dreams or marvellous coincidences. They corresponded to his wavering standard of the credible and probable, which generally excluded what seemed physically impossible. For instance, he positively refuses to believe that statues assumed a sitting posture.[21] He duly records the story that a certain man dived under water a distance of several miles. It was the private opinion of Herodotus that that man arrived in a boat.[22]

Perhaps the story of the miraculous deliverance of Delphi from the Persians[23] may be taken to illustrate the ill-defined limits of his faith. Their oracle declared to the Delphian priests that the god would himself provide for the safety of his sanctuary, and when the Persians came they were repelled, with great havoc, by lightning and by the fall of huge boulders from Parnassus. Herodotus relates this without any hint of scepticism, though he emphasizes the miraculous nature of the events. Now you observe that there is nothing impossible in the alleged physical occurrences; the marvel lies in the opportunity of the coincidence and the fulfilment of the oracular announcement. Against a marvel of this order Herodotus had no prejudice. But another miracle was said to have happened on the same occasion. Certain sacred arms, which were preserved within the shrine and were too sacred to be profaned by human touch, were suddenly discovered lying in a heap in front of the temple. A rationalist—Euripides, for instance—would find no difficulty in such an occurrence, assuming the fact to be certain. Herodotus accepts it as a genuine marvel, without any suggestion that human agency, notwithstanding Delphic asseverations to the contrary, might have been concerned in the matter; and the notable thing is that he considers it less wonderful than the intervention of the physical forces which overwhelmed the Persians. If such a phenomenon as the removal of the arms presented itself to us for criticism—supposing the fact were assured beyond a doubt, and supposing human agency were absolutely excluded by the circumstances—we should regard it as something incomparably more extraordinary than the unquestionably wonderful coincidence of the storm of lightning.[24] Here, in fact, Herodotus has failed to draw the line at what is physically impossible. The truth is that his faith and doubt are alike instinctive; he had never thought the problem out for himself; he had never clearly defined the border between the domains of the credible and the incredible. And so in this episode he has no sooner given us a lesson in faith than he relapses into reserve. For there was yet another marvel to be told. It was said that two armed warriors of superhuman stature pursued the flying Persians and dealt death among their broken ranks. But Herodotus carefully avoids the responsibility of accepting this story. He gives it on the authority of the Persians; he qualifies it by the phrase "as I am informed"; and he adds that the Delphians identified the two warriors with local heroes.

The contrast of the *naïveté* of Herodotus with his scepticism imparts to his epic a very piquant quality. Credulity alternates with a cautious reserve, which is especially noticeable when he is aware of more than one version of an occurrence. He is an expert in the art of not committing himself. He says in one passage, "I am bound to state what is said, but I am not bound to believe."[25] Of the tale that Zalmoxis lived for three years in a subterranean chamber, he professes agnosticism;" I do not disbelieve nor do I absolutely believe it."[26] Occasionally he criticizes and rejects a story, for instance the charge against the Alcmaeonids of treachery at Marathon; but his common practice is to state conflicting accounts and leave the matter there. This method, as it happens, is much more satisfactory to a modern critic than if Herodotus had selected one version, or had attempted to blend different versions together. But it shows him in the light of a collector of historical material, and an accomplished artist in arranging and presenting it, rather than as what we mean by a historian, who considers it his business to sift the evidence, and decide, if possible, between conflicting accounts.

We are often tempted to think of Herodotus as an Ionian, although he was not a native of Ionia. He wrote in Ionic; and he cannot be severed from the school of the Ionian historians, to whom his work owed a great deal more than appears on the surface. But if he had heard himself described as an Ionian writer, he would have been vastly indignant. He is at great pains to dissociate himself from Ionia and Ionian interests. In his account of the Ionian revolt and of the part which the Ionians played in the war with Xerxes, he shows a hardly veiled contempt for a people which, as he says, had been thrice enslaved. He tells us that the name "Ionian was one of no great repute." He is careful to record, without any comment, the Scythian opinion that the Ionians were the most cowardly and unmanly people in the world.[27] He takes frequent opportunities of criticizing adversely the views of Ionian writers. Now I think we may say that this antagonistic attitude was not due entirely or principally to the fact that he belonged by birth to Dorian Halicarnassus. He does indeed insist on the difference of Dorian and Ionian, but the contrast on which his anti-Ionian feeling depended was one within the Ionian race itself—the distinction of the Athenians from the Ionians of Asia. We saw that Herodotus was at Athens before he went to Italy, and his connexion with Athens impressed its mark on his political views. He was a warm admirer of the Athenians, and looked with favour and enthusiasm on their empire. He participated in their experiment of colonising Thurii, became a citizen of their daughter-city. But even if we had not this external proof of his political sympathy, his work testifies to it abundantly. The whole account not only of the Marathonian campaign but of the war with Xerxes is one that redounds to the glory of Athens and flatters Athenian pride. It is, in fact, written mainly from the Athenian point of view, and represents largely, though not exclusively, the Athenian version. The Spartans and the part they took in the war are often handled with irony—for example, they were always arriving too late because they were celebrating a feast. The Corinthians are treated almost with malice. The story would have had a very different complexion if it had been written in the Spartan interest; and even though we have no philo-Spartan historian of the time, a very good case has been made out for the view that Sparta showed as true heroism as Athens.[28] Further, Herodotus takes opportunities to set forth the mythistorical claims of Athens to a hegemony of the Greeks, and represents

Athens as asserting those claims at the time of the Persian war.[29] This is an anachronism. At that time Sparta was admittedly the leader and dictator; Athens was a member of the Peloponnesian confederacy, and the strife for supremacy had not begun. Thus the situation is construed in the light of the sequel; history is distorted in the interest of politics; and the grounds of the claim to hegemony which Herodotus ascribes to the Athenians of that time are the stock arguments which we find used in Athenian funeral orations to illustrate and justify the Athenian empire. In the Epitaphios which Pericles pronounced over the citizens killed in the Samian war (439 B.C.) these arguments from myth and history were doubtless marshalled; and that Herodotus was present and listened to it is a conjecture of Eduard Meyer, which has some plausibility, since we find that a famous picturesque phrase used by the orator, likening the dead soldiers to the spring taken out of the year, was adopted by the historian and placed in a new setting.[30]

Admiration for the Athenian empire in the third quarter of the fifth century meant admiration for Pericles, the chief inspirer of Athenian policy, and the sympathy of Herodotus with Pericles is revealed in the single passage in which he mentions him, where he records the anecdote of his mother's dream that a lion would be born to her.[31] It is revealed, too, in sympathy with the Alcmaeonid family.[32]

His strong phil-Athenian feelings cannot be disconnected from his tone of prejudice and disparagement in treating the Ionians. When the immediate danger of Persian subjection was over, and the Ionian cities which had been leagued with Athens as an equal were brought to submit to her as a mistress, there was little love lost. The Ionian record of the war was one which would have failed to satisfy Athenian patriots as certainly as the Herodotean narrative must have failed to please the Ionians. Herodotus expressly argued that the Athenians were "truly the saviours of Greece";[33] but he did more: he gave currency and authority to a story which embodied Athenian tradition and justified Athenian empire, and with such cunning and tact that it has been permanently effective. His admiration for Athens was bound up with his belief in democratic freedom. Until the Peisistratids were overthrown, he says, Athens was an ordinary undistinguished city; but when the Athenians abolished the tyranny and won their freedom, they became by far the first state in Greece.[34]

Herodotus then was a phil-Athenian democrat. If the story is true that the Athenians bestowed on him ten talents (about 12,000 dollars) in recognition of the merits of his work, it was a small remuneration for the service he rendered to the renown of their city.[35] But that he did this service does not degrade his work into anything that could be described as a partisan publication in the offensive sense. It was pragmatical; it reflected the author's political beliefs, and exhibited a strong bias in the preference given to Athenian sources. But it was the work of a historian who cannot help being partial; it was not the work of a partisan who becomes a historian for the sake of his cause.

Something more particular must be said about the Herodotean story of the Persian invasion. A self-flattering version of the war had become a tradition at Athens. We have an early sketch of it, in a poetical form, in the *Persae* of Aeschylus (472 B.C.); but Herodotus was probably the first to write it down in a historical form, some twenty years later. Oral traditions (gathered at Athens, Sparta, Delphi, and elsewhere) appear profusely in his work, as every one knows. But he could not have constructed his history of the course of the war from oral traditions alone, or composed such a narrative of events, in which he was too young to take part, thirty years or so afterwards, without the help of some earlier record. We have seen that he depended on Hecataeus for Egypt, though this was just one of the portions of his work where autopsy, and information collected orally, might have sufficed. There is little doubt that Hecataeus was his main guide for early oriental history, and that the same writer was also used for the descriptions of Scythia and Libya, along with other geographical works of the Ionian school. When we come to the invasion of Darius and Xerxes, we find, as we might expect, clear indications that Herodotus here too had a written guide.

Throughout the narrative, in the last three Books, of the events after Marathon to the end of the second invasion, the historian has naturally to pass backwards and forwards from the Persians to the Greeks. Now there is a remarkable contrast between the character of the narrative when the writer takes us to Susa or to the Persian camp, and when he transports us to the cities or tents of the Greeks. In the accounts of what the Greeks did, we are constantly confronted with more than one story, representing various oral traditions which reflect different local interests. But when we follow the movements of the Persians, we have a continuous chronological narrative, by no means always credible, but all of a piece and marked by enumerations and details which point to a more or less contemporary written source, and a source of which Persian, not Greek, history was formally the subject. This source contributes the main thread of the narrative, round which Herodotus has wrought all the additional supplementary and illustrative material he managed to collect. The chronology of Persian events after Marathon is orderly and distinct, contrasting with the uncertainties which beset the digressions on Greek history, such as that on the Spartan kings Cleomenes and Demaratus. Now we know of a history of the Persian war prior to Herodotus, the book of Dionysius of Miletus. I spoke of it in the last lecture, and I also pointed out that the Persian history of Charon of Lampsacus may, not improbably, have come down to the invasion of Xerxes. Either of these books would satisfy the condition that the war was treated as an episode in Persian, not Greek, history, so that it is not unlikely that one of these may have been the source of Herodotus.[36]

Into the warp thus furnished by an older writer is wrought a woof of Athenian tradition, varied here and there by tissue from other sources. And it is noteworthy how in the last three Books, comprising the invasion of Xerxes, the imminence of a divine direction of human affairs is strongly accentuated. The sceptical tone is less apparent here than in other parts of the work. From the beginning of the seventh Book the dominant note is changed, at least this is the impression I receive; the atmosphere becomes charged with a certain solemnity; it is, I think we might say, rather Athenian than Ionian. Is this difference due to the influence of those Athenian dramas which had glorified the subject, the tragedies of Phrynichus and Aeschylus? The catastrophe which befals the Persian expedition is not conceived as the work of jealous gods annoyed by the conspicuous wealth or success of mere mortals. It is rather a divine punishment of the insolence and rashness that are often born of prosperity. This is the Aeschylean doctrine:

> Ζεύς τοι κολαστὴς τῶν ὑπερκόμπων ἄγαν
> φρονημάτων ἔπεστιν εὔθυνος βαρύς[37]
> Zeus is a judge who visits heavily
> All whose self-glorious spirit vaults too high.

This Athenian influence in the last Books of Herodotus accords with my conjecture that Athens was his headquarters during a part of the ten years or so which elapsed between his banishment and his sailing for Italy.

Herodotus then made a considerable use of older writers[38]— of whom he only names Hecataeus, and usually for the purpose of hinting something uncomplimentary. As the works of these writers have perished, it is very difficult to form a fair estimate of the achievements of Herodotus himself as a historical investigator— apart from his transcendent gifts as an artist and man of letters. His great service consisted probably in the collection of unwritten material concerning modern Greek history; this floating matter he wrought with masterly skill into a framework of facts constructed by predecessors. His maxims of historical criticism may be set down as three: (1) Suspect superhuman and miraculous occurrences, which contradict ordinary experience. But this, in his application of it, leaves a wide room for portents, and it does not cover oracles and dreams. (2) When you are confronted by conflicting evidence or differing versions of the same event, keep an open mind; *audi alteram partem*. But this does not save him from a biassed acceptance of Athenian tradition. (3) Autopsy and first-hand oral information are superior to stories at second hand, whether written or oral.[39] This tends to take the naïve form, "I know, for I was there myself," and it placed the historian at the mercy of the vergers and guides in Egyptian temples.

I may illustrate by a couple of examples how Herodotus was sometimes unfortunate in his information gathered on the spot. When he visited Egypt he saw on the great Pyramid inscriptions which disappeared in the Middle Ages. Probably they were of religious import, appropriate to a royal tomb. But Herodotus tells us that they enumerated the sums of money which were expended on the onions and leeks consumed by the workmen who built the pyramid. This was the interpretation with which the guide satisfied the Greek traveller's curiosity.[40] The other instance I will quote appertains to Babylonian history. Herodotus saw at Babylon the great buildings of a king, with whose name even those of us who have not studied Babylonian annals are probably familiar— King Nebuchadnezzar. He is correctly informed as to the time at which they were built—five generations after the reign of Queen Sammuramat whom he calls Semiramis. But autopsy did not keep him from falling into a droll error about the potentate who built them. Nebuchadnezzar has had rather bad luck. In the book of Daniel he is metamorphosed into a beast of the field; in Herodotus he is forced to masquerade as a woman. We have to discover his identity under the mask of Queen Nitocris.[41]

We must give full credit to Herodotus for having recognised the principles of criticism which I have indicated, though his application of them is unsatisfactory and sporadic. They are maxims of permanent validity; properly qualified they lie at the basis of the modem developments of what is called historical methodology. But notwithstanding the profession of these axioms of common sense, he was in certain ways so lacking in common sense that parts of his work might seem to have been written by a precocious child. He undertook to write the history of a great war; but he did not possess the most elementary knowledge of the conditions of warfare. His fantastic statement of the impossible numbers of the army of Xerxes exhibits an incompetence which is almost incredible and is alone enough to stamp Herodotus as more of an epic poet than a historian. It matters not whether he worked out the arithmetic for himself or accepted it entirely on authority; this is a case in which to accept is as heinous as to invent. Heinous for a historian; and if we judge Herodotus by the lowest standard as a historian of a war, this case invalidates his claim to competence. But as an epic story-teller he escapes triumphantly. His catalogue of the Persian host is a counterpart to the Catalogue of the *Iliad:*

μῦθον δ' ὥς ὅτ' ἀοιδὸς ἐπισταμένως κατέλεξας.

His incompetence in military matters is shown, in another way, in his account of the campaign of Thermopylae and Artemisium. The key to their actions lay—and it required no technical training or experience to discern this—in the close connexion and interdependence of the Persian land army and the Persian fleet, a fact which governed the Greek measures for defence. Herodotus, though he mentions several things which imply this and enable us more or less to penetrate the strategy of the combatants, fails completely to realise the situation and treats the naval and the land operations as if they were independent.

In his relation of the Persian war, Herodotus does not neglect the chronology, and it is perhaps as satisfactory as we could expect. But it may fairly be questioned whether the credit for this is not to be imputed to an earlier writer—Dionysius or Charon—whom he had the discretion to follow. It is significant that he does not give any formal date which a Greek reader could easily interpret, until he mentions, almost by the way, that the Persian invasion of Attica occurred in the archonship of Calliades.[42] But while chronology fares pretty well in the last three Books, the whole work shows that, while the author copied the dates which his sources supplied, he never attempted to grapple with the chronological difficulties of Greek history, although so many of the episodes which he related raised the problem of synchronizing Hellenic tradition with oriental records. We have no reason to suppose that he avoided the problem because he judged it insoluble; his indifference to it is another manifestation of his epic, quasi-historical mind.

The first phase of Greek historiography culminates and achieves its glory in Herodotus. He reflects its features — its eager research into geography and ethnography (the indispensable groundwork of history), and its predominant interest in the East. He adopts from Hecataeus a critical attitude towards the ancient myths, aided by a rudimentary comparative mythology. But these elements are transfigured by the magic of his epic art and the spell of a higher historical idea. He was the Homer of the Persian war, and that war originally inspired him. His work presents a picture of sixth-century civilisation; and it is also a universal history in so far as it gathers the greater part of the known world into a narrative which is concentrated upon a single issue. It is fortunate for literature that he was not too critical; if his criticism had been more penetrating and less naïve, he could not have been a second Homer. He belonged entirely in temper and mentality to the period before the sophistic illumination, which he lived to see but not to understand. Before his death, the first truly critical historian of the world had begun to compose. Our attention will next be claimed by Thucydides.

LECTURE III

THUCYDIDES

§ 1. *His life and the growth of his work*

THUCYDIDES belonged by descent to the princely family of Thrace into which Miltiades, the hero of Marathon, had married. He was thus a cousin of the statesman Cimon, and he inherited a rich estate with gold mines in Thrace. And so, while he was an Athenian citizen and connected with a distinguished family of Athens, he had an independent *pied à terre* in a foreign country. His mind was moulded under the influence of that intellectual revolution which we associate with the comprehensive name of the Sophists, the illumination which was flooding the educated world of Hellas with the radiance of reason. Without accepting the positive doctrines of any particular teacher, he learned the greatest lesson of these thinkers: he learned to consider and criticize facts, unprejudiced by authority and tradition. He came to be at home in the "modern" way of thinking, which analysed politics and ethics, and applied logic to everything in the world. We might illustrate how intense and deep-reaching the sophistic movement was, in the third quarter of the fifth century, by pointing to the difference between Herodotus and Thucydides. If you took up the two works without knowing the dates of their composition, you would think there might be a hundred years' development between them. But then consider the difference between Sophocles and Euripides.

Thucydides must have been at least twenty-five years old, some think he was as much as forty, when the Peloponnesian war broke out in 431 B.C. At the very beginning he formed the resolution to record it, and in the first years of the war, at least, the composition of the history was nearly contemporary with the events. In 424 B.C. he was elected to the high office of a strategos and appointed to command in Thrace; and the loss of Amphipolis led to his condemnation and banishment. For twenty years he did not see Athens, and, while he probably lived for the most part on his Thracian estate, he also travelled to collect material for his work. It seems certain that he visited Sicily, for his narrative of the Athenian expedition could not have been written by one who had not seen Syracuse with his own eyes.[1] After the end of the war he was allowed to return to Athens in 404 B.C. (by the decree of Oenobius). He did not die before 399 B.C.; perhaps he was no longer alive in 396 B.C.; and he left his book unfinished.[2]

It is evident how these biographical facts, and they are almost all we know about the man, bear upon his historical work. His family connexion at Athens provided him, perhaps, with exceptional facilities for obtaining authentic information, while his military training and experience qualified him to be the historian of a war. His second home in Thrace gave him an interest independent of Athens, and helped him to regard the Athenian empire with a certain detachment which would have been less easy for one who was a pure-blooded citizen and had no home outside Attica. His banishment operated in the same direction, and afforded him opportunities for intercourse with the antagonists of his country. The intellectual movement which invaded Athens when he was a young man was a condition of his mental growth; if he had belonged to an earlier generation, he could not have been Thucydides.

But if all these circumstances helped and conditioned the achievements of a profoundly original mind, which always thought for itself, we must seek the stimulus which aroused the historical faculty of Thucydides in—the Athenian empire. If it was the wonder of the Greek repulse of the Persian hosts that inspired the epic spirit of Herodotus, it was the phenomenon of the Empire of Athens, a new thing in the history of Hellas, — an empire governed by a democracy, a new thing in the history of the world—that captured the cooler but intense interest of Thucydides. He did not take up his pen to celebrate; his aim was to understand, — to observe critically how that empire behaved in the struggle which was to test its powers. It has not, I think, been sufficiently realised what an original stroke of genius it was to form the idea of recording the history of the war at the very moment of its outbreak. Contemporary history in the strictest meaning of the term was thus initiated. Thucydides watched the events for the purpose of recording them; he collected the material while it was fresh from the making. Further, he designed a history which should be simply a history of the war and of the relations of the militant states, which should confine itself to its theme, and not deviate into geography or anthropology or other things. Thus he was the founder of "political" history in the special sense in which we are accustomed to use the term.

Widely divergent views are held as to the way in which the work of Thucydides was constructed and the stages by which it reached its final though incomplete state. This question is not one of merely meritorious curiosity which may be left to the commentator as his exclusive concern; it affects our general conception of the historian's point of view, as well as his art, and no study of Thucydides can evade it.

The history falls into two parts. The first ends with the Fifty Years' Peace of 421 B.C., which at the time seemed to conclude the war and terminate the author's task. The second part is formally introduced by a personal explanation, in which Thucydides announces the continuation of his subject down to the capture of Athens in 404 B.C. He explains that though we may divide the whole period 431–404 B.C. into three parts—the first war of ten years, then seven years of hollow truce, and then a second war, — the truer view is that there was only one war lasting twenty-seven years, for the hollow truce was truly nothing less than war. This passage was written after 404 B.C. and naturally suggests that Thucydides had only recently recognised that the indecisive war which he had recorded was only a portion of a greater and decisive war, and had determined to extend the compass of his work to the whole twenty-seven years. On the other hand, his statements[3] seem to make it evident that during his banishment he had followed the course of events and travelled with a view to continuing his work. This continuation was prompted by the Athenian expedition to Sicily, and was intended to be the history of what then seemed to him a second war. I conclude then that there were three stages in his plan. After the Fifty Years' Peace of 421 B.C., his book was to be simply a history of the war of ten years. The course of the Sicilian expedition began a new war which he determined also to record, as a chronologically separate episode. Then the catastrophe of 404 B.C. set in a new light the significance of all that had happened since the original outbreak of hostilities in 431 B.C., and imparted to the whole series of events a unity of meaning which they would hardly have acquired if the struggle had been terminated in 404 B.C. not by the fall of Athens but by a second edition of the Fifty Years' Peace. Hence Thucydides rose to the larger conception of producing a history of the whole period of twenty-seven years.

Accordingly he found on his return to Athens that he had three things to do. He had to compose the history of the ambiguous interval between the Fifty Years' Peace and the Sicilian war. Secondly, he had to work up the rough copy and material of the last ten years. This was done[4] fully and triumphantly for the Sicilian episode, but of the rest we only possess the unrevised draft of the years 412 and 411, known as Book VIII., for which, perhaps in respect to its literary shape, and certainly in respect to its matter (by means of supplementary information procurable at Athens), much had to be done. In the third place, it was desirable and even necessary to make some additions and alterations in the original, completed but still unpublished, history of the first ten years, so as to bring it internally as well as externally into the light of the higher unity. This was a natural thought, and it appears to me the only hypothesis that explains the facts without constraint.[5]

§ 2. *His principles of historiography: accuracy and relevance*

In his Introduction Thucydides announces a new conception of historical writing. He sets up a new standard of truth or accurate reproduction of facts, and a new ideal of historical research; judged by which, he finds Herodotus and the Ionian historians wanting. He condemns them expressly for aiming at providing "good reading," as we should say, rather than facts, and for narrating stories, the truth of which cannot possibly be tested. He does not seek himself to furnish entertainment or to win a popular success, but to construct a record which shall be permanently valuable[6] because it is true. He warns his readers that they will find nothing mythical in his work. He saw, as we see, that the mythical element pervaded Herodotus (of whom, evidently, he was chiefly thinking) no less than Homer. His own experience in ascertaining *contemporary* facts taught him, as nothing else could do, how soon and how easily events are wont to pass into the borders of myth; he learned thereby the most effective lesson of scepticism in regard to historical tradition. It was indeed of inestimable importance for the future of history that Thucydides conceived the new idea of recording the war at its commencement. It made all the difference to his work that he formed the resolve in 431 B.C. and not after the war was over.

Writing the history of the present is always a very different thing from writing the history of the distant past. The history of the distant past depends entirely on literary and documentary sources; the history of the present always involves unwritten material as well as documents. But the difference was much greater in the days of Thucydides than it is now. To-day a writer sitting down to compose a history of his own time would depend mainly on written material, — on official reports, official documents of various kinds, and on the daily press. He would supplement this, so far as he could, by information derived personally from men of affairs, or by his own experience if he had witnessed or taken part in public events; but the main body of his work would depend on written sources. The ancient historian, on the contrary, in consequence of the comparative paucity of official reports and the absence of our modern organization for collecting and circulating news, would have to be his own journalist and do all the labour of obtaining facts orally from the most likely sources; and his success might largely depend on accidental facilities. His work would rest mainly on information obtained orally by his own inquiries, supplemented by such documents as were available, such as the texts of treaties or official instructions or letters; whereas the modern work is based principally on printed or written information, supplemented by such private information as may be accessible. It is clear that the ancient conditions made the historian's task more difficult, and demanded from him greater energy and initiative. Few things would be more interesting than a literary diary of Thucydides, telling of his interviews with his informants and showing his ways of collecting and sifting his material. But it was part of his artistic method to cover up all the traces of his procedure, in his finished narrative. He had to compare and criticize the various accounts he received of each transaction; but his literary art required that he should present the final conclusions of his research without indicating divergences of evidence. It is probable that he suppressed entirely details about which he could not satisfy himself. He was very chary of mentioning reports or allegations concerning which he felt in doubt; in the few cases in which he disclaims certainty we may suppose that he accepted the statement as probable.[7] He does not name his informants; nor does he even tell us on what occasions he was himself an eye-witness of what he describes. We may make guesses, but we can only speak with assurance of the operations which he conducted as strategos.

We are able, however, to gain a slight glimpse into the historian's workshop because some parts of his work have been left incomplete. The eighth Book is only a preliminary draft. In it we find accounts emanating from different informants, Athenian and Peloponnesian, written out so as to form a continuous narrative, yet containing contradictions as to matters of fact as well as differences in tendency. It is possible, for instance, to detect that some of the Peloponnesian informants were favourable to Astyochus the Lacedaemonian commander, and others were not. It is evident that we have material which has only been provisionally sifted. Again, the texts of the three successive treaties of alliance between Persia and Sparta are given *verbatim*,[8] and if we consider the transitory significance of the first two, it seems improbable that Thucydides intended to reproduce them *in extenso* in his final draft. They were material —material, according to a plausible conjecture, furnished by Alcibiades. These facts, and the unsatisfactory nature of the account of the oligarchic revolution, as compared with the finished portions of the work, confirm what the style and the absence of speeches had long ago suggested, that Book VIII. was a first draft which, if the writer had lived, would have appeared in a very different shape.

In the fifth Book it may also be shown that there was still revision to be done, though this section was in a more advanced state than Book VIII. Here we find a whole series of documentary texts. Now it was not in accordance with the artistic method of Thucydides, or of ancient historians in general, to introduce into the narrative matter heterogeneous in style; and it is almost incredible that he would have admitted texts not written in Attic Greek. We must, I think, conclude that we have here material which was to be wrought in during a final revision.

In the finished part of the history we can sometimes penetrate to the source of information. It is easy to see that he consulted Plataeans as to the siege of Plataea, and that he received information from Spartans as well as from Athenians about the episode of Pylos and Sphacteria. We can sometimes divine that he has derived his statements from the official instructions given to military commanders; and it has been acutely shown that his enumeration of the allies of the two opposing powers at the beginning of the war was based on the instrument of the Thirty Years' Peace.[9] Sometimes the formulae of decrees or treaties peer through the Thucydidean summary.[10]

We have then to take the finished product, which Thucydides furnishes, on trust. We have not any considerable body of independent evidence for testing his accuracy, but so far as we can test it by the chance testimonies of original documents, he comes out triumphantly (in those parts which he completed), and there can be no question that the stress which he laid on accuracy was not a phrase.[11] The serious criticisms which can be brought against him in regard to facts concern not what he states but what he omits to state. For instance, the important measure which Athens adopted in 424 B.C. of raising the tribute of the subject states is passed over entirely, though it is a pertinent fact in the story of the war; we have learned it in recent years by the discovery of parts of the stone decree. We cannot discern his reasons for recounting some passages of military history at great length and passing over others (such as the attempt of Pericles on Epidaurus) with a bare mention. But in other cases his silence is a judgment. He rejects, for instance, by ignoring, the connexion which the gossip of the Athenian streets alleged between the private life of Pericles and the origin of the war. But it must be allowed in general that, in omitting, Thucydides displays a boldness and masterfulness on which no modern historian would venture.[12]

His omissions are closely connected with a general feature of his work. If the first fundamental principle of his ideal of history was accuracy, the second was relevance; and both signify his rebound from Herodotus. Discursiveness as we saw was the very life-breath of the epic history of Herodotus; the comprehensiveness of the Ionian idea of history enabled him to spread about through a wide range, to string on tale to tale, to pile digression on digression, artfully, yet as loosely as the structure of his Ionic prose. Thucydides conceived the notion of political history, and he laid down for himself a strict principle of exclusion. His subject is the war, and he will not take advantage of opportunities to digress into the history of culture. He excludes geography, so far as brief notices are not immediately necessary for the explanation of the events recorded. He disdains personal gossip and anecdotes; he had no use for the spicy memoirs of Ion and Stesimbrotus. He rigidly abstains from dropping any information about the private life of Pericles, Cleon, or any other politician; and the exception which he makes in the case of Alcibiades only serves to show the reason for the rule; because those sides of the life of Alcibiades which Thucydides notices had, in his view, distinct political consequences in determining the attitude of the Athenians towards him. Further, he excludes the internal history of the states with whose political inter-relations he is concerned, except when the internal affected directly, or was bound up with, the external, as in the case of the plague and of the domestic seditions. He does not give any information about the political parties at Athens, though some of his statements imply their existence, till he comes to the oligarchical revolution. His outlook, as Wilamowitz has observed, is not bounded by the Pnyx, but by the Empire.

There are, of course, digressions in Thucydides, but with hardly an exception they are either closely relevant or introduced for some special purpose.

The history of the growth of the Athenian empire is in form an excursus; but we might fairly say that it properly belongs to the prolegomena; it is distinctly relevant to the subject of the book, and had the special purpose of supplementing and correcting Hellanicus. The digression on the fortunes of Pausanias is also a relevant, though certainly not necessary, explanation of the Athenian demand that the Lacedaemonians should expel a pollution; but the account, which follows, of the later career of Themistocles is wholly unconnected with the Peloponnesian war. I will however show hereafter that the author had a special motive in introducing it. The valuable chapter on early Athens, with its archaeological evidence,[13] is strictly to the point, for its purpose is to illustrate the historian's acute remark that the distress of the country people at coming to live in the city was due to habits derived from the early history of Attica. A sketch of the early history of Sicily was almost indispensable for the elucidation of the narrative; a knowledge of the island and its cities could not be taken for granted in the Athenian public. The description of the Odrysean kingdom of Sitalces[14] was unquestionably due to the author's personal interest in Thrace; but it had the object of suggesting a contrast between the power and resources of Thrace and Scythia with those of the Greek states.

The story of the fall of the Athenian tyrants (in Book vi.), which is an excursus in the true sense of the word, was introduced to correct popular errors. The other passage in which Thucydides seems for a moment non-Thucydidean is where he sketches the history of the fair of Delos, quotes from a Homeric hymn, and deviates into the history of culture. I cannot help suspecting that here too he is correcting some current misapprehension. If he may legitimately be criticized for turning aside from his subject to correct errors which may seem trivial enough, and if he is sometimes reprimanded for having elsewhere captiously noted a couple of small blunders in Herodotus, it must be remembered that it was of importance to illustrate his doctrine that tradition cannot be taken on trust, and that the facile methods of current historiography inevitably led to inaccuracy.

The digressions then in Thucydides which can fairly be called digressions are different in character from the digressions and amplitudes of Herodotus. The critic Dionysius considered it a point of inferiority in Thucydides, as compared with Herodotus, that he pursued his subject steadily and kept to his argument, without pausing by the way and providing his readers with variety; and he supposed that in "the two or three places" where the historian did digress, his motive was to relieve the narrative by a pleasant pause. The criticism would have been more elucidating if Dionysius had pointed out that, while Herodotus was influenced by the epic, the artistic method of Thucydides must rather be compared with that of the drama. Thucydides adheres as closely to his argument as a tragic poet, and such variety as was secured in tragedy by the interjection of choral odes, he obtains by the speeches which he intersperses in the narrative. His first consideration was accuracy; he had to follow events and not to mould them into correspondence with an artistic plan, and his strict chronological order excluded devices of arrangement. But occasionally we can detect deliberate management for the sake of a calculated effect. It may be pointed out that the long section on the origin and growth of the Athenian empire, placed where it is, between the two Assemblies at Sparta, has the effect of interrupting a series of speeches which coming together would have been excessively long. Again, it has been well shown by Wilamowitz-Möllendorff how the delays of Archidamus, in the first invasion of Attica, in the hope that Athens might give in at the last moment, are reflected in the form of the narrative, which is arranged to produce the impression of a slow and halting march; and the archaeological deviation into the early history of Athens has the value of assisting in this artistic effect.

§ 3. *Modern criticisms on his competence*

In common with other ancient historians, Thucydides may be taken to task for not having recognised the part played in human affairs by economic facts and commercial interests. That he was not blind to economic conditions is shown by the leading significance he attributes to want of material resources in the early Greek communities; and he fully realises the importance of finance. But it may be said that he should have furnished a detailed explanation and analysis of the commercial basis on which the Athenian power rested, and of the mercantile interests of other states which were affected and endangered by her empire. It is however only in quite recent times that economical and commercial factors in historical development have begun to receive their due, and, perhaps it may be said, rather more than their due. They have come so much to the front that some writers are tempted to explain all historical phenomena by economic causes. This illustrates how the tendencies of the present react upon our conceptions of the past. These factors, of such immense importance in the present age, certainly did not play anything like the same part in the ancient world, and if the ancient historians considerably underrated them, we may easily fall into the error of overrating them. We may be sure that the interests of Athens presented themselves to statesmen, as to Thucydides, primarily under the political, and not the economical, point of view. Thucydides created political history; economic history is a discovery of the nineteenth century.

Perhaps the gravest accusation which has been brought against the competency of Thucydides is that he misunderstood, if he did not intentionally misrepresent, the causes of the Peloponnesian war. The charge has been formulated and pressed in different ways by a German and by an English scholar.[15] Their indictments do not appear to me to be successful. The historian's account, which can only be refuted by proofs of internal discrepancy or of insufficiency, seems to be both consistent and, with certain reserves, adequate.

It will not be amiss to make a preliminary observation on two words which Thucydides uses in the sense of cause — αἰτία and πρόφασις. αἰτία has almost the same history as the Latin equivalent, caussa. Its proper sense was "grievance" or "ground of blame," "charge," and in Thucydides it generally[16] either means this or, even when we can most appropriately translate it by cause, implies a charge or imputation. πρόφασις is an alleged reason, which may be either true or false; ultimately it became virtually restricted to a false or minor reason, and so equivalent to "pretext." In Thucydides it is not so restricted; he employs it in both ways. And from meaning an alleged reason, it is evident how easily it could come to mean a reason, whether alleged or not; in other words, a "motive" or an "occasion," so that here it approximated very closely to the sense of "cause." This various use of the word does not imply any confusion of thought; we use the word "reason" with similar elasticity; the context decides the sense.

When a war breaks out, there are two things to be explained which must be kept distinct: why the aggressors go to war at all, and why they go to war at the time they actually do. This distinction is crucial, for instance, in the case of the outbreak of the Franco-Prussian war of 1870. In some cases, the answer to both questions is the same; there may be no reason for the war, beyond the particular circumstances which lead immediately to its declaration. In the case of the Peloponnesian war, Thucydides is careful to insist that this was not so. There was a permanent motive for hostility, of such a kind that war, sooner or later, might be counted on as a certainty; there were also particular transactions which determined its actual outbreak at a particular moment. When the Lacedaemonians took steps to break the peace, of course they did not mention the permanent and really impelling motive, namely, jealousy of Athenian aggrandisement, but rested their declaration on certain recent actions on the part of Athens. Thucydides puts it thus: "The true motive (πρόφασις), though it was not expressed in words, I consider to have been the fear which the growth of the Athenian power caused to the Lacedaemonians; but the publicly alleged grounds of complaint (αἰτία) which provoked the war I will proceed to explain," and he enters upon the stories of Corcyra and Potidaea. Thucydides accepted the convictions expressed both by the Corcyraean ambassador in his speech at Athens and by Pericles that a war was unavoidable, and that it was merely a question how long it might be postponed; and we certainly cannot prove that this judgment was wrong.

The distinction then between the real motive of the Lacedaemonians, in the absence of which they would not have declared war, and the particular actions which brought matters to a head and determined the beginning of a war at a certain date, is perfectly clear and valid. The further question can be raised, whether in his account of the affairs which moved the

Peloponnesian alliance to hostile action at a given moment, Thucydides estimated rightly their proportional gravity. The charge is that he has not given its due importance to the Megarian business, whether failing to realise its meaning, or deliberately keeping it in the background in order to devolve the responsibility for the war from the shoulders of Pericles who was responsible for the Megarian policy. The second insinuation I need not consider; for I will show hereafter (in the next Lecture) that the historian's attitude to Pericles and his policy is detached. I will only observe here that if he had wished to shield that statesman from the alleged responsibility, it was clumsy of him not to suppress or explain away the fact that in the final negotiations the Lacedaemonians made Megara the test-question, and said they would be satisfied if Athens yielded on that point.

This ultimatum of the Lacedaemonians may indeed appear, at first sight, inconsistent with the subordinate rôle which the Megarian grievance plays in the historian's narrative of the circumstances which led to the war; and it has been urged that instead of keeping it in the background he ought to have assigned it the most prominent place in the foreground. But a careful examination will show, I think, that the narrative is completely consistent, and embodies a closely reasoned account of the causes and motives at work.

The most casual reader receives the unmistakable impression that the Corinthians were the prime instigators of the war, driving the Lacedaemonians into action. The two affairs in which their interests were exclusively involved, the affair of Corcyra and the affair of Potidaea, are those which the author designates as the direct occasion of the war; and the leading part taken by Corinth is emphasized by the reproduction of two Corinthian speeches, voicing Peloponnesian dissatisfaction. If the deepest concern of Corinth was the action which Athens had taken in regard to Megara by excluding her from the markets of the Athenian empire, and thereby threatening her with economic ruin, then it must be allowed that Thucydides was entirely misinformed. In their speeches at Sparta, the Corinthian envoys do not mention the Megarian name, and the author expressly states that their eagerness to have war declared immediately was due to their anxiety for Potidaea. Can we discover any proof as to the real interest of Corinth in the Megarian question?

When the Corcyraean affair occurred, Corinth was so far from being anxious for war that she did all she could to secure the goodwill and neutrality of Athens. And she did not come with her hands empty. She did not merely urge her claims on Athenian gratitude for past services. She proposed a deal (433 B.C.). Some time before this, Athens had already initiated new designs on Megara by a decree excluding Megarian wares from Athens itself. Corinth now said to her in effect: Leave us a free hand in dealing with Corcyra, and we will leave you a free hand in dealing with Megara. The Corinthian ambassador put this diplomatically, at least in his speech before the popular Assembly.[17] He did not say: You have improper designs on Megara, and we will connive. He said: Your conduct in regard to Megara has been open to suspicion; you can allay these suspicions by doing what we ask. It came to the same thing.

This proposition on the part of Corinth shows that in her eyes the independence of Megara was not of crucial importance. Her interests there weighed much less than her interests elsewhere. It was the alliance of Athens with Corcyra, followed by the affair of Potidaea, that determined the collision of Corinth with Athens, and it was this collision that precipitated a war which would in any case have come later. The Megarian decrees did not determine the action of Corinth, and it was Corinth's action which was decisive. On the other hand, once war was decided on by Corinth and the war-party at Sparta, the grievance of Megara formed an imposing item in the list of Peloponnesian complaints and the general indictment of Athenian policy. In this indictment, the alliance of Athens with Corcyra, though it had been the first of the effective causes which led to the war, could not appear at all; it could not be represented as either illegal or immoral. The attack on Potidaea could form a count; but it arose out of a complicated situation, and a great deal could be said on both sides. It was therefore an obvious stroke of diplomatic tactics to move the Megarian question into the foremost place, and represent the cruelty of Athens to Megara as the principal of her offences. The Lacedaemonians said: Yield on this question and there will be no war. It was a demand which no proud state, in the position of Athens, could have granted, and concession would have been simply an invitation for further commands. The reply was: We deny your right to dictate; but we are perfectly willing to submit all your complaints to arbitration in accordance with the instrument of the Thirty Years' Peace.

This is a perfectly consistent and intelligible account of the origin of the war; is there any reason for supposing that it is not true? The only positive evidence to which an appeal can be made for rejecting it is that of Aristophanes, who attributes the outbreak to the second Megarian decree. This was the natural, superficial view, on account of the prominence which had been given to that decree in the final negotiation; and it is not inconsistent with the Thucydidean account, in so far as that, if Athens had yielded, the war might have been avoided, or rather postponed. Further: in evaluating the statement of the comic poet, which doubtless reflected the current opinion of the Athenian market-place, we must not leave out of account the Athenian feeling against the war a year or so after it had broken out, a feeling which sought to lay the entire blame on Pericles and wove legends round the Megarian decree.[18] But the popular opinion, expressed by Aristophanes, does not really contradict the causal perspective of Thucydides. It was precisely the notion which in the given circumstances was most likely to be left in the popular mind, if the occurrences were such as Thucydides represents them.

There is another consideration which must not be neglected. Unless we hold the doctrine that all the speeches are entirely free inventions of his own, as purely Thucydidean throughout in argument as they are in style, — a doctrine which is untenable in face of his express statement, — and that he adapted the speeches of the first Book to a preconceived construction of his own, the speeches were a most important part of his material for forming his conclusion as to the causes and motives of the war. He probably heard those delivered at Athens; he was informed of the tenor or heads of those delivered at Sparta; and he has reproduced the drift of these important pieces of evidence. Both in what they say, and in what they do not say, they bear out the justice of his construction and his perspective.

It is a distinct question, What were the guiding motives of the Athenian policy in regard to Megara? Thucydides does not consider it, because it did not seem to him to have determined the outbreak of the war, and was therefore, in a narrow sense, irrelevant; a modern historian would not venture to treat it in this way. The object of Athens was undoubtedly to recover control of the Megarid which she had in recent times won and lost; and, to do this without violating the Thirty Years' Peace, she resorted to economical pressure which would starve her neighbour into voluntary submission. Megara had a double value. Her control would give Athens the power of blocking the land route between the Peloponnesus and Boeotia, and would also secure to her a direct access to the Corinthian Gulf, for her commerce or her troops.[19] We cannot say which of these consequences of the geographical position of Megara counted more with Athenian statesmen, in their unarmed aggression against a neighbour with whom their relations had long been unfriendly; whether they were actuated rather by the "long view" of the use of a port on the Corinthian Gulf, for adding a western to their eastern empire, or by the more obvious view of erecting a barrier against the Peloponnesus. At Sparta, we may be sure, it was the second danger which would create more alarm. But however this may be, there is nothing to show that if there had been no affair of Corcyra and no affair of Potidaea, the Megarian question by itself would have caused the outbreak of the war at the time.

But the criticism to which Thucydides has been exposed illustrates the disadvantages of his method, when it is pressed too far. His principle is to mention only effective policies, and to mention them for the first time when they begin to become effective.

If Megara was a pawn in Athenian schemes of aggrandisement in western Greece, it was never moved; and in saying nothing of this aspect of the Megarian question, the historian is true to his method. If, in 433 B.C. or before, some Athenian politicians had their eyes on Sicily and Italy, the policy had no results till 427 B.C., and therefore in passing over with a bare mention the fact that Athens, in accepting the Corcyraean proposals in 433 B.C., recognised Italy and Sicily as within the range of her interests, he is again true to his method.

§ 4. *His treatment of non-contemporary history*

Thucydides not only showed Greece how contemporary history should be studied and recorded; he also gave a specimen of a new way of handling the history of past ages. He prefixed to his work a general sketch of the history of Hellas which Dionysius of Halicarnassus, who by no means appreciated its merits, justly described as equivalent to an independent work. This sketch is amazing in its power and insight. We must remember that it is confined strictly to one side of the historical development. It is intended to answer a definite question: how it was that before quite recent times no large and powerful state had arisen in Greece; and to explain the small scale of the military and political enterprises of the past. It does not touch on constitutional history at all, and the "period of the tyrants" is only emphasized because their non-aggressive policy was a relevant point in the exposition. Within the limits to which it strictly adheres, this outline is a most closely reasoned argument and was the revelation of a totally new way of treating history. We cannot endorse it all; and of the Homeric and pre-Homeric civilisation in Greece we have come to know within the last thirty years more than Thucydides could discover. But criticism of details is not to the point; his sketch remains a shining example of sheer historical insight and grasp. Rising with easy mastery over the mass of legends and details which constituted the ill-ordered store of Greek tradition, he constructs a reasoned march of development, furnishing the proofs of his conclusions. He draws broad lines of historical growth, elicits general and essential facts from the multitude of particulars, and characterizes periods by their salient features. He calls attention to the importance of considering conditions of culture, and suggests the text for a history of Greek civilisation. He turns the daylight of material conditions on the mythical period, and discovers in the want of resources the key to certain sides of the development of Hellas.

He accepts, of course, like Herodotus and every one else, the actual existence of heroes such as Pelops, Agamemnon, Minos, for whom the genealogies seemed to vouch.[20] He did not question the fact of the Trojan war; but he inferred that such a fact meant the eminence of a leading state in Greece at the time, and showed that an examination of the traditions about it pointed to a general lack of resources. He accepted Minos; and his instinct in emphasizing the Cretan thalassocracy seems to be justified by the recent discoveries in Crete. When he comes to a later time, he seizes with a sure eye as the greatest and most important fact of the two centuries before the Persian war the revival of nautical powers and the growth of navies.

In his acute arguments he employs methods which may be called modern. For instance, he points to the culture of backward parts of Greece as a survival of a culture which at one time in the past prevailed generally. He quotes Homer as a witness for the conditions of his own age without any reserve; but when he quotes him in evidence for facts about the Trojan war, he adds a clause of caution. His proof of a Carian population in the islands is not literary but archaeological—Carian tombs which were discovered in his own day when Delos was purified.

The outline of the growth of the Athenian empire after the Persian wars is an exercise of a different kind. No history of this period existed except what was furnished by the brief chronicle of Hellanicus. The account of Thucydides is an original contribution and embodies the results of his own inquiries. He comments on the work of Hellanicus, noticing its inadequacy and alleging that it was chronologically inaccurate. Hellanicus, as we saw, found a place for every event in an archon year, and I gave an instance of the errors into which he fell through pretending to know too much. Thucydides gives no absolute dates and very few chronological indications of any kind. It looks at first sight as if Hellanicus might have retorted on Thucydides that he had a curious notion of chronological precision. But the point of the Thucydidean criticism was just this, that there were no certain or sufficient data for such precision, and that the chronological exactness of Hellanicus was an illusion. We may suspect further that in the order in which he placed some of the events, he corrected his predecessor. How far his corrections, for which he must have relied on the memories of older men, were right, we cannot say. But in any case, here too, he gave his contemporaries a salutary lesson in scepticism. He pointedly abstains from referring at all to the archon years.[21] In his view the archon years, which ran from July to July, were inconvenient and unsuitable for a chronicle of military events, and liable to lead to serious inaccuracies. For this reason he based his own military history on the natural division of the year into summer and winter. That strict chronology was indispensable for accurate history, Thucydides was fully convinced. He proved it by casting his own work into the form of annals. He was an artist, and he could not have failed to see as clearly as his critics (like Dionysius of Halicarnassus) that the annalistic frame was an awkward impediment to any plan of artistic construction. The two claims of chronological accuracy and a pleasing literary arrangement are not irreconcilable, as other historians, like Gibbon, have shown; but Thucydides did not attempt to combine them, and it was characteristic that he should have preferred the demand of historical precision to the exigencies of literary art. His artistic powers were displayed not in the architecture of his work, but in a certain dramatic mode of treatment which will be considered in the next lecture.

LECTURE IV

THUCYDIDES (CONTINUED)

§ 1. *The Speeches*

THE historian has to do more than chronicle events. It is his business to show why things happened and to discover the forces which were at work. In order to understand the meaning of historical facts, he has to measure the characters and penetrate the motives of the actors, as well as to realise the conditions in which they acted. A psychological reconstruction is thus always involved in history, a reconstruction carried out in the mind of the individual historian, and necessarily affected by his personal temperament and his psychological ability. Some one has said that a writer who could draw a perfectly true and adequate portrait of Napoleon's complex character would be a man whose own soul was a counterpart of Napoleon's. This of course is an extreme way of putting the case, for there is such a thing as psychological imagination. But the subjective process can never be eliminated. It has different aspects in the cases of contemporary and non-contemporary historians. The contemporary historian lives in the same milieu, in the same sphere of ideas, and thus has more points of common sympathy with the political actors of his time; but, on the other hand, he cannot generally avoid the bias of personal views of his own. The historian of a past epoch may hope to be more impartial, but he cannot hope to divest himself, beyond a certain point, of the standards and measures of his own age; they are inwoven in the tissue of his mind and they must affect his attempts to reconstruct the past.

Thucydides has concealed this inevitable subjective element by his dramatic method. The persons who play leading parts in the public affairs which he relates reveal their characters and personalities, so far as is required, by their actions and speeches. The author, like a dramatist, remains in the background, only sometimes coming forward to introduce them with a description as brief as in a playbill, or to indicate what men thought about them or the impression they made on their contemporaries. His rule is to commit himself to no personal judgments, and to this rule there are very few exceptions.

The characters of some of the political personages are partly indicated in the speeches, of which I must now speak. They are an essential feature of the Thucydidean art. Herodotus had set the example, but Thucydides used speeches for different purposes and on a different scale, and adapted them to a different method. He states explicitly how the speeches are to be taken and what they represent. In some cases he heard speeches delivered, but it was impossible for him to remember them accurately; and in other cases he had to depend on the oral reports of others. His general rule was to take the general drift and intention of the speaker, and from this text compose what he might probably have said. It is clear that this principle gave great latitude to the author, and that the resemblances of the Thucydidean speeches to those actually spoken must have varied widely according to his information. They are all distinctly Thucydidean in style, just as the various characters in a play of Euripides all use similar diction. Homogeneity in style was a canon of most ancient men of letters; they shrank from introducing lengthy quotations or inserting the *ipsissima verba* of documents. Occasionally Thucydides has probably indicated personal mannerisms. For instance, in a speech of Alcibiades there are one or two expressions which are intended to suggest his characteristically "forcible" style.[1] But this has been done with great reserve. Thucydides in his portraiture does not depend on mannerisms. The speeches of Pericles produce the effect of the lofty earnestness of a patriotic statesman who is somewhat of an idealist; the speech of Cleon is that of a bullying pedagogue. But the diction is the same. So in Aeschylus, the nurse maunders, though she speaks Aeschylean; and the *naïveté* of the policeman in Sophocles is sufficiently revealed though he does not speak a policeman's language.

But though Thucydides is always Thucydides, yet within the compass of his style there are remarkable variations. It is outside my scope to enter upon this subject in any detail; to do justice to the styles of the writers who come before us would require another set of lectures. But in the case of Thucydides, I suspect that his different styles have a certain meaning for the treatment of his subject. It is patent to any reader that there is a difference between the narrative and the speeches, and that there are marked differences in the speeches themselves. Obscurity is a reproach which has constantly been brought against him and of which he cannot be acquitted. But it is not true of his work as a whole. The narrative is generally clear and straightforward. If it stood alone, we should never dream of describing him as obscure. Nor is this description true of the speeches indiscriminately. Some are lucid and simple; others excessively obscure; in others again we have perfectly simple passages beside sections which, with Dionysius, we may designate as conundrums or as darker than dark sayings of Heracleitus.[2] I have taken obscurity and difficulty—difficulty which the Greeks felt no less than we— as a rough test of distinction. But on what does this difficulty depend? It depends on stylistic technique. There is no doubt that Thucydides was influenced by the rhetorical school of Gorgias, though he was not dominated by it. He modified it by peculiarities of his own; but the affinity is unmistakably shown in the artificial balancing of clauses, the artificial verbal antitheses, the poetical phrase. Generally he keeps this tendency well in hand, but in some passages he deliberately allows it to run riot, and then he becomes obscure because the grammatical constructions have to be twisted unnaturally to subserve verbal effects. Some of these crooked passages produced upon a Greek ear almost the effect of dithyrambs released from the bonds of metre. Dionysius in his instructive criticism takes two passages as conspicuous for this fault (as he considered it), — the dialogue of the Athenian and Melian diplomatists, and the reflexions upon the psychological and social aspects of civil sedition. Both might be described as elaborate studies in this kind of technique — the "obscure and contorted style." It is unnecessary, nor have I time, to illustrate it at length, but I will give one brief example. It is said in the Funeral Oration of Pericles, about soldiers who had fallen in battle: οἷς ἐνευδαιμονῆσαί τε ὁ βίος ὁμοίως καὶ ἐντελευτῆσαι ξυνεμετρήθη.[3] To express the meaning in tolerable English we have to render somewhat like this: "Whose days were so measured that the term of their happiness was also the term of their life." But this is a paraphrase, and it does not give the effect of the Greek. The literal translation is: "For whom life was made commensurate, to be happy in and to die in, alike." (Even this fails to bring out the force of the aorist tense ἐνευδαιμονῆσαί which suggests the familiar Greek saying, that a man's life cannot be judged happy till after his death.) But if the English is obscure and intolerable, to a Greek ear, such as that of Dionysius, the Greek was hardly less so.

Now is there any significance in this remarkable variation in style? Is it purely capricious? Does Thucydides break into dithyrambic prose just when, and simply because, he is in the mood? Such caprice would not be artistic, and it would not be Greek. If the difference in style corresponded to the distinction between narrative and speeches, the explanation would be ready. The speeches, in any case, serve the artistic purpose of pauses in the action; they introduce the variety which Herodotus secured by digressions; they fulfil somewhat the function of choruses in the drama. And so we should not be surprised to find a corresponding variety in the diction and technique. But the difference in style extends into the speeches themselves.

The explanation which I would submit to you is that when Thucydides adopts what we may fairly call his unnatural style, when he is involved and obscure, he is always making points of his own. In support of this view, I allege the following considerations. (1) The meditation on the party - struggles in Greek states, though not a speech, belongs to this category. It interrupts the action; it is, in fact, a speech of the author. And it is one of the flagrant examples of the unnatural style, and is commented on, as such, by Dionysius. Here then the author undisguisedly adopts this style for his own reflexions. (2) Secondly, take the Melian dialogue. Now whether we think, as some do, that such a conference was never held, or believe—and this is my opinion— that it was held, all agree that the actual conversation is in the main fictitious. I will return to this dialogue in another connexion. I would point out now that it is a clear case in which the unnatural style is employed for a political study of the author. Contrast it, as Dionysius contrasts it, with another dialogue, that between Archidamus and the Plataeans. This is in the natural style, and obviously gives the simple tenor of what passed on the occasion. (3) My third proof lies in the contrast between two of the speeches of Pericles. The speech he delivered before the war is so lucid and straightforward in style as to have satisfied Dionysius; and at the same time it is perfectly appropriate to the situation, and no doubt gives the general drift of the Periclean argument. On the other hand, the speech which he delivers in self-defence, when he became unpopular, is marked in part by those obscurities which excited the censure of Dionysius, and is also distinguished by unsuitable statements which could not have been addressed by any statesman to a public whose favour he desired to recover.[4]

I infer that when Thucydides writes in the unnatural style, he intends the reader to understand that he has here to do with the author himself—that the author is making points. When he writes in the natural style, he is producing documentary evidence. The speech of Pericles on the eve of the war is virtually a document.

Let me make an application of this inference, which I think has some interest. The *Epitaphios* of Pericles is composed on the whole in the unnatural style.[5] It enshrines, as I believe, some utterances of Pericles himself; but the style is generally contorted and obscure, though we forgive, or may even find a certain pleasure in, this, so lofty is the spirit and so fine the thoughts. Now it is to be noted that, unlike other speeches, this funeral address does not cast any direct light on the events of the war, and that its tone is out of keeping with the occasion.[6] There was no great action, no conspicuous deed of valour, in the first year of the war, yet this oration over the Athenians who fell in it is pitched in a key which would be appropriate to the burial of the heroes of a Thermopylae. My view is that Thucydides has seized this occasion to turn the light on Pericles himself. The Athens which Pericles here depicts is an ideal; and the purpose of the historian is to bring out the fact that he was an idealist. The very incongruity between the occasion and the high-pitched strain of the orator heightens the calculated impression that Pericles, along with his political wisdom, possessed an imagination which outranged realities.

If you were asked to translate into ancient Greek "he is an idealist," you could not, I think, find a more exact equivalent than ζητεῖ ἄλλο τι, ὡς ἔπος εἰπεῖν, ἢ ἐνυ οἷς ζῶμεν. This expression is applied by Cleon (in his speech about Mytilene[7]) to the Athenians in general, to whom it was hardly appropriate; it was, I take it, a covert hit at the *ethos* and character of Pericles. Now both this speech of Cleon and the counter-speech of Diodotus are, by my criterion, largely composed of matter which is purely Thucydidean. The speech of Diodotus contains, you remember, reflexions on the general theory of punishment—the earliest discussion of the subject in literature; and we know from other evidence that this was a question which had a special interest for Pericles. I venture therefore to think that one of the points which Thucydides wishes to make in these speeches is, that the more lenient treatment of the rebels of Mytilene was in accordance with the *spirit* of Periclean policy. With the spirit; but it might have been argued that it was not in accordance with the letter and the logic; and this, I think, is one of the points which Cleon's speech is intended to suggest. It is notable that while the speaker makes, as I think, an oblique hit at Periclean idealism, and strikes an anti-Periclean note in his dispraise of knowledge and criticism, at the same time he iterates phrases which occur in the Periclean speeches: "Empire means tyranny"; "Do not play the virtuous." Thucydides is here studying not only the contrast between the two politicians, but also the difficulties inherent in the Periclean imperialism.

§ 2. *Dramatic treatment of the* historiae personae

The speeches in general served two purposes. In the first place they were used by the author to explain the facts and elements of a situation, as well as underlying motives and ideas. In some cases the speech was only a dramatic disguise of a study of his own. Thus, the characters of the two protagonist cities, Athens and Sparta, are delineated in a speech of a third party, the Corinthians: the author of this famous comparison was unquestionably Thucydides himself. But in other cases he uses the actual expositions of politicians,—genuine political documents so far as the main tenor went,—as the most useful means of explaining a situation. The comparative advantages of the two contending powers for the coming war are stated in two speeches from opposite points of view.[8] The prospects and difficulties of the Sicilian expedition are set forth by the same means.

The speeches had the second function—and here I return to the point from which I set out—of serving the objective dramatic method of indicating character which Thucydides chose to adopt.[9] The speeches of Pericles, Cleon, Brasidas, Nicias, and Alcibiades, taken in conjunction with their actions, reveal as much of their characters as seemed to the author necessary for the matter in hand; that is, those sides of their nature which in his opinion governed their public actions or affected their political influence. The general plan was that the men, as well as the events, should speak or be made to speak for themselves, with little or no direct comment from the writer.

This method produced the illusion that the actors showed themselves to the reader independently of the author. It really meant that the author had framed a psychological estimate of them, as a dramatist constructs his characters: an estimate founded on his knowledge of their actions, but nevertheless no more than his own subjective interpretation. The reader is here almost as completely in the author's hands as in a drama. He has not the means of forming a corrective judgment for himself; for he does not know how the historian has arrived at his results.

The application of the method may be observed in the cases of Cleon and Nicias. Thucydides held a distinct view of the character of Cleon as a politician. He allows us to see it reflected from Cleon's actions and from the opinions of people about him. When he describes Cleon as an influential leader of the demos, who was very violent, namely in manner and speech, he only states a fact which was undoubtedly notorious and admitted. The oration of Cleon on the Lesbian question exhibits his fashion of rating the people like a pedagogue. The drastic judgment that, if Cleon's command at Pylos ended in disaster, this would be a great blessing, for it would rid the city of Cleon, is not recorded as the historian's own sarcasm; it is mentioned as the opinion of some people at Athens. But as the people who thought so are called "sensible" (σώφρονες), the disguise is here very thin; the writer permits his own assent to be visible. No reader of the scenes in which Cleon appears would be left in any doubt that Cleon in the author's estimation was a pestilent demagogue; but in one passage[10] Thucydides entirely abandons his dramatic reserve and ascribes the worst motives to the politician for his unwillingness to bring the war to a close.

The portrait of Nicias, the conscientious patriot, an embodiment of respectability, cautious and experienced, but unendowed with first-rate talent, afraid of responsibility, afraid of the Ecclesia, is perhaps the most successful achievement of Thucydides in dramatic art. All this comes out in his actions and speeches. But in this case too the author once comes forward himself and directly construes the motives which actuated Nicias in working in the interests of peace. They were of a selfish nature: he thought of his own reputation; he desired "while he had suffered no reverses and was held in repute, to preserve his good fortune; he wished for rest himself as well as to give the people rest; he hoped to leave his name to posterity as of one who had never brought calamity on the city; and he thought that the best means to secure this was to trust as little as possible to fortune and to keep out of danger, which would be avoided by peace."[11] The irony is unmistakable. Again, in the last scene, when Nicias has been executed at Syracuse, the historian appears before the curtain for a moment and pronounces an epitaph, the point of which posterity has frequently misunderstood. It is generally taken as an encomium; it is really *malice*. In my opinion, says Thucydides, Nicias deserved such an end less than any other Athenian, considering his conventional virtue.[12] In other words, a man of such conventional virtue was unsuited for such an unconventional end. That is irony of a kind in which Thucydides rarely indulges; behind it lurks the suppressed judgment that Athens was unfortunate in the trust which she reposed in Nicias, the model of irreproachable respectability.

In the case of Alcibiades the historian dwells on the extravagance and display of his private life, because they had a direct influence on the feelings of the Athenians towards him, and affected his public career and the course of the war. But here too the character is revealed in actions and words; insolence and ambition come out in his orations, and, as I have already observed, some strong phrases seem to be characteristic of his manner. Thucydides refrains from commenting on his character, but points out his services and shows that the Athenians regarded him with a suspicious apprehension which prevented them from profiting by his ability.

In the cases of Themistocles, Pericles, and Antiphon, the author departs from his usual practice, and gives characterising judgments of his own. In the case of Themistocles this might be considered a necessary exception, as he does not come into the main narrative and cannot reveal himself dramatically. The same reason might be held partly to apply to Pericles, since the greater part of his lifework was over when he comes on the stage. The favourable notice of Antiphon's ability might also be explained by the fact that he had hardly appeared in the political arena before the year of the revolution, and his appearance then was so brief. The eulogy on Antiphon indeed has a personal note, which betrays perhaps a friendship. It is, however, futile to seek to explain or explain away these exceptions. The truth is that in general Thucydides is dramatic, but he has not carried his method to extremes.

It is noteworthy that nearly all the judgments which he pronounces concern intelligence and political ability. This is the case with Themistocles, Pericles, Antiphon, Theramenes, and Hermocrates. They all receive greater or less praise for political capacity, which in the case of Themistocles is said to have amounted to genius.

The case of Hyperbolus demands a few words, because it illustrates the method of Thucydides and his political leanings. In the years between the Fifty Years' Peace and the Sicilian Expedition, the division of parties under the opposing leaders Nicias and Alcibiades paralysed the foreign policy of Athens and hindered continuity of action. The situation was so serious that the only way out seemed that proposed by the demagogue Hyperbolus — a trial of ostracism, which would expel one of the rivals and secure unity. Alcibiades frustrated this device by combining, if not with his rival, at least with a sufficiently large oligarchical faction, to procure the ostracism of Hyperbolus. Thucydides does not say a word about this affair, though of course he was perfectly aware of the facts, and though they had an immediate bearing on the foreign policy of Athens. We must suppose that as the purpose of the ostracism was defeated and the relative positions of the two leaders were not altered by the vote, he considered it superfluous to record the occurrence. It will be admitted, however, that a modern historian who allowed himself such an omission or carried his principle of exclusion so far, would not escape censorious criticism. But in another connexion, Thucydides refers to the ostracism, without dating it, or in any way suggesting its significance. Hyperbolus was killed in 411 B.C. at Samos. Thucydides records this and mentions that Hyperbolus had been ostracized. This is the only place where he names the demagogue, who in the years following Cleon's death had been one of the most influential speakers in the Ecclesia. We might suspect that in ignoring this politician, just as he ignored men of the same type like Eucrates and Lysicles, he exercised a reserve which was equivalent to an adverse criticism, a negative expression of contempt; but no doubt is permitted by the words in which he paints his memory black. Hyperbolus was ostracized, we are told, not because he was esteemed dangerous, but because he was an unprincipled scoundrel and a disgrace to the city. The same epithet ($\mu o \chi \theta \eta \rho \acute{o} \varsigma$) is here applied to Hyperbolus which was applied to him by Aristophanes.[13] We may note how Thucydides violates here his own principle of relevance. At this moment, Hyperbolus is not interesting or important, and in holding up his character to reprobation the historian is deviating from his narrative. Again, what he says of the cause of the ostracism is untrue. Hyperbolus was not ostracized because he was a disgrace to the city, whether he was so or not. He would not have been ostracized if the supporters of Alcibiades had not been instructed to write his name on the sherds instead of that of the virtuous Nicias. We know very little about Hyperbolus; but this judgment of Thucydides cannot be taken as objective or impartial. It is quite clear that he had a profound antipathy to popular leaders like Cleon and Hyperbolus, and that he was incapable of doing them whatever justice they deserved. And such antipathy is sufficient to account for the treatment of Cleon, without invoking a further motive of personal resentment for any part Cleon may have taken in procuring the condemnation of the historian.[14]

§ 3. *Rationalistic view of history*

It is by his practice of allowing his characters to reveal themselves by their actions and words, while keeping himself in the background, although he does not adhere to this plan with pedantic consistency, that the art of Thucydides may be appropriately called dramatic. The description of "dramatic" has indeed been claimed for his history on another ground. It has been thought that he viewed the whole war under the scheme of a tragedy, in which the Sicilian expedition was the *peripeteia* or "reversal" of fortune for Athens. This idea has recently been developed in a new shape by Mr. F. M. Cornford, in a brilliant study which seeks to establish that the historian read Aeschylean conceptions into the events of the war and mounted it, like a tragedy, with the dark figures of Tyche, Hybris, Peitho, and Eros, moving in the background and prompting the human actors. That such a conception should be read by an ingenious scholar in a work which impresses the ordinary reader as entirely matter of fact in its treatment of political transactions, illustrates what a wonderful book the history of Thucydides is. The truth is, I think, that the style of Thucydides was influenced by the Attic drama, no less than by the rhetoric of Gorgias, and it is one of the merits of Mr. Cornford's monograph to have illustrated this influence. But that the tragic phrases and reminiscences, and the occasional use of tragic irony, cannot be held to have more than a stylistic significance, and that Thucydides did not intend to cast the war into the typical scheme of a tragic development, will be apparent if we consider his own clear statements.

His view of the causes of the collapse of Athens displays the difference between his own outlook on human affairs and that of Herodotus. The older historian pourtraying the collapse of the Persian power discerns, in the development of the plot, imminent above the actors a superhuman control and the occult operation of nemesis. The only external influence recognised by the younger writer appears in the form of the incalculable element which he calls *Tyche,* Chance. Herodotus interpreted history and life, in the sense that the decline of a state or of a man from a post of commanding eminence was due to the action of a supernatural power which would not tolerate the exaltation which invariably leads to immoderate elation of soul and often to acts of insolence and rashness. In one of the speeches in Thucydides this anthropopathic idea is translated into the dry formula: "It is the nature of human things to decline." But it can hardly be said that he believed unreservedly in this principle (which may be found in Ionian philosophers) as a certain fact. And his analysis of the course of the war and his explanation of its issue show that the operation of the incalculable element of chance need not be decisive. It contributed to the decline of the Athenian power, but that power might have survived and defied its outrages, if it had not been for human mismanagement.

In the early stage of the war there were two cases of the play of the incalculable. There was first of all the plague. But though severe, maiming and weakening more than anything else the offensive power of the State for years to come, it was not crushing, it did not spell doom; one of its gravest consequences was the psychical effect upon the Athenians, for which Pericles suffered. The other surprise of fortune was a kind one, the combination of circumstances which helped the Athenians to their stroke of luck at Pylos. This elated them, as the pestilence had cast them down. Instead of grasping the opportunity of making advantageous terms and bringing to an end a war which they would gladly have concluded on any terms a few years before, they were incited to hopes of new conquest. But the consequences were by no means disastrous; the Peace of 421 B.C. left the balance of power much the same.

They had recovered from the effects of the plague and the war when they undertook the conquest of Sicily in 415 B.C. The catastrophe of that enterprise was the beginning of a gradual decline, which was determined by domestic dissensions in Athens, and afterwards by the intervention of Persia. A modern historian has designated the Sicilian expedition as an act of insanity, an instance of a whole people gone mad, analogous to the case of England in the Crimean war. But this was not the opinion of Thucydides. He says, and he is speaking in his own name, that it was not an error of judgment in the design or in the calculation of strength, and would have been a success, if it had been properly supported and carried out. The verdict of the modern writer was influenced partly by ethical considerations; the verdict of Thucydides did not take ethics into account; he only contemplates the question whether, judging the strength of Athens and the resistance offered to her, the ambition of extending her empire to Sicily was reasonable or foolish. The failure of the enterprise and the reverses of the ensuing years he imputes to the dissensions at home; and in the same way he explains mismanagement in the earlier period of the war by the jealousies of rival politicians. In other words, the key to the decline of Athenian power was the fact that Pericles had no successors. The city began to fall away from her eminence when her government was no longer controlled by an able leader.

Even after the Sicilian expedition, the situation might have been retrieved; for there was a man marked out to be a leader like Pericles, if the Athenians had trusted him. This was Alcibiades. That this was the view which Thucydides formed of Alcibiades can, I think, admit of little doubt. The distrust of the Athenians, he says, contributed heavily to the fall of the city; Alcibiades conducted the war with masterly ability.[15] In other words, things would have turned out very differently, if the conduct of affairs had been entrusted to him. The distrust is attributed to the somewhat insolent display and splendour of his private life, which excited envy and the suspicion of tyrannical designs. Nicias taunts him with this λαμπρότης, Alcibiades glories in it.[16] Now the career of Alcibiades had remarkable points of resemblance with that of a great Athenian statesman of a former age, Themistocles. They were both banished from Athens; both conspired with her enemies against her; and

Alcibiades like Themistocles became a trusted adviser of the Persians. But another point of likeness is indicated by Thucydides, λαμπρότης. It is not for nothing that he describes Themistocles and Pausanias as the most magnificent or luxurious of the Greeks of their time (λαμπροτάτους). That was a weak point in the case of Themistocles as in that of Alcibiades; it led to the suspicion of tyranny. This parallel suggests that one motive of the digression on Themistocles was to point it. At all events it throws light on the view of the historian. Athens produced three men who had the faculty, which cannot be learned by study, for guiding the affairs of a great state, Themistocles, Pericles, and Alcibiades. Two of them fell into the snare of luxurious splendour, which ruined their careers. Pericles avoided that pitfall, and won and retained the public confidence. This contrast, I would observe, gives special point to a famous phrase in the *Epitaphios*. Pericles himself was φιλόκαλος μετ' εὐτελείας, he was not λαμπρός, he indulged his private tastes without undue or obtrusive expense.

This analysis, which is furnished by the historian's own comments, eliminates entirely the dim superstitious notions of doom and nemesis, which do duty for Providence in Herodotus and dispense the spectator from any deeper study of the course and causes of events. Thucydides deals with purely human elements; human brains bear the ultimate responsibility. There is nothing mysterious about the fact that events cannot be foreseen. The course of events, says Pericles, may sometimes be as incalculable by reason as the thoughts of a man's mind. Thucydides does not regard the plague as a divine dispensation. It was simply an occurrence which could not be foreseen, exactly as you may not foresee the moves of your enemy. Herodotus credits the oracles with mysterious knowledge; Thucydides occasionally refers to oracles, but their sole significance for him lies in the psychical effect they produce on those who believe them. Of the oracle which predicted that the war would last twenty-seven years, he drily observes that it is the only one to which people who put their faith in oracles can point as having been certainly fulfilled. Here he was at the same standpoint as Anaxagoras and Pericles.[17] The philosophers who had established the reign of law had not written in vain for Thucydides.[18] Chance means for him the same kind of thing that it means for us; it does not signify the interference of an external will or caprice; it simply represents an element which cannot be foretold. He recognises the operation of the unknown; he does not recognise the presence of "things occult." And he reduces the unknown to its minimum of significance for human life. The great philosopher, Democritus of Abdera, had said: "Chance is an idol which men fashioned to excuse their own mental incapacity. As a matter of fact chance seldom conflicts with wisdom. In most affairs of life, an intelligent mind can exercise clairvoyance with success."[19] These words of Democritus might serve as a motto for Thucydides.

The elements for the conception of the war as a tragedy, in the proper sense of the word, were absent from his interpretation of the course of history. There was no mysterious controlling force, no doom or retribution, no inevitable decree of fate, no moral principle at stake. The lessons which the catastrophe conveyed were not moral or cathartic. The war was full of instructive lessons for statesmen and generals; but those lessons were assuredly of a very different order from the lessons of Aeschylus and Sophocles. And the occasional use of phraseology, which the tragedians charged with meaning, should not mislead us. Just as a writer of the present day who is completely innocent of any traffic with the supernatural may employ such terms as fate, doom, nemesis, so Thucydides could borrow the personified abstractions of tragedy for purposes of expression, without meaning to suggest anything occult. If I say that I have been prompted to do something by an imp of mischief or by a demon of unrest, you will not impute to me a belief in demons or imps. If Thucydides has sometimes expressed psychological observations in the language of tragic poets, this does not prove that he looked at history from a tragic poet's point of view.

§ 4. *Political analysis*

Attempts have inevitably been made to peer behind the scenes and discover the personal political views or tendencies of this singularly reserved historian. Dionysius, a critic who is usually instructive though never profound and often obtuse, stigmatizes in Thucydides a lack of patriotism so marked as to amount to positive ill - will both towards Greece and towards Athens. "He began at a point where the Greek world had begun to decline. A Greek and Athenian should not have done this, especially one who was no outcast but had been honoured by the Athenians with high command. He was so malicious that he imputed to his own city the open causes of the war, though he might have found means to attach the responsibility to other cities. He could have *begun* not with the Corcyraean affair but with the supreme successes of his country after the Persian war, and could have shown that it was through jealousy and fear, the consequence of these successes, that the Lacedaemonians, alleging other reasons, began the war."[20] When this criticism is examined, it will be found that it mainly touches the *arrangement* of the first Book,[21] but it shows that the narrative produced upon Dionysius the impression that Thucydides was unpatriotic.

On the other hand, it is held by some modern critics that the account of the beginnings and first years of the war is virtually a defence of the policy of Pericles, and it is even insinuated that the author manipulated facts, concealing some and mitigating others, with the purpose of presenting that policy in a favourable light. This view evidently contradicts that of Dionysius; it implies that Thucydides sympathized with Athens during the Periclean régime and at the outbreak of the war.

The fact that the narrative can convey two such contradictory impressions is a certificate of the author's critical impartiality. The censure of Dionysius is based on the conventional principle of later times that it is a historian's duty to be patriotic at all costs, to sacrifice his critical judgment; and it is superfluous to refute his charge of ill-will. On the other hand, the theory that Thucydides was an unreserved admirer of Pericles and deliberately intended to exalt and defend his policy, almost as a partisan, has some *prima facie* plausibility, and, as it has a direct bearing on the writer's attitude to history and politics, we must consider it more particularly.

We have seen how Thucydides speaks in the highest terms of the political ability of Pericles, and was convinced that, if he had lived or had a successor as able as himself, the war would have terminated favourably for Athens. But this general conviction would be quite compatible with discriminating criticism. The tribute which he has paid to Pericles does not imply that he saw eye to eye with the statesman in all things or held his political faith. There are proofs, in my opinion, that he exercised here, as in other cases, a cold independent judgment, and had no scruples in exhibiting weak points.

The speeches of Pericles claim our special attention. I may begin by pointing out that the praise which Pericles bestows in the *Epitaphios*[22] on the democratic constitution of Athens, implying that it was an ideal form of government, is not in accordance with the view of Thucydides, who expressly states that in his opinion the short-lived *politeia* which was established in Athens after the fall of the Four Hundred was not merely superior to democracy, but was the only good constitution that Athens had enjoyed in his lifetime.[23] In other words, he did not consider democracy a good constitution. In the second place, we may feel confident that the eloquent and fascinating portrait of Athens, drawn by Pericles, did not in the historian's opinion correspond to reality. It was the Periclean ideal. And Thucydides knew perfectly well that the claim that Athens was the school of liberal education for Greece would have been scouted by other states; and, as a matter of fact, it did not become anything of the kind till after the Peloponnesian war. Again, it seems more than doubtful whether Thucydides approved of the Periclean policy of bringing all the inhabitants of Attica into the city. The length at which he dwells on the unpleasant consequences of this arrangement, his pains in showing how distasteful it was to the people, suggest that he considered it a measure of highly questionable wisdom.

He certainly looked on Pericles as the most successful states-man who had recently guided the counsels of Athens. But he saw him, like all his other *dramatis personae*, in a dry light, and, as I have suggested, he has presented one side of the statesman's mind with a certain veiled irony.

The dramatic detachment of Thucydides readily produced the impression that he was unpatriotic. He allows every party to state their case as strongly and persuasively as possible. But while he wrote not as a patriot but as a historian, it is Athens, not Sparta, the Athenian Empire, not the Peloponnesian Confederacy, in which the interest of the narrative centres throughout. As to the questions at stake and the issues involved in the war, what we may hope to discover is not what political views the historian held, but *what was his attitude of mind in observing political events.*

His interest centres in the Athenian empire. In the passage in which he offers a general explanation of the result of the war he writes from the Athenian side entirely. Now as to the nature of the Athenian empire he has no illusions. In the first Book he unfolds the unscrupulous way in which it was acquired, with per-fect candour. He states that it was generally unpopular, and he allots a speech to an indictment of it by one of the subject states. That it was a despotism based not on right but on might is not merely alleged by the opponents of Athens but is emphasized by Athenian speakers. The Athenian diplomatist who spoke at the Congress of Sparta characterizes it without any reserve as having been won from motives of self-confidence and ambition; and the justification assigned is that it is a law of human nature that the weaker should be constrained by the stronger. Pericles is still more candid and emphatic. "The Empire you possess," he says, "is a tyranny; it may have been unjust to acquire, it is perilous to relinquish it." Again: "That man is truly wise who incurs odium for the highest stakes. Hatred does not balance the present mag-nificence and the future fame." Here power, wealth, and glory are assigned as a justification of an unjustly gotten and unpopu-lar empire. Arguing against the peace-party — οἱ ἀπράγμονες — who have scruples about justice, Pericles takes the same line, though with more cynicism, as a modern British chauvinist contemptuous of those whom he calls the Little Englanders. He sneers at their conscience, which, he suggests, is a cloak for cowardice. Alcibiades in advocating the Sicilian expedition points out the necessity to imperial states of an active and aggressive policy. Hermocrates, the enemy of Athens, does not complain of such a policy on grounds of morality; he says: "I can fully pardon the Athenians for their grasping policy; I do not blame those who seek empire, but those who are ready to submit; for it has always been the natural instinct of man to rule him who yields and to resist the aggressor."

The excuse which both Hermocrates and Athenians urge for the acquisition of empire is the instinct of human nature. But Pericles also attempted what may be called a justification on higher grounds. In the Funeral Oration he draws a picture of the grandeur and the *culture* of Athens. There, he so much as says, is the ideal which our city, by winning power and wealth, through an empire which was certainly *not* built on foundations of justice, has realised for the admiration and imitation of Hellas. Such things cannot be achieved by timid justice and stay-at-home piety. This is the *leit-motif* of the Funeral Oration.

Thus the historian kept before himself, and keeps before us, the fact that the empire cannot be defended on grounds of justice, that it could not be maintained except by *force majeure*, and that if slavery was an extreme word for the condition of the subject states, they were generally reluctant under the yoke. It is further to be observed that when Thucydides makes occasional reflexions of his own, he never takes justice or morality into account, from which we may infer that in his estimation those conceptions did not illuminate the subject. He recognised that the ideal of justice was an actual psychological force and could not be neglected by statesmen, any more than popular religion. But he did not consider it worth while to apply the standard of justice in estimating political transactions, just as he did not ask whether an action was pleasing to the gods.

The speech of Diodotus, advocating lenient treatment for the rebels of Mytilene, is interesting in this connexion. As the speaker played no part in history except here, the harangue must be introduced solely for the sake of its arguments. Its chief interest is that it repudiates the intrusion of justice into the question; the speaker reproaches Cleon for having dragged in so irrelevant a consideration, and bases his own view entirely on reasons of state. Thucydides with his usual reticence abstains from comment, though the tone of his narrative suggests that he sympathized with the lenient policy; but the fact that he chose these speeches of Cleon and Diodotus for working up, and that he has worked them up largely in the style which he employs when he is not documentary, shows that *his interest lay in the logic of policy.*

In the light of the debate on Mytilene we may consider the notorious debate of the Athenian and Melian representatives. Melos, you remember, was an independent state. Athens had made an attempt to force her into her empire in 426 B.C.; the idea was not resumed till 416 B.C., but in the meantime the relations of the two states had been hostile. When the expedition reached the island, the generals sent envoys to demand submission. They were admitted to a round-table conference with members of the Melian government, and Thucydides gives in the form of a dialogue what purposes to be the tenor of the debate. That such a conference was held, there cannot be a reasonable doubt, nor is it improbable that Thucydides had something to work upon. There is no difficulty in supposing that he might have heard enough from some one who knew to furnish him with a text.

The note of the dialogue is the elimination of justice from the discussion, by the Athenians. "Lass unsern Herr Gott aus dem Spass." The field of the argument is confined to policy and reason of state. When the Melians essay to find an issue from this restricted ground by observing that, being innocent of wrong, they expect a heaven-sent chance to intervene in their favour, the Athenians retort that gods as well as men recognise it to be a law of nature that the weaker should be ruled by the stronger. Now this is nothing more than what had already been said by Hermocrates and the Athenian envoy at Sparta. The attitude of the Athenians on this occasion is exactly the same as that of Diodotus in arguing for leniency towards Mytilene. Both alike are ruthlessly realistic; both alike refuse to consider any reason but reason of state. The conscience and feelings of the readers of Thucydides have been shocked by the tone of the Athenians at Melos because they sympathize with Melos; whereas they are not shocked by Diodotus because they sympathize with Mytilene. Yet Diodotus in 427 B.C. regarded Mytilene just as Athens in 416 B.C. regarded Melos, merely as a pawn in the game of empire. It is also important to observe that the discussion in the Melian council-chamber before the siege has nothing to do with the rigorous treatment of the people after the capture of the city. A few years before, Athens had meted out the same treatment to Scione; all the adult males were killed, the women and children enslaved. Thucydides makes no comment in either case. But if Athens had contented herself with reducing Melos to the condition of a tributary, the notorious dialogue would have been equally to the point. The policy of annexing Melos was one thing, the policy of punishing was another; Thucydides does not express his views on either. But it has been supposed by various critics that he introduced a cynical dialogue for the purpose of holding up to obloquy the conduct of Athens, and even of making it appear an ill-omened prelude to the disastrous expedition against Sicily. This theory will not, in my opinion, bear examination. Thucydides, as we have seen, did not consider that the Sicilian expedition was ill-advised in principle, and he does not hint that any consequences, bad or good for Athens, ensued from the conquest of Melos.

The truth is, I think, that Thucydides took the opportunity of the round-table conference to exhibit, pure and unvarnished, the springs of political action. The motives and arguments of the Athenians, whether wisely or unwisely applied in this particular case, were nothing new; they were the same which lay at the foundation of all their empire-building. This was the first case of a new annexation since the outbreak of the war, and it was the first occasion offered to the historian to analyse imperial policy from the point of view of aggression; he had already examined it from the point of view of preservation. The Melian dialogue only develops more undisguisedly and expressly—and the circumstance that no public was present gave the author the artistic pretext for candour—what is to be found in all the argumentative speeches: that not justice but reason of state is the governing consideration which guides the action of cities and claims the interest of historians.

We are now in a position to understand the attitude of Thucydides. *His object in to examine and reveal political actions from an exclusively political point of view.* He does not consider moral standards; his method is realistic and detached; he takes history as it is and examines it on its own merits. This detached analytical treatment is illustrated by the earliest political prose pamphlet we possess, written by a contemporary of the historian in the early years of the war; I mean the short tract on the Athenian Constitution. The author was an oligarch and declares without reserve his personal hostility to the democracy; but it is not a polemical work. He detaches himself from his own feelings, places himself at the point of view of democrats, and examines democracy exclusively in this light. Applying his acute logic, he demonstrates that the institutions of Athens could hardly be improved upon. The writer is intellectually allied to Thucydides in the detachment of his attitude and the logical restriction of the issue under a particular point of view.

Now when Thucydides offers reflexions *in propria persona* on events, his criticisms, on the policy of Athens, for instance, or on the value of an Athenian politician, are generally determined by the consideration whether they were conducive to success or failure in the war. In his appreciation of Brasidas, he places himself at the point of view of Sparta, and recognises that this general's conduct, policy, and character were conducive to the extension of Spartan power in competition with Athens. He takes the objects of the conflicting states as given, without approving or condemning; and in recording acts and methods his rare verdicts of praise or blame are confined to the question whether those acts and methods were calculated to achieve their object; just as in characterizing a man he refers only to his intellectual powers. He offers no opinion whether the aims were justifiable or admirable; he applies no ethical standard to policies or politicians.

Of course, he was fully conscious of ethical questions which arise in connexion with high politics, and these questions raise their heads in the dramatic parts of the work. In the speeches, justice and expediency are frequently distinguished and opposed. A speaker, for example, according to circumstances, is concerned to show that a course which is just is also expedient, or that expedience ought to be preferred to justice. Sometimes the consideration of justice is briefly dismissed as irrelevant. It appears as a psychical factor actually operative in international transactions, a principle to which at least homage of the lips was paid, by which praise and blame were popularly awarded, and which therefore had to be taken into account. But its rôle was slight and subordinate: the dramatist could not ignore it, though he allows it as small a range as he can; the thinker dismissed it.

There is not, so far as I can discover, any reason for believing that Thucydides thought or intended to suggest that an uncompromising policy of self-interest conduced to the fall of the Athenian empire, or that her wrong and unwise actions were wrong and unwise because they were guided by considerations of expediency alone. There is no ground for supposing that he would have had a thought of censure, if he had lived in our own days, for statesmen like Cavour and Bismarck and Disraeli, who were guided exclusively by reason of state, and are therefore blamed by moralists for having debased the moral currency in Europe. If, instead of a history, Thucydides had written an analytical treatise on politics, with particular reference to the Athenian empire, it is probable that he would occupy a different place from that which he holds actually in the world's esteem; he would have forestalled the fame of Machiavelli.

Thucydides simply observes facts; Machiavelli lays down maxims and prescribes methods; but the whole innuendo of the Thucydidean treatment of history agrees with the fundamental postulate of Machiavelli, the supremacy of reason of state. To maintain a state, said the Florentine thinker, "a statesman is often compelled to act against faith, humanity, and religion." In Thucydides, reason of state appears as actually the sovran guide in the conduct of affairs. But the essential point of comparison is that both historians, in examining history and politics, abstracted from all but political considerations, and applied logic to this restricted field. Machiavelli—the true Machiavelli, not the Machiavelli of fable, the *scelerum inventor Ulixes*—entertained an ideal: Italy for the Italians, Italy freed from the stranger: and in the service of this ideal he desired to see his speculative science of politics applied. Thucydides had no political aim in view; he was purely a historian; his interest was to investigate the actual policy of Athens in maintaining and losing her empire. But it was part of the method of both alike to eliminate conventional sentiment and morality.

A certain use of the term ἀρετή by Thucydides has an interest in this connexion. It is sometimes said that he did not assign great importance to the action and rôle of individuals. This seems to me a mistake, due to the circumstance that he does not draw personal portraits in the manner of subsequent historians. For it is evident that he considered the brains and wisdom of him whom he calls "the first man" as largely responsible for the success of Athenian policy before the Peloponnesian war. We can read between the lines that in his view the Peisistratids, Themistocles, and Alcibiades were also forces which counted for a great deal. The pre-eminent significance of the individual was a tenet of Machiavelli and his contemporaries (a classical feature of the Renaissance); it was a prince, an individual brain and will, to which he looked for the deliverance and regeneration of Italy. Both writers conceived the individual, as a political factor, purely from the intellectual side. Now Thucydides has used ἀρετή in his notice of the oligarch Antiphon, to express the intelligence, dexterity, and will-power of a competent statesman, in sharp contradistinction to the conventional ἀρετή of the popular conception. The only appropriate equivalent by which we can render in a modern language this Thucydidean ἀρετή is a key-word of Machiavelli's system, *virtù*, a quality possessed by men like Francesco Sforza and Cesare Borgia.[24]

It must be understood that this attitude of Thucydides only concerns international politics, the subject of his work. Domestic politics lie, except incidentally, outside his scope. When he turns aside to describe the disintegrating influence of party faction on the internal conditions of Greek states, he recognises the important operation of ethical beliefs and religious sanctions in holding a society together. But where national aims are at stake and international rivalries are in motion, no corresponding beliefs and sanctions appear, possessing the same indefeasible value for the success and prosperity of a state. There is irony in his remark that the Lacedaemonians, after the first war had come to an end, ascribed their own want of success to the fact that they had refused the Athenian proposition to submit the Peloponnesian grievances to arbitration, in accordance with the Thirty Years' Peace. It is noteworthy that in the Funeral Oration of Pericles, where he pourtrays the qualities of his countrymen, there is not a single word about those conventional virtues in which Nicias shone. The Athenians are praised for their political intelligence and versatility, for their adventurous activity, for enlightened freedom in their intercourse with strangers, and for other excellent things. Not a word is said of their piety, and they were certainly pious. We are told that they have accomplished much and reached the heights by their own talents and their own toil. There is not a word, not a single perfunctory phrase, of assistance or favour from heaven. Of religion, or of morality in the conventional sense, there is not a syllable from the beginning to the end of this brilliant speech. Pericles could hardly have avoided at least some conventional reference to the gods, in the speech he actually delivered at the sepulture; that Thucydides overlooked it is significant.

If this appreciation of the historian is sympathetic, I hope you will not suppose that I belong to the band of devotees who make a cult of Thucydides and can see no defects in their idol. Such devotees existed in ancient as well as in modern times, and the historian's ancient indiscriminating admirers received a very proper rebuke from Dionysius of Halicarnassus. I have already suggested that he carried his method of exclusion and omission too far. His treatment of individuals displays a more serious limitation in his idea of historical reconstruction. Thucydides does not seem to have grasped fully that in estimating the action of an individual in history his whole character must be taken into account; he is a psychical unity, and it is not possible to detach and isolate certain qualities. Psychological reconstruction is one of the most important as well as delicate problems which encounter the historian, and Thucydides failed to realise all that it means. In his impatience of biographical trivialities, he went to the extreme of neglecting biography altogether. Take, for instance, his silence concerning the personality of Pericles. This statesman was one of the forces which operated in bringing about the war, and to understand his actions we want to know more about his personality. Thucydides is content to note his consummate political ability and his indifference to money, and to indicate his idealism. This does not enable us to realise what manner of man Pericles was; we still feel, and modern criticism illustrates this, that he is in many respects an unknown or at least ambiguous quantity.

The work of Thucydides has limitations which we must beware of underrating; but it marks the longest and most decisive step that has ever been taken by a single man towards making history what it is to-day. Out of the twilight in which Herodotus still moved wondering, he burst into the sunlight where facts are hard, not to wonder but to understand. With the Greeks historical study never acquired the scientific character which it was reserved for the nineteenth century to impress upon it. But within the limits of the task he attempted Thucydides was a master in the craft of investigating contemporary events, and it may be doubted whether within those limits the nineteenth century would have much to teach him. If he had admitted his readers into the secrets of his workshop, if he had more clearly displayed his raw material and shown how he arrived at his conclusion, if he had argued and discussed, he might have exercised a greater influence than he did on the *methods* of subsequent Greek historians. His incomplete work, posthumously published, had an immediate and far-reaching result in establishing political history; and in the next lecture we shall see how men of the younger generation received a stimulus from him. But, although the value and greatness of his work were at once recognised, and he always remained the one and undisputed authority on the period he had treated, yet, for several centuries after his immediate successors, his history seems to have been little read except by scholars; he was a great name, not a living influence as a teacher or a model. His style, with its "old-fashioned and wilful beauty,"[25] repelled, and other ideals of history, sharply opposed to his, came into fashion. It was not till the first century B.C., with the return to Attic models, that the interest in his work revived; and from that time we can trace his influence on leading writers[26] down to one of the latest Byzantine historians, Critobulus. But this influence was of a superficial kind: it concerned style and phraseology; it was generally a mere mechanical imitation.[27] And the historians whom he would himself have most esteemed were not those who came under his own influence.

LECTURE V

THE DEVELOPMENT OF GREEK
HISTORIOGRAPHY AFTER THUCYDIDES

§ 1. *The generation after Thucydides*

THUCYDIDES had set up a new standard and proposed a new model for historical investigation. He taught the Greeks to write contemporary political history; this was the permanent result of his work. But the secret of his critical methods may be said to have perished with him; it has been reserved for modern students fully to appreciate his critical acumen, and to estimate the immense labours which underlay the construction of his history but are carefully concealed like the foundation stones of a building. Influences came into play in the fourth century which drove history along other paths than those which he marked out; the best of the principles which his work had inculcated did not become canonical; and his historical treatment was not sympathetic under the new intellectual constellations.

The age succeeding his death was perhaps not favourable to the composition of political history.[1] The engrossing intellectual interest was then political science, and the historical method had not been invented. The men who might otherwise have shone as historians were engaged in speculations on the nature of the state. They were eagerly seeking an answer to the speculative question: What is the best constitution? Only three historians of note arose in this period; they were more or less under the influence of Thucydides, but at long intervals behind.

Of these the only name familiar to posterity is Xenophon, who was probably the least meritorious of the three. To the circumstance that he is one of the very few classical Greek historians whose work has survived, he owes a prominence to which his qualities do not entitle him.[2] In history as in philosophy he was a dilettante; he was as far from understanding the methods of Thucydides as he was from apprehending the ideas of Socrates. He had a happy literary talent, and his multifarious writings, taken together, render him an interesting figure in Greek literature. But his mind was essentially mediocre, incapable of penetrating beneath the surface of things. If he had lived in modern days, he would have been a high-class journalist and pamphleteer; he would have made his fortune as a war-correspondent; and would have written the life of some mediocre hero of the stamp of Agesilaus. So far as history is concerned, his true vocation was to write memoirs. The *Anabasis* is a memoir, and it is the most successful of his works. It has the defects which memoirs usually have, but it has the merits, the freshness, the human interest of a personal document. The adventures of the Ten Thousand are alive for ever in Xenophon's pages.

He took up the story of the Peloponnesian war where Thucydides had left it, and he carried down the history of Greece from that date to the fall of the Theban supremacy, in the work which we know as the *Hellenica*. By this work his powers as a historian must be judged. Some of its characteristics are due to the superficial lessons which the author learned from the founder of political history. In the first portion of the book[3] he employed strictly the annalistic plan of Thucydides. He adopted the device of introducing speeches, and the objective method of allowing the actors to reveal themselves in their acts and words. He does not himself pourtray their characters, as he pourtrays Cyrus and the generals in the *Anabasis*. But he never goes down below the surface of events; he never analyses the deeper motives; and he writes with little disguise of his own predilections. His history is an apotheosis of Agesilaus; he does not conceal his strong philo-Laconian leanings or his hatred of Thebes;

he pointedly ignores Epaminondas. His ideas about historical happenings were those of the average, conventional Athenian; and he ascribes the fall of the Spartan supremacy to divine nemesis, avenging the treacherous occupation of the Theban citadel. He cannot resist the commonplace attraction of commonplace moralising; he tells anecdotes which his austere predecessor would have disdained; but he has learned from Thucydides to keep to the matter in hand.

Other works of Xenophon had more influence than the *Hellenica,* on subsequent historiography; or, as it would probably be safer to say, reflected an interest which was to become not only permanent in literature but a conspicuous feature in history. I am referring to biography. Interest, deliberate and serious interest, in individual personalities, had been awakened by the sophistic illumination; and Euripides probably did as much as any single man to heighten and deepen it. A new branch of literature, biography, emerged; and the word βίος, life, acquired a new meaning, charged with the whole contents of a man's actions and character. Biography was founded by Isocrates and the pupils of Socrates. The earliest biography we possess is the *Evagoras* of Isocrates, and it is to this model that we owe the second, the *Agesilaus* of Xenophon. In other works of Isocrates also there are biographical sketches, and perhaps the portraits in the *Anabasis* were due to his influence.[4] We can see too that the original personality of Socrates, which made a deep impression on his disciples, was effective in helping to establish this kind of literature; most of them used their pens; and the incidental portraiture of Plato, and the *Memoirs* of Xenophon, which are not a Life, have their significance for the rise of biography. I have not to follow its further development or to show how it was stimulated by the Peripatetic school.[5] As a literary art ancient biography reached its highest perfection in Plutarch's gallery of great men. That series is invaluable to us, because the author consulted many books which are now lost; but he was not a historian; his interest was ethical. What we are here concerned to note is that, after Xenophon and Isocrates, historians generally considered sketches of character and biographical facts to be part of their business. It was a feature which was flagrantly liable to abuse, and often led to irrelevancies, which would have shocked Thucydides. But although, in practice, ancient character-portraits tended to be conventional and uninstructive, it was in principle an important advance to recognise that the analysis of character and personality has historical value, and cannot be confined within the limits which Thucydides had allowed.

The continuation of Thucydides was taken up by another writer who seems to have had a truer calling than Xenophon to exercise the historian's trade. Cratippus was one of the obscurest figures in literature, and till a few months ago we had not even a fragment to indicate the character of his work. But a passage of Plutarch might suggest that his history possessed more than ordinary merit. "If there were no men of action," Plutarch observes,[6] "there would be no historians. Abolish Pericles, Phormio, Nicias, and the rest, and you eliminate Thucydides. Abolish Alcibiades, Thrasybulus, and Conon, and you abolish Cratippus." Here Cratippus is singled out as the leading historian of Athens for the years subsequent to the termination of Thucydides, and as one whose loss would be acknowledged to be an impoverishment of historical literature. The passage also leads us to infer that Cratippus carried his continuation as far as the naval victory of Cnidus, 394 B.C., which enabled Athens to win back an independent and eminent position in the Greek world. Egypt, which has yielded so many invaluable relics of classical literature to the indefatigable explorations of the eminent Oxford scholars, Grenfell and Hunt, has recently enriched us with a treasure, which, I have little doubt, is a portion of the work of Cratippus. This substantial fragment covers a part of the year 396 B.C. and most of the year 395, so that it may represent more than a twentieth part of the whole history. Some eminent scholars claim for it the authorship of Theopompus; but the weight of evidence, in my opinion, is entirely against that theory; while there is nothing inconsistent with the authorship of Cratippus (the only other admissible claimant[7]), which was advocated by Blass. As no relics of the work of Cratippus have been preserved in literature, we have no direct positive evidence for the identification. The case rests (1) on the argument by exclusion; the claims made for other candidates cannot be reconciled with the character of the fragment; (2) on the circumstance that the few things we know about Cratippus correspond to the indications of the new text. The narrative bears the stamp of an original composition by a contemporary (like that of Thucydides, and even more so than Xenophon's *Hellenica*), not compiled from books. We can see that it was written without knowledge of Xenophon's work. The lower limit of its date can hardly be later than about 350 B.C.[8] Now Cratippus, we know, was a younger contemporary of Thucydides,[9] and his literary activity must have been subsequent to the death of Thucydides (*c.* 396 B.C.) whose work he continued; so that chronology as well as subject accords with the hypothesis of his authorship. There are no speeches, and one of the things we know about Cratippus is that he disapproved of the speeches in Thucydides and considered the absence of them in the last Book a proof that Thucydides had come to regard them as undesirable.[10] The narrative is lucid and simple, unadorned by rhetorical phrases and free from didactic commonplaces. It is also extremely dull; but it would be illegitimate to judge from this particular section that the work as a whole could not have evoked the praise implied by Plutarch. If nothing were left to us of Thucydides but, say, the last thirty chapters of the third Book, with the tedious account of the Acarnanian operations of Demosthenes, what a dull writer we should esteem him. We can see that the author was not given to passing personal criticisms; no hard words are said of any one; a slight approbation is accorded to an act of Conon; and one much-mutilated passage contains apparently a characteristic of a statesman, whose identity can hardly be determined.[11] This evidence does not enable us to decide whether Cratippus adopted the objective method of Thucydides in regard to the personalities of the historical actors. But in other matters at least he condescended to his readers. He explains the relations and actions of political parties; he traces the growth of anti-Spartan feeling in Greece; and of the constitution of Boeotia he gives as clear an account as could be desired in a handbook, an account which shows us that we were ignorant of its real nature. The general impression I gain from the fragment is that if the work had survived it would occupy a distinctly higher place than the *Hellenica* of Xenophon, though the author did not possess Xenophon's technical knowledge of warfare.

The discovery of Grenfell and Hunt has added to our knowledge of facts, but for our present purpose its interest lies in showing on what lines the writing of contemporary history, founded by Thucydides, might have developed in the hands of men, not endowed with his brain-power and originality, but competent and diligent, if it had not been diverted from an independent path by forces which I will presently notice.

The influence of Thucydides was probably more marked in another contemporary historian, who moved in another part of the world and had a different horizon, Philistus of Syracuse. Like Thucydides, he had experience of public affairs, and suffered exile, and lived to be recalled. He did not confine himself to contemporary history, as Thucydides did, for he related the story of Sicily from the very beginning down to the time of his own youth — he had been an eye-witness of the Athenian expedition. But his more important work was the history of the two tyrants Dionysius, father and son, a record of events in which he had himself played an active part both as politician and military commander. He enjoyed the posthumous distinction of being the only historian whose works followed Alexander, along with the great poets, to Further Asia, and, as Freeman says, "the reason of the choice is plain enough. Nowhere could Alexander find reading more to his taste than in the history of Dionysius, the first man who carried on war on a scale and after a fashion at all approaching to his own."[12] Philistus made Thucydides his model,[13] not by a slavish imitation of his style, but rather in temper and method, and we may suspect that of all Greek historians he was most Thucydidean. He is thus appraised by Cicero, who, though he lived in a day when other styles of history were in fashion, had a keen literary sense. "Philistus," he writes to his brother Quintus, who was engaged in reading the Sicilian author, is "a writer of the first rank, pithy, sagacious, concise, almost a miniature Thucydides."[14] Cicero's portrait suggests that Philistus displayed Thucydidean qualities beyond conciseness and the faculty of keeping strictly to the point; and this we know from other evidence. The court of the old fox (*veterator*) Dionysius the Elder, of whom he was an intimate confidant before his disgrace, was a school of statecraft and political casuistry, in which the imitator of Thucydides could well learn to study political phenomena from the non-moral attitude of his exemplar. But the mere fact that Philistus undertook to write in detail the early history of Sicily raises a presumption that he was less sceptical than the Athenian; and as a matter of fact he did not disdain to record wonders and omens, such as the appearance of a swarm of bees alighting on the mane of a horse, which was taken to presignify the reign of Dionysius.[15]

§ 2. *The influence of rhetoric*

During the period in which these three historians, Philistus, Cratippus, and Xenophon, wrote, the educated Greek world was succumbing to the spell of two influences, towards which Thucydides had been detached and independent. I refer to rhetoric and philosophy. You are all familiar with the immense influence which Isocrates exerted on literature and education. He was not a man of genius, yet at no age, perhaps, can we find a single man who in this sphere held such a magisterial position. Greeks from every part of the world repaired to his school at Athens, and his rules for style were canonical. I need not illustrate this, but will go on to show how he affected the development of historiography and especially through two eminent admirers, Ephorus and Theopompus.

And first of all I may point out how the political view of which Isocrates was the most conspicuous exponent affected history. The rise of Macedon in the middle of the fourth century, and the gradual fulfilment of the aspiration for the union of Greece, under Macedonian direction, brought to the front what was virtually a new conception of Hellenic history. Hitherto, history had been either sectional, the histories of particular states or groups, or had been concerned with particular episodes, such as the joint efforts of the Greek states against the Persian or inter-Hellenic wars. But the idea of Greek unity preached by Isocrates, and taking the special form of unity under Macedonian leadership against Persia, reacted upon history, and no fewer than three works were written in the days of Philip and Alexander, which were inspired by the idea of the unity of Greek history. Two of them have vanished, leaving not a trace except the mere record of their existence. One was by Zoilus, whose name is better remembered for his carping criticisms of Homer which earned him the nickname of *Homero-mastix*, Homer's scourge.[17] The other was by his pupil Anaximenes, who was one of the teachers of Alexander. Both these historians were submerged in oblivion by the success of the third, Ephorus of Cyme. He is said to have been a pupil of Isocrates, but I do not think that this is established.[18] The work to which he devoted his life, beginning with the mythical origins of Greece and embracing the barbarian peoples with which the Greeks came into contact, was probably intended to terminate with the year 334, when Alexander crossed into Asia, but only reached as far as 356, in consequence of the author's death. It became and remained one of the standard works of antiquity, and established what has been aptly described as "the vulgate of Greek history." It is usual to designate this book, which, although it has perished, is inwoven in the narratives of our later authorities, so that we know a good deal about it indirectly, as the first universal history; and so it is described by Polybius. But it is important to discriminate the precise sense in which we can admit this description. We must always remember that the Greeks had never formed a nation; they were never united even in an all-embracing federation; they had no national history in the proper sense of the word. The bond of community among them was the general homogeneity or unity of their civilisation. Now the novelty of the work of Ephorus lay in this, that, recognising this unity of culture which contained potentialities of a real Hellenic nation, he brought together the particular histories of all Greek-speaking communities, and thus produced what might be called a quasi-national history. But it was distinctly a history of Greece, *Hellenica,* not a history of the world; non-Greek peoples only came in so far as they were connected with Greek history; and the title "universal" can be applied, not on the ground that the author, like Herodotus, comprised portions of non-Greek history, but in the limited sense that all the Greeks were embraced. To some extent the chronicles of Hellanicus had been an anticipation of this idea of Ephorus and his contemporaries.

It became the fashion at this time to divide large works into books. The history of Ephorus consisted of twenty-nine Books, of which each was a unity in itself and had a preface of its own.[18] Thus it was not constructed on the annalistic method. The author seems to have had a wide acquaintance with the whole range of historical and geographical literature, and he did not copy uncritically. He was fully conscious of the value of first-hand information, and we may note his acute observation, wondering how far he applied it, that in the history of modern times the most detailed accounts are the most credible, but for ancient history those who profess to know most particulars are the least worthy of belief. His critical principles led him formally to throw over the purely mythical period and begin with the return of the Heracleidae; but he did not carry out consistently this counsel of wisdom; in the course of his narrative he introduced myths and indulged in the crude methods of rationalising which had been initiated by the Ionians.

I cannot enter into a detailed account of the work of Ephorus, and must be content just to mention characteristics for which the influence of Isocrates is responsible. Among them may be noticed the interruption of the narrative by moralising platitudes; the introduction of elaborate Isocratean speeches, even when an army was facing the enemy; and the passion for panegyrics. These features, and his conventional battle-scenes, which conformed more or less to a model scheme, manifest the same tendency to sacrifice truth to effect. History is becoming epideictic, like oratory and poetry, and desires to show off. And this is what is meant by saying that historiography was drawn under the pernicious influence of rhetoric. One does not mean by that, the cultivation of a clear, agreeable, and rhythmical style; one means the tendency to seek first of all and almost at any cost what may be called rhetorical effects.

The other famous historian of the Isocratean school, Theopompus, continued the work of Thucydides in his *Hellenica,* which covered the same period as Cratippus and for which he must have derived his material mainly from older works, such as those of Cratippus himself and Xenophon. His more important effort was the *Philippica,* a history of Greek affairs in the time of Philip, and here he was in the full sense an original contemporary writer.[19] He, too, was affected by the national idea of Isocrates; he saw in the Macedonian power a unifying principle, and he made it the pivot of his contemporary history. But it is notable that he called that history, not Macedonica, but Philippica. It was a new thing to treat a period as "the age of Philip."

He was probably the most interesting historian of the fourth century. But some have even pronounced him truly great, worthy to rank near Thucydides. The evidence is sufficient to disprove such a claim.[20] The Isocratean features which were common to him with Ephorus are decisive. And if we observe that he was more concerned with the private morality of men of action than with their political or military capacity, that he served up miracles and fables, and related a figment of his own invention concerning the imaginary land of Merope beyond the ocean, where the golden age is still a reality,[21] we may see that any comparison with Thucydides is almost ludicrously inappropriate. He seems to have been a man of restless vanity, endowed with what we might call an epideictic temper. While Ephorus devoted his life to study without personal ambition, Theopompus travelled about, eager to cut a figure in the world, like Gorgias and others of the early sophists. He had a "temper," revealed in his writings and infusing a spice, which was lacking in the flavourless works of Ephorus and Cratippus. He was a psychological analyst, and he was more inclined to be censorious than panegyrical. The critic Dionysius says that his great aim was to dive into the profundities of the human soul and discover the secret wickedness almost invariably lurking beneath the semblance of virtue.[22]

In judging these new tendencies to which history succumbed under the Isocratean régime, we must bear in mind that they responded to the taste of the public which Isocrates did much to educate. In old days Homer and the epic poets satisfied the requirements of a large public. Herodotus similarly appealed to public taste and public interest. Thucydides had a different object in view. He formed a standard of historical truth, and deliberately renounced the idea of making his book a popular success. We may conjecture with high probability that the works of his successors Cratippus and Philistus had a very small and select circle of readers. Ephorus and Theopompus determined to win the public ear. It was not enough to write; they wanted to be read. From this point of view they represented a reversion to the days before Thucydides. But they had a different audience to please from that which listened to Herodotus, and they captured votes by accommodating history to the rhetorical effects for which the public cared. This was a natural instinct of self-preservation. At all events, the craving for the achievement of popular success dominated historiography henceforward; the exceptions to the rule are few.

Under Isocrates, Athens had been the educational and literary centre of Greece. The primacy passed away from her in the greater Greece created through the conquests of Alexander; she was no longer the arbitress of taste or the leader of intellectual fashion. In the field of history, Timaeus of Tauromenium illustrates the transition from Attic to Hellenistic literature. He lived through vast political changes. Born two years before Chaeronea, he survived the outbreak of the First Punic war. Driven from Sicily by Agathocles for political reasons in his youth, he found a new home at Athens, where he devoted the rest of his long life[23] to a history of Sicily and Italy. He not only ransacked literature, but travelled for the purpose of his work, sparing neither time nor money to gain accurate information about the ill-known western nations, Iberians, Celts, and Ligurians. He made a special investigation of chronology, and was the first to introduce into Greek historiography the clumsy, inconvenient method of reckoning time by the Olympiac years. His work (in thirty-three Books) came down to 320 B.C., but he continued it in a history of Agathocles, and in a later book which reached to 264 B.C. and included the campaigns of Pyrrhus. Timaeus was not only used extensively by subsequent historians, especially by Diodorus, but his history was recognised as an authoritative storehouse of information by the scholars and poets of Alexandria, such as Apollonius, Lycophron, Callimachus, and Eratosthenes. The material furnished by this means has enabled Geffcken to restore the general construction of the first two Books of his chief work, dealing with the mythical history and geography of Sicily and Italy. For us his merit lies in his industrious collection of ethnographical facts and local legends, material which is still of value; but this merit would never have sufficed to secure him the popularity and authority which he enjoyed for many generations after his death, if his history had not possessed other features which we should mark as his weak points. When he came to Athens he studied rhetoric under a pupil of Isocrates, and his work had characteristics which we expect from the Isocratean school, such as speeches packed with commonplaces, and the conventional administration of praise and blame. He had also weaknesses of his own. He was a thorough pedant, without sense of proportion or the faculty to discriminate weighty from trivial things; interested in disconnected details; fond of fables and marvels. He was also something of a mystic. He sought to show, for instance, that to every sinner punishment, unmistakable as such, was meted out, and that coincidences of date had a transcendent significance; he was ever on the watch for the revelation of mysterious or daemonic influences in historical events. Again, his history of the contemporary period must have been far from impartial. His extravagant admiration of Timoleon was the counterpart of his failure to recognise any but the worst qualities of Agathocles, whom he hated on account of his own banishment, which had embittered his mind.

Living in the Attic atmosphere and trained in Isocratean rhetoric, we should expect to find Timaeus conforming to the canons of Attic style. But it appears that he adopted a new kind of writing which bade farewell to the traditions of Attic taste. It is impossible to decide whether he struck out this new way for himself, or came under the influence of Hegesias of Magnesia, who is always designated as the founder of the famous school of style which came to be known as the Asianic. As we do not know the precise dates of the life of Hegesias, we cannot say whether he and Timaeus were independent of each other. The literary parentage of this new style is to be sought in the prose of the elder sophists, like Gorgias and Alcidamas; but it outdid anything that Gorgias in his most frigid moments had been tempted to essay. It produces the impression of a bacchic revel of rhythms and verbal effects. This Asianic movement triumphed; the general public lost the power of appreciating Attic measure and Attic sanity; and the new style was predominant for two hundred years. Nor did it disappear when the reaction came and Attic models again came into fashion. On the contrary, as Norden has shown, the two styles, the archaic and the modern, contended for mastery throughout the ages of the Roman Empire. For instance, in the fourth century A.D. we have a great archaic rhetorician, Libanius, thrilling Antioch with his eloquence, while a great modern sophist, Himerius, was teaching the art of style at Athens.

Of the modern style, in its early or Asianic period, we have very few specimens, but we know that it comprised two distinct kinds — the pretty style and the bombastic style. The bombastic

suited the taste of grandiose Hellenistic princes, and it so happens that the one considerable example we possess of it is a
long inscription of Antiochus of Commagene (discovered in
1890), in which the King describes his achievements. It is, as
Norden says, a prose dithyramb. But the other, the pretty style,
was the more popular and more important; it was the style in
which Timaeus experimented and which Hegesias established.
It is not easy to reproduce the effect of this style in a modern
language, because it depends so much on rhythm; but in
order to show the sort of thing you would find in the most
popular works of the lost literature of the third and second
centuries B.C., I will quote a passage of Hegesias, who wrote a
history of Alexander the Great. The historian makes the following comment, shall I call it? or dirge, on that monarch's
destruction of Thebes:[24]

> In rasing to earth Thebes, O Alexander,
> Thine hand a deed has done,
> Such as Zeus would do
> Were he to cast the moon utterly
> Out from yon heaven's section;
> For the sun as a fitting symbol I keep for Athens.
> Verily these cities twain were visual orbs of Hellas;
> So that now for the one of the pair in pain I travail.
> For Hellas hath lost half her vision, one eye knocked out,
> Even the Theban town.

This means in plain language: Athens and Thebes are in
Greece what the sun and moon are in the sky; or they may be
likened to the two eyes of Greece, and Alexander in destroying
Thebes has deprived Greece of one eye. I have made an attempt
to imitate the rhythm, though it is indeed impossible to catch
the effect in another language, or perhaps to appreciate it even
in the Greek. But the example will illustrate the poetical character of the Asianic style. Is not this passage what one might look
for in the chorus of a third-rate historical tragedy?

The popularity which Timaeus enjoyed for a couple of centuries mirrors the public taste, and he would hardly have
enjoyed it if he had adhered to the canons of Attic style, which
drew a sharp line between poetry and prose. But there was
another school of historical art bidding for public favour in the
days of Timaeus. It was initiated by Duris of Samos, a pupil of
Theophrastus. He became, through some stroke of luck, tyrant
of Samos, and he wrote a history of Greece from 370 B.C. to 281,
a biography of Agathocles, and a chronicle of his native city. He
declared war on what I may call the conventional school of
Ephorus and Theopompus, asserting that these writers failed to
excite the pleasure which history, differently treated, is capable
of affording. They lacked, he said, *mimêsis*. *Mimêsis* is the nearest
Greek equivalent of "realism"; and we shall not be far from the
mark if we say that what Duris demanded was realism, and if we
call his school the realistic school. Duris was intensely interested
in the theatre; he wrote books on tragedy and the history of art;
and it was this interest in drama that inspired him with the idea
that historians should aim at producing the same kinds of effect
as dramatists. He required, for instance, that they should introduce their personages dressed in the costumes appropriate to
the time and circumstances. But his chief point of insistence was
that the feelings of the readers should be moved and harrowed
by highly wrought pathetic scenes, conjured up by the writer's
imagination; while they were also to be entertained by anecdotes and gossip and amorous stories. He achieved a success
with the public, and naturally his success was followed up by
others. For example, Phylarchus, who wrote an important history
of the years 272–220 B.C., is blamed by Polybius as "feminine"
because he aimed at moving his readers to tears.[25] That was the
influence of Duris.

There was a good deal to be said for the instinct of Duris in
his reaction against conventionalism. The power of realising and
vividly describing scenes of the past is a high merit in a historical
writer, provided he has the material necessary for constructing a
true picture. But this proviso is sure to be overlooked when the

writer's first consideration is not truth, but effect. And so it was with Duris. His school, like the conventionalists, subordinated history in the Thucydidean sense to literary art. The conventionalists appealed to taste, the realists appealed also to the emotions. The former edified, the latter excited. But for both alike history was simply a branch of rhetoric.

We may regret this corruption, as we call it, of history. But it is more to the purpose to understand the Greek point of view. It is not easy for us to realise the importance which the art of rhetoric possessed for the Greeks, as a purveyor of aesthetic pleasure. Indeed, the history of Greek rhetoric testifies, perhaps as impressively as the history of Greek plastic, to the large part which aesthetic pleasure played in Greek life. For the later Greeks, the declamations of rhetoricians, which we find intolerably tedious to read, had as intense an aesthetic value as the Homeric poems for their remote ancestors, and were listened to with as eagerly attentive and as critical ears. People went to hear a rhetorical display just as we go to hear a symphony. And this interest lasted down to late Graeco-Roman times. Greek prose was always an art in as full a sense as the poetry from which it sprang, regulated by principles and canons, which have no counterpart in modern languages, even in French, and required prolonged study and practice. And rhetoric came to fulfil for Greek audiences the same rôle which had been once fulfilled by the epics. Just as the historians, or as we should say mythologers, of the Homeric age were epic poets, so the later historians were rhetoricians. If the historian were not trained in the school of the rhetorician he would have had few readers.

Again, history and geography were the great field from which light reading was provided for the educated public. The later historians helped to satisfy the same need of entertainment which had formerly been met by the tales of the epic poets or the historical anecdotes of the sixth and fifth centuries. There was no special literature yet of romances and novels, and the functions of our modern novelists were to a great extent fulfilled by the historians. History had to answer the purpose now answered by fiction, and it is not surprising if it tended to partake of the nature of fiction.

The knowledge of strange lands won by the conquests of Alexander the Great stimulated the appetite for marvels and provided abundant food. It was not necessary to imagine, as Theopompus did, a land of Merope; there was now an actual background and there were actual adventures; history could appear without excuse as romance, and romance could mask as history. The sober and veracious relations of Alexander's achievements, the political Memoir of Aristobulus and the military Memoir of Ptolemy, fell dead; and four centuries elapsed before the excellent Arrian composed the first history of the Macedonian hero's conquests that was based on these and some other trustworthy sources,[26] with a rigorous rejection of the literature which was written πρὸς ὄχλου καί θέατρον, not only, I am afraid, as we say "for the gallery," but for the stalls too. The great popular success was won by Cleitarchus, a rhetor of Colophon,[27] who made the most of the possibilities of his theme and captured his public by fantastic descriptions of the gorgeous East. This quasi-historical work became the standard book on the subject, and seems to have exerted a deep influence on the traditional history of Alexander.

But while such romances captivated the public, those plain veracious reports of Ptolemy, Aristobulus, and Nearchus have an important place in the development of historiography. They founded a new branch of historical literature,[28] which in the next generations was represented by the Memoirs of Pyrrhus and of Aratus, to be succeeded in Roman days by the Commentaries of Julius Caesar, the Memoirs of Corbulo, and Trajan's history of his Dacian wars. The Commentaries of Caesar fulfilled indeed, in a most subtle way, the function of political pamphlets, but the plain businesslike, unadorned relation has its literary parentage in the memoirs of the generals of Alexander. And it is not, I think, unreasonable to conjecture that these memoirs were the model or inspiration of an exceptional work of this period, which fulfilled, as it would appear, the demands which Thucydides made on historiography. Hieronymus of Cardia, a soldier and statesman, who had served under Eumenes and Antigonus Gonatas, wrote a history of the Diadochi and Epigoni from the death of Alexander to about 266 B.C. His sole concern seems to have been to record facts accurately; he used official despatches, and in general he told only what he knew of his own knowledge or from credible information. But his style was careless; he disdained rhetoric. The Greeks would not read what did not gratify their aesthetic sense; and a work like that of Hieronymus had no more chance in competition with Duris than the Memoir of Ptolemy against the sensational and rhetorical story of Cleitarchus. Speculating on what we casually learn about this lost book, we may suppose that if it had survived we should regard Hieronymus as a third in a triumvirate of Greek historians, along with Thucydides and Polybius.

We saw in the first lectures how the Persian conquest of Asia Minor and invasion of Greece played a determining part in the rise of history. Similarly, the Greek conquest of the Persian empire had a decisive influence on its development. I have pointed out some of the ways in which this second great stimulus from the Orient operated. Just as it was in consequence of the destruction of Miletus and the Persian war that the intellectual primacy in Greece passed from Ionia to Athens, so it was a consequence of the expansion of Hellas by Alexander that the primacy passed away from Athens to Alexandria and other places—passed back, we might say, to the East; and this affected history as well as other branches of literature. Again, the opening up of the distant countries of Asia stimulated and ministered to the romantic history which gratified the popular appetite for sensation. On the other hand, the reports and "blue-books" of Alexander's generals founded a new kind of history which eschewed rhetoric, addressed no appeal to the public, and had very few exponents. Another result of Alexander's work was the rise of the idea of the *oecumene*,—the realisation of the inhabited world as a whole of which account must be taken.[29] This idea had indeed no immediate influence on history. We can trace its influence in the Stoic philosophy, and it gave rise to the conception of the Romans that their dominion was potentially conterminous with the *orbis terrarum*. As a historical principle, it then began to become effective, as we can see in the universal histories of the first century B.C., and it prepared the way for the Christian conception of world-history.

§ 3. *The influence of philosophy and the rise of antiquarianism*

I have traced the influence of rhetoric on history; we must now consider the influence of philosophy. In the first half of the fourth century, a period of intense practical, as well as theoretical, interest in problems of government and social organization, we find, beside Isocrates the sophist, who wrote for the hour, Plato the philosopher, who wrote for the ages. Different as they were, they both represented from different sides the same interest in political speculation, and both alike gave it an ethical direction, the effects of which were permanent. Both these masters, the man of genius and the man of talent—the programmes of the one and the ideals of the other—set historical tasks to the next generation. While Isocrates set in motion Theopompus, Ephorus, and Androtion, the greatest pupil of Plato found it necessary, in investigating political philosophy, to trace the histories of the political constitutions of Hellenic states.

We should understand many points in the political speculation of Plato as well as in the political pamphlets of Isocrates if we possessed the mass of political literature which inundated Athens during the period of the Peloponnesian war. Of that literature we have one early specimen in the anonymous book on the Athenian Constitution. We have only a few fragments of the publications of Antiphon, Thrasymachus, and Critias, the most distinguished names. Some papyrus fragments of the *Apologia* of Antiphon have been published the other day by Nicole, but, welcome though they are, they do not amount to very much.[30]

It has been happily observed by Wilamowitz[31] that these political pamphlets, of which the book of Stesimbrotus was one of the first, were the prose successors of the Elegies of Solon and Theognis. The most effective and important flysheets emanated from the men who were dissatisfied with the democracy and desired to substitute oligarchy or polity; they were dealing with burning questions and they did not spare persons. The book of Stesimbrotus, which seems to have been entitled *Concerning Themistocles, Thucydides, and Pericles,* had struck the personal note. The Athenian history of the fifth century was perverted by these writers into a history of demagogues; and this perversion had a decisive influence on Athenian thinkers of the following century. The pupils of Socrates were only too ready to adopt a view which held up to obloquy the democracy which had taken the life of their master. We have the scheme of the Athenian demagogues in Plato's *Gorgias,* in the *Politikos* of Antisthenes, in the *Dialogues* of Aeschines, in the *Philippika* of Theopompus, in the *Athenian Constitution* of Aristotle. It was somewhat as if the sources of the American history of the nineteenth century were lost, and a reactionary publicist wrote a book to make out that a series of demagogic Presidents was the key to the history of the United States.

This literature, contemporary with Thucydides, must have had a considerable effect in creating an interest in Athenian history. It corrupted history, but it also quickened it. It was the object, for instance, of Theramenes and his followers to prove that polity, the form of government which they desired, was not an innovation but the true and original Athenian constitution, the πάτριος πολιτεία,[32] and that the existing democracy was a perversion which had been generated and fostered in the interests of demagogues. The historical question, what was the nature of the πάτριος πολιτεία and the Solonian reform, thus became a question of burning political interest. We may illustrate it by the controversies, not yet extinct, as to the nature of the Reformation in England, between Church parties which, in the interests of their own ecclesiastical views, place different interpretations upon historical events.

Aristotle's *Constitution of Athens* may itself be regarded from one point of view as belonging to the political literature of the fourth century. To describe it as a pamphlet[33] is as absurd as it would be so to describe the work of Herodotus. Its main purpose was scientific; but the author was deeply interested in the politics of the day, and his book had an intentional bearing on the contemporary situation.[34] It was due to his own views as a politician, and not to his curiosity as a historian, that he used as authorities flysheet literature, especially a polemical pamphlet dating from the last years of the fifth century and expressing the anti-democratic conception of Athenian history which prevailed in the circle of Theramenes.

But the *Constitution of Athens* is only one of 158 Greek constitutions and some not Greek, which were compiled by Aristotle or under his direction. Their purpose was to supply actual material for a scientific study of political phenomena. And thus Aristotle possesses the great significance that he was the founder of constitutional history, the precursor of Waitz and Stubbs. The *Constitution of Athens,* the only one of the collection we possess, was the one most likely to be affected by Aristotle's political prejudices. Its weaknesses are evident. It consists of two parts—a sketch of the constitutional changes to the end of the fifth century, and a description of the existing constitution. His main thread in the former was the local history of Athens as described by Attic chroniclers who came after Hellanicus;[35] just as his main guides for other states were probably the local histories which had been industriously consulted by Ephorus. So far, so good; and he also displayed historical instinct in using the poems of Solon for his account of the economic conditions of that statesman's time. But he completely neglected the material on which a modern historian would base his investigation, the stones and the archives. And it is clear that he did not comprehend the working of the constitution in the fifth century; his critical faculty did not resist the spell of the polemical literature of the extraordinarily clever publicists who had invented their own version of Attic history. When he has recorded the overthrow of the Council of the Areopagus, instead of pointing out that the actual power and government were in the hands of the Council of Five Hundred, he intimates that the conduct of the state rested entirely with Pericles. The truth is that Aristotle seems to have reflected very little on the subject, or rather to have confined his reflexions within very narrowly drawn lines. The formalism of his conception is most evident in the way in which he treats, or fails to treat, the Athenian empire. To a modern student, who should undertake to write a constitutional history of Athens, one of the most important problems would be to examine how the democracy governed the empire and how the empire reacted on it. Aristotle dismisses the empire in about four lines (c. 24). Moreover, although he has traced the constitutional changes in relation to the political crises which brought them about, he has, in general, his eye merely on the dead machinery; he tells us the names of the parts, but he does not show how the machine worked. Even when we come to the democracy of the fourth century, we get only a full account of the official organization and the formal procedure; no effort is made to gain an insight into the political efficiency of the institutions. It is doubtful whether even here he consulted the laws themselves, or rather used an analysis written by somebody else.[36] And if in this historical treatise he fails to show the actual working of the constitution and to explain the unwritten *Staatsrecht,* his scientific treatise, the *Politics,* does not supply this want.

Plato troubled himself little with history, but it is not improbable that one of his speculations suggested the idea of the first history of civilisation. In the *Laws,* where he descends to lower heights, nearer to the actual conditions of terrestrial society, Plato has sketched a reconstruction of the development of the human race. It is governed by the idea of cataclysms, such as deluges or pestilences which wiped out the human race, leaving only a remnant, which had to begin at the very beginning and weave civilisation, like the web of Penelope, all over again. The latest of these periodic cataclysms was a deluge, and the few survivors who had gained safety on the tops of high hills found themselves without the means of travelling and without arts; the metals had disappeared and there were no means of felling timber. "The desolation of these primitive men would create in them a feeling of affection and friendship towards one another; and they would have no occasion to fight for their subsistence; for they would have a pasture in abundance"; also abundance of clothing, bedding, and dwellings, and utensils; so that they were not very poor. And they were not rich, as there was no gold or silver. But "the community which has neither poverty nor riches will always have the noblest principles; there is no insolence or injustice, nor, again, are there any contentions or envyings among them."[37] Plato draws here the picture of an age which is ethically golden; although he does not use the expression. He then sketches the patriarchal government of primitive societies, appealing to Homer's description of the Cyclôpes; the rise of agriculture and of city-life; the beginnings of legislation which became necessary when men who had different laws in their separate life came to live together. He shows how this gathering into large communities suspended patriarchal rule and brought about a monarchical or aristocratic government.

Up to this point we suppose that we are reviewing the general development of mankind throughout the whole earth. Then suddenly, by a sort of legerdemain, the philosopher changes this universal scene to the plain of Troy, and continues the imaginary record from the foundation of Ilion. The rest is a curious commentary on the history of Greece. It turns on the idea that the Heracleidae missed a great opportunity. The object of the Dorian institutions which they introduced was, Plato alleges, to protect the entire Hellenic race against the barbarians, and, if they had only legislated with more far-sighted wisdom, they might have secured a permanent union or confederacy of the Hellenic world, strong to resist all assaults of the barbarians. As history, this is absurd; the interest lies in Plato's reflexion of the national Hellenic idea which was preached by Isocrates. Nor indeed does Plato intend it to be taken more literally than the previous imaginary reconstruction of the progress of man from his primeval conditions.

This slight sketch, which represents the primitive age as ethically golden, but materially rudimentary, must, I fancy, have been present to the mind of Dicaearchus when he decided to compose the earliest *Culturgeschichte* or history of general civilisation, his Βίος Ἑλλάδος in which, starting from conditions like those indicated by Plato, he traced the progress of Greece in public and private institutions and in the arts. It is remarkable how the speculations of the Greeks on primitive civilisation were bounded by that tradition of a decline from a golden age, which Hesiod expressed in his scheme of the Five Ages.

But if Dicaearchus found his text in Plato, his work was a characteristic product of the Peripatetic school to which he belonged. It was the merit of that school to promote specialism, and it produced a considerable historical literature on all kinds of special subjects, such as the history of philosophy, the history of drama, the biographies of sculptors. Demetrius of Phaleron played an active part in establishing in the Greek world the Peripatetic idea of collecting and classifying facts of every order. For it was largely due to his stimulus and influence, after he retired from Athens to Egypt, that under the auspices of Ptolemy I. books were collected at Alexandria which formed the nucleus of the two great libraries formally founded by Ptolemy II.[38] Political history indeed was not much written by the savants of Alexandria, whose great achievements were in the sphere of philology; but the antiquarian tastes which found their fullest satisfaction there, and afterwards at Pergamon also, in the shadow of large libraries, were introduced by the Peripatetic movement, and did not fail to affect historiography. We can notice this influence in the work of Timaeus, who, though he was thoroughly incapable of philosophical ideas and made scurrilous attacks on Aristotle, shared with the Aristotelian school the passion for collecting facts of all kinds, and was so trivial in its indulgence that he was called an "old rag woman" (γραοσυλλέκτρια).

The creation of antiquarian study is one of the numerous precious services of the Greeks to the progress of human culture. Its distinction is that, apparently and in its immediate aspect, it is disinterested. The Greeks described it as πολυπραγμοσύνη, attending to what is not one's business, a singularly felicitous phrase for a sphere which has no relation to human life. The Roman word for antiquarianism had a similar significance: *curiositas*, superfluous care for what is practically unimportant, or, in fact, the love of useless knowledge. But although *curiositas* came to be an instinct in men who could not have assigned any reason of utility for their pursuits, it must be remembered that it sprang from a certain side of the general philosophical theory of Aristotle, and, thus having a place in a system, had originally a justification outside itself. It may be called useless in a narrow sense of the term, but from another point of view, as I will show in a subsequent lecture, it has a human value and is therefore ultimately not disinterested.

Although the ancient antiquarians tended to be rather learned than critical, and in criticism to be rather minute and finical than luminous, there were brilliant exceptions; such as Eratosthenes, the greatest and most original geographer of the ancient world. His studies in physical science helped him to prosecute his antiquarian researches with freshness of insight. I would, in particular, point out his attitude to Homer. One of the most serious impediments blocking the way to a scientific examination of early Greece was the orthodox belief in Homer's omniscience and infallibility—a belief which survived the attacks of Ionian philosophers and the irony of Thucydides. Eratosthenes boldly asserted the principle that the critic in studying Homer must remember that the poet's knowledge was limited by the conditions of his age, which was a comparatively ignorant age.[39] This was an important step in historical criticism.

Ancient antiquarians did not work out principles of method, nor did they, beyond the collection of libraries, provide facilities for research, like the bibliographies and innumerable works of reference which are compiled for the convenience of modern students. It is somewhat surprising that archives were not systematically transcribed, and official documents collected. The idea was not unknown. Craterus, who seems to have been a contemporary of Theophrastus, compiled a corpus of the Attic decrees of the fifth century, arranged in chronological order. The traveller, Polemon of Ilion, was such a diligent copyist of inscriptions that he earned the name of stone-rapper (*stêlokopas*). Among the Romans, Mucianus, the friend of the Emperor Vespasian, collected and edited a large corpus of official documents, probably including reports of the proceedings of the Senate (*acta senatus*) during the last age of the Republic.[40] As this collection included reports of public speeches by leading orators and statesmen, the motive of Mucianus in compiling it may have been an interest in oratory rather than in history. Such labours were in any case exceptional.

Greece did not create scientific philology any more than scientific history. But the movement set on foot by the Peripatetic school was invaluable, both for preserving the records, and exploring the recesses, of the past; and however uncritical or crude the methods of ancient antiquarians may appear to us, they represent a prominent stage in the advance of knowledge. But while their disinterested passion for research affected the reconstruction of past history, contemporary history was composed by men who subordinated truth to rhetorical effect. There were few exceptions, conspicuously Hieronymus, whom I have mentioned, and Polybius, to whom the next lecture will be devoted.

LECTURE VI

POLYBIUS

THE life of Polybius covered about the first eighty years of the
second century B.C. (c. 198–117 B.C.) — the period of the great
political process which linked together the destinies of Greece
and Rome. He was born in the Hellenistic world, a noble repre-
sentative of its civilisation, to become the herald of the new
Graeco-Roman world into which he witnessed the Hellenistic system passing. You will remember that having played a public part
in the politics of the Achaean League of which his father
Lycortas was then the leading statesman, and having served as a
commander of cavalry, he had been taken with other hostages,
after the battle of Pydna (168 B.C.), to Rome, where he was
placed in the house of the victorious general Aemilius Paullus.
There he enjoyed the intimate society of Scipio Aemilianus, and
had exceptionally good opportunities of gaining a first-hand
knowledge of Roman affairs and of studying the character of the
governing class and the working of the constitution. There he
became reconciled to the fate of his country. He lived sixteen
years at Rome before he was allowed to return to Greece, and
during that time he conceived the idea of his work and wrote a
considerable part of it (at least fifteen Books). His original
design was to relate the history of the advance of Roman conquest, through a period of fifty-three years from the eve of
the Second Punic war (220 B.C.) to the Roman conquest of
Macedonia (168 B.C.). He explains very fully why he chose his

121

starting-point. There broke out almost at the same moment three great conflicts: the war of Rome with Carthage, the war of the Leagues in Greece (in which the Achaeans and Philip were ranged against the Aetolians), and the war in the East between Antiochus and Ptolemy Philopator. Up to that epoch, events happening in the various quarters of the world were unconnected and did not bear upon each other either in their purposes or in their issues. But from this time Italian and African affairs begin to come into relation with Asiatic and Greek affairs, and history begins to assume the form, not of strewn *disiecta membra,* but of a single organic body ($\sigma\omega\mu\alpha\tauο\epsilon\iota\delta\hat{\eta}$).

But, while Polybius marks this date as the proper beginning of his work, he goes back farther in a long introduction, filling two Books, in which he sketches the earlier history of the relations of Rome with Carthage, including the First Punic war and the previous history of the Achaean League. Thus, so far as the lands of the Western Mediterranean are concerned, his history began where Timaeus had left off, as he expressly notes.[2]

He signalises the *motif* of his work in imposing phrases. "Our own times have witnessed a miracle, and it consists in this. Fortune moved almost all the affairs of the world towards one quarter and constrained all things to tend to one and the same goal. And so it is the special note of my work to bring under one purview for my readers the means and the manipulations which fortune employed for this end. This idea was my principal motive and stimulus. It was an additional reason that in our time no one had attempted a universal history."[3]

Subsequent events, the fall of Carthage and the annexation of Greece in 146 B.C., led Polybius to extend his plan and fix this later year as the term of his history. In its augmented form it reached the considerable bulk of forty Books, of which only the first five have been preserved completely, though of many of the others we possess long excerpts. He seems to have finished the composition of the whole work about the year 134, but he continued to insert many additions and corrections up to 120 B.C. These supplements are often in contradiction with other passages, for he died without submitting the book to a systematic revision. Indeed, he had allowed the original introduction, which expounded the first scheme of his history, to remain unchanged, and simply inserted a statement of his revised plan.[4] Of the later additions the most interesting are those which were suggested by the author's visit to Spain about 133 B.C.,[5] and those which allude to the revolutionary movement of the Gracchi. Of the latter I shall have something more to say.

I have observed that the history of Polybius follows on to that of Timaeus, and it is to be noted that in his chronological arrangement he has adopted the awkward reckoning by Olympiads which Timaeus introduced, but he supplements it by the years of the Roman Consuls and other marks of time.[6] In the first portion of his work, up to the year of Cannae (216 B.C.), he pursues continuously the history of each of the various states without interruption; but after that, he adopts the annalistic method and synchronizes events in different parts of the world under the same year.

The arrangement of his immense work displays conspicuous skill; but whether the forty Books can be reduced to the scheme of a symmetrically grouped work of art, like the history of Herodotus, is a question which we can hardly answer with confidence, considering that of many of the Books we possess only a few fragments. Nissen has attempted the discovery of a symmetrical plan.[7] He holds that it was divided into seven parts, each of which contained six Books, except one which contained four. These groups, he thinks, correspond to definite stages in the development of Roman dominion: "The first group," he says, "contains the introduction; the second the culminating years of the contest between Rome and Carthage; the third begins with the war in Africa, and ends with the destruction of the Macedonian hegemony; the fourth traces the history of the Roman hegemony, and the fifth its transformation into an empire of client states; the sixth (which is the exceptionally small division) forms the transition to the last rising of the Mediterranean states against Rome, which is the subject of the seventh." In support of this design, he points out that three Books which are devoted to long digressions—VI. on Roman Institutions, XII. on the work of Timaeus, XXXIV. on Geography—come each at the end of one of these main divisions. Moreover, the addition of a fortieth Book, containing a *résumé* of the contents, is urged as an argument in favour of the alleged construction, on the ground that it was required to complete the last hexad. The theory has a certain plausibility, but we have to remember that Polybius changed and enlarged his plan in the course of its composition, and I find it difficult to believe that, if he had deliberately adopted a definite scheme of this kind, he would have failed to draw attention to it in the preface to his first or third Book. His solicitude that the reader should fully grasp his plan and arrangement is hardly reconcilable with his silence on such a leading point. The symmetry is not clearly convincing as in the case of Herodotus.

But whether this incomplete symmetry is due to the design of the author or only to the discernment of an ingenious reader, Polybius has shown a fine artistic sense of propriety in fixing the place which he chose for his account of the institutions of Home. The third Book concludes with the defeat of Cannae, which set the mistress of Italy face to face with the prospect of the extinction of her power. How was it that, brought to bay, she baffled the triumphant invader, recovered Italy, and conquered Carthage? The historian emphasizes the problem. Of course, the measures her government adopted after the disaster were wise. But a sagacious policy at the last moment would not have availed if Home had not been what she was. The explanation lay, Polybius believed, in her institutions. And so he interrupts the narrative of the Punic war at this point to describe the institutions which saved Rome.[8] He has seized the instant at which the reader's interest is most fully prepared and awake to learn the lessons which those institutions have to give.

Polybius is not less express than Thucydides in asserting the principle that accurate representation of facts was the fundamental duty of the historian. He lays down that three things are requisite for performing such a task as his: the study and criticism of sources; autopsy, that is, personal knowledge of lands and places; and thirdly, political experience. He was himself a man of action, and had acquired political and military experience before he became a historian, so that he fulfilled the third condition; and he was most conscientious in endeavouring to satisfy the two other self-imposed requirements. He possessed a wide acquaintance with historical literature, and criticized the authorities whom he used with fearless independence of judgment. He was not taken in by "authority," and he declined to render unreserved credit to a writer on the ground that he was a contemporary or a man of character. For instance, he criticizes the views of the Roman historian Fabius on the causes of the Punic war. "There are some," he observes,[9] "who think that because he lived at the time and was a Roman senator he should be believed without more ado. Whereas I consider his authority high, but not absolute or such as to dispense the reader from forming his own judgment on the facts themselves."

Polybius was also a traveller, and he travelled for the purpose of historical investigation in accordance with his belief that topographical autopsy was a primary qualification for writing history. He passes severe criticisms on Timaeus, who, he says, always "lived in one place," and on Zeno of Rhodes, for the blunders they committed through ignorance of geography. He was intimately acquainted with Greece itself;[10] his description of the battle of Sellasia was censured by Delbrück, but has been successfully defended by Kromayer. He travelled in Italy and Sicily; he visited Africa in an official capacity; he went with Scipio to Spain, and explored the coast of the Atlantic, returning to Italy by Southern Gaul and the Alps.

The historians of whom Polybius seems to have most highly approved were Ephorus and Aratus. The Memoirs of the Achaean statesman naturally appealed to him as an Achaean politician, but also because they satisfied his doctrine that history is a practical and not an antiquarian study. Written by a man of action, whose interests were directly practical, they gave the kind of instruction which it was the main function of history, in the esteem of Polybius, to give. On the other hand, Ephorus appealed to him as a universal historian, "the first and only writer who undertook to write universal history."[11] Thus Aratus and Ephorus displayed severally the two great features of the work of Polybius, on which he constantly insists. His view of history is *pragmatical* and it is *universal*. The word pragmatical (πραγματικός) has been sometimes misunderstood. By a pragmatical man he means a practical politician, and by pragmatical history he means history which bears on political actualities and furnishes practical instruction. In an interesting passage he says[12] that this kind of history has always been useful, but is more than ever opportune now, "because in our times science and art (ἐμπειρία καὶ τέχνη) have made such great advances that theoretical students can deal, as it were on methodical principles, with the situations that occur." He insisted very strongly on the point that, in order to serve such pragmatical uses, a mere narrative of events is inadequate, and the historian must investigate and explain the causes and the inter-connexions. The whole value of history, he said, lies in a knowledge of causes. Some exponents of Polybius have applied the term "pragmatism" to his work, in the particular sense that he investigated the causal nexus of events. This is a misuse of the word, and is not countenanced by his language. "Apodeictic" is the term which he uses of his history in so far as it traces causes.[13] His history is pragmatical, and because it is pragmatical, it is also apodeictic.

Now, what does Polybius understand by causes? He is careful to enlarge on the distinction between cause and beginning (αἰτία and ἀρχή), and he illustrates it by examples. For instance, while the beginning of the Persian war of Alexander the Great was his crossing over into Asia, the causes are sought by Polybius as far back as the expedition of Cyrus and the wars of Agesilaus.[14] But it cannot be said that he goes very deep into the question of historical causes. He conceives causation in an external and mechanical way, and he does not proceed beyond the idea of simple onesided causation to the idea of reciprocity, or of action and reaction, which is often required to express adequately the relations of historical phenomena.

The view of Polybius on causation in general is more interesting than his applications of it to particular cases. Until he was well on in years and had virtually completed his work, he shared the popular belief that, apart from the regularly operating natural and human causes, a superhuman power, which men call Tyche, exerts a control over events and diverts them in unexpected ways. This popular view had been presented in a quasi-philosophical dress by Demetrius of Phaleron, whose treatise Περὶ τύχης[15] doubtless made a deep impression on the mind of Polybius, for its influence on a number of passages in his work has been proved by von Scala. The event of 167, the fall of the Macedonian monarchy, the new step in the resistless advance of the western world-power, in whose chariot wheels Polybius himself and his country were caught up, might well seem a powerful confirmation of the theories of the wise man of Phaleron. Though Polybius traces the causes of the success of Rome to its history and constitution, he writes as follows in the preface to the original plan of his work: "Fortune has caused the whole world and its history to tend towards one purpose — the empire of Rome. She continually exercises her power in the lives of men and brings about many changes, yet never before did she achieve such a labour as she has wrought within our memory."[16] Thus the Roman conquests produced upon Polybius the same impression which the Macedonian conquests had produced upon Demetrius. Elsewhere Polybius quotes the very words which Demetrius had used.[17] "Fortune, who exhibits her power in compassing the unexpected, is even now, I think, displaying it to the world, having made the Macedonians the inheritors of Persian prosperity. She has lent them these blessings, till she forms a new resolution on their destiny." In many other places, too, Polybius recognises the active operation of Fortune, and comments on her instability, her paradoxes, her caprices, quite in the tone of Demetrius.

But there are other passages in which Polybius sounds a very different note. Thus he finds fault with writers who ascribe public calamities or private misfortunes to Fortune and Fate, and only allows that when it is impossible or difficult for man to discover causes, as in the case of storms or droughts, he may in his embarrassment refer them to God or Fortune, "but when you can discover the cause of an event it is not, in my opinion, admissible to impute it to God."[18] Before you pray for rain, it is wise to look at the barometer. Again, he deprecates the practice of ascribing to fortune or the gods what is due to a man's ability and prudence. These and other similar observations are not perhaps ultimately inconsistent with the doctrine of Demetrius, but the note is different; they show a desire to restrict the operation of the external power within as narrow limits as possible. But there are other assertions which are directly opposed to that doctrine. When he inquires into the causes of the power and eminence attained by the Achaeans, a people who were not numerous and lived in a small country, "it is clear," he says,[19] "that it would be quite unsuitable to speak of Fortune; that is a cheap explanation; we must rather seek the cause. Without a cause nothing can be brought about, whether normal or apparently abnormal." When he wrote this, he had reached a point of view diametrically opposed to that which he had learned from Demetrius. Further, he applied his new doctrine to the empire of Rome. If, in the words which I quoted a few moments ago, he had claimed Rome's successes as a supreme illustration of the mysterious dealings of Fortune, he now, with equal confidence, repudiated the theory that Fortune had anything to do with the making of Rome's greatness. "It was not by fortune, as some of the Greeks think, nor causelessly, that the Romans succeeded; their success was quite natural; it was due to their training and discipline; they aimed at the hegemony and government of the world, and they attained their purpose."[20]

Thus it appears that Polybius, having originally started with the conception of an extra-natural power, directing the world and diverting the course of events from its natural path, was led by wider experience of life and deeper study of history to reduce within narrower and narrower bounds the intervention of this *dew ex machina*, until he finally reached the view that it was superfluous for the pragmatical historian. But it would be rash to assert that he ultimately embraced a theory of pure naturalism. All we can say is that he came to entertain the view that nothing happens without a natural cause, and the operation of Tyche or chance is, in general, an invalid assumption.

It is probable that Stoicism had something to do with his change of view. It is certain that he came under the influence of the new school of liberal Stoics, through intercourse with Panaetius, who, like himself, was an inmate of the house of Scipio at Home. "I remember," says a speaker in Cicero's *De Republica*,[21] "that you, Scipio, often conversed with Panaetius in the presence of Polybius, two Greeks the most deeply versed in politics" (*rerum civilium*). Polybius did not become a Stoic, but he assimilated some Stoic ideas, as in his earlier life he had been influenced by the Peripatetics.

In his actual treatment and presentation of historical events, the fluctuation in his views on this question probably did not make much difference. A change in his views as to the freedom of the will would have affected his treatment far more deeply. I know for myself that on days when I am a determinist I look on history in one way, and on days when I am an indeterminist, in quite another. Polybius was an indeterminist, like most Greeks; he believed in free-will. The particular Stoic influences to which he submitted did not touch this doctrine. For Panaetius did not share the doctrine of Chrysippus and older Stoics, that the world is governed by laws of iron necessity which exclude free-will.

We can see the results of his contact with Stoicism in the account which Polybius gives of the rise and fall of political constitutions.[22] He adopts the newer Stoic version of the theory of a cyclic succession of forms of government. When the human race is swept away (this has happened, and may be expected to happen again) through deluges, plagues, or famines, and a new race takes its place, the work of civilisation has to begin afresh;

monarchy is the first form in which society constitutes itself; this passes through successive corruptions and revolutions (tyranny, aristocracy, oligarchy, democracy) into an anarchical democracy which Polybius calls *cheirocracy*, the rule of might; from which a dissolving society can only be rescued by a return to monarchy, and then the cycle begins again. In the interval between two cataclysms there may be any number of such cycles. Polybius accepts catastrophic occurrences not as a mere ancient tradition or philosophical speculation, but as a proved scientific fact.[23]

The theory of a recurring cycle of political constitutions which comes from Plato and the Stoics is an application of the cyclical theory of the world-process which was propounded by early philosophers. Such a theory is more or less implied by Anaximander and Heracleitus, but it was clearly formulated, in very definite terms, by the Pythagorean school.[24] You remember the passage in Virgil's Fourth Eclogue where a new Argonautic expedition is contemplated and a second Trojan war:—

atque iterum ad Troiam magnus mittetur Achilles.

That is the cyclical doctrine, and logically it applied to small things as well as great. I may illustrate it in the vivid manner of the philosopher Eudemus. According to the Pythagorean theory, some day I shall again with this manuscript in my hand stand here in this hall and lecture on Polybius, and you each and all will be sitting there just as you are this evening; and everything else in the world will be just as it is at this moment. In other words, the cosmical process consists of exactly recurring cycles, in which the minutest occurrences are punctually repeated. We do not remember them—if we did, they would not be the same.

But the cyclical doctrine was not, perhaps, generally taught in this extreme form.[25] Polybius does not appear at first to have held even the universal validity of the law of growth, bloom, and decay. He considered that it holds good of simple constitutions, pure monarchy, for instance, or pure democracy, but he thought that the setting in of decay could be evaded by a judicious mixture of constitutional principles. He has submitted to a minute analysis the Spartan and the Roman systems of government, as eminent examples of the union of the three principles of monarchy, aristocracy, and democracy, compounded in such a way that they balanced one another and mutually counteracted the separate tendencies of each to degenerate. The Spartans owed the idea of their mixed constitution to the happy divination of the genius Lycurgus, the Romans attained to theirs through the school of experience. In other words, the Spartan constitution was an invention, the Roman was a growth. From these premisses, which are largely untrue, Polybius deduced the exceptional permanence of the institutions of Sparta and Rome, and evidently thought that they defied the law of degeneration. It may be noticed that the superiority of a mixed constitution was not a new idea.

In other passages, however, Polybius speaks in a different tone. He sacrifices the theory that Rome owed everything to her mixed constitution, by admitting that her government was aristocratic when she reached her greatness in the time of the Second Punic war. It was a mechanical and wholly inadequate theory, even if the facts on which it was based had been correct —even if Rome *had* possessed a constitution in which the equilibrium of the three constitutional principles was maintained. In abandoning it Polybius was forced to recognise that the secret of life did not lie in a mechanical adjustment of the parts of the state, and to admit that there was no guarantee that Rome herself would not decline. But what induced him to abandon it? Undoubtedly his observation of the revolutionary movements in the time of the Gracchi. These movements came as a great surprise to him; nothing could have seemed to enjoy a more secure stability than the fabric of the Roman state in the days when he began writing his book. But the Gracchan revolution opened his eyes. Its significance was brought home to the friend of Scipio by Scipio's assassination. These stormy years flashed a lurid light on the past, and Polybius could now look back with illuminated vision and see in the agrarian law of

Flaminius (232 B.C.) the beginning of the degeneration of the people.[26] Without touching what he had written before, he introduced into his work new paragraphs which meant the surrender of his former belief in the permanence of the constitution. He now recognised that Rome, too, was destined to decline, and he could consequently accept unreservedly the principle of anacyclosis. Stoic teaching may have gradually prepared him for this change of theory; and Scipio assuredly had not been blind to the signs of the times. The revolutionary outbreak illustrated the melancholy prediction which he heard from the lips of his friend on the ruined site of Carthage: —

> ἔσσεται ἦμαρ ὅταν ποτ' ὀλώλῃ Ἴλιος ἱρὴ
> καὶ Πρίαμος καὶ λαὸς ἐυμμελίω Πριάμοιο.
> Some time will come the day
> Of doom for Troy divine and Priam's sway,
> And Priam and his folk shall pass away.

More than an epitaph on Carthage, it was a prophecy on Rome.

Both Polybius and Thucydides, as I have already observed, held with equal conviction that the first obligation of a historian is to discover and relate facts as they actually occurred, and herein they both represented a reaction against the history which held the field. Each alike feels that the purpose of his work is to be instructive and not to be entertaining. Polybius is fully aware that for the majority of the reading public his work will have no attractions;[27] it is intended for statesmen, not for antiquarians or people who want to be amused. Just as Thucydides is conscious that his conception of how history should be written is opposed to that of Herodotus, so Polybius repudiates the fashion of historiography which was in vogue, and denounces the rhetorical effects or exciting sensations of the works which were most popular, such as those of Timaeus and Duris. He is severe upon Phylarchus for introducing into history effects which are appropriate to tragedy.[28] Phylarchus was always "forcing the note." He was ever attempting to arouse the pity and sympathy of the readers by pictures of despairing men and dishevelled women, children and aged parents, embracing, weeping and making loud lamentation, in the extremity of woe. Tragedy and history, says Polybius severely, have different objects. The aim of tragedy is to move the soul; but the aim of history is to instruct the mind. Again, just as Thucydides ignores all the gossiping anecdotes which memoir-writers like Ion and Stesimbrotus collected, so Polybius condemns writers of a later day for retailing what he calls the "vulgar babble of a barber's shop"—what we should call the gossip of the clubs, or the canards of the daily press.[29]

Polybius then represents a return, though not a conscious return, to the principles of Thucydides and a reaction against some of the most conspicuous tendencies which had marked historiography in the interval. But Thucydides exercised no direct influence upon him, and the extant parts of his work indicate that he was not one of the historians with whom he was familiar. Polybius has been affected by the speculations in political science and by the schools of philosophy, no less than by the changes in the political world which had come to pass since the lifetime of Thucydides. Any one who turns from one to the other is struck by the salient contrasts between their methods of treatment. Thucydides is an artist, Polybius is a teacher. Thucydides, as we saw, employs the objective treatment of a dramatist, and rarely comes forward himself to address directly to the reader brief criticisms or explanations. Polybius on the contrary is entirely subjective. He is always on the stage himself, criticizing, expounding, emphasizing, making points, dotting the *i*'s and crossing the *t*'s, propounding and defending his personal views. Thucydides did all his constructive work beforehand, and presents to the reader only the syntheses and results. Polybius takes the reader fully into his confidence, and performs all the processes of analysis in his presence. Thucydides states in a few sentences the plan of his work, indicates in a few lines his principles of historiography; and his rare criticisms on other historians are confined to a word or two. Polybius devotes pages to an exposition of the scheme of his history, at the outset, and reiterates it in another place. At the end of his work he gave a chronological scheme of the whole plan. He had commenced with the intention of supplying an epitome of contents at the beginning of each Book, but afterwards preferred to place at the beginning of each Olympiad a summary of the events which occurred in it.[30] He thus showed a kindly solicitude that the reader should fully understand the construction of his work. He goes, at length, into the proper principles and methods of history, frequently returning to the subject, and he digresses into elaborate criticisms of other historians, such as Timaeus and Phylarchus, Ephorus and Theopompus. He is unsparingly didactic and his diffuse explanations are often wearisome. This feature, as to which he stands in marked contrast to the early historians, may partly be set down to the influence of popular philosophy, which tended to promote a didactic style. We might indeed say that the history of Polybius contains the material for a handbook of historical method; and this adds greatly to its value for us.

Like Thucydides and the ancients in general, Polybius believed in the eminent significance of the individual in history. He reiterates the platitude that one mind is more efficacious than a mass of men, quoting the saying of Euripides, "One wise plan prevails over many hands."[31] He takes a deep interest in the characters of the men who appear on his scene. On the other hand, he sees that there are potent forces at work besides great men. A student of the history of Rome, which had won her supreme position, unsteered by single men of transcendent powers, could not be blind to this. Polybius recognises the importance of national character. He considers the influence of climate upon it, and finds a key to a nation's character in its institutions and political life. We have seen the importance which he ascribed to the mechanism of political constitutions. But he had no idea of history as a continuous progress, no eye for what we call historical tendencies, no notion of the way in which historical changes are brought about by the innumerable and almost invisible activities of thousands and thousands of nameless people. He possessed a knowledge of the facts and conditions of his own age, and of the men of his own age, to which we could not attain even if we had his whole work in our hands. Yet, fragmentary as our knowledge is, we can say with some confidence that we have a deeper insight than he into the tendencies of his time, and of the time immediately preceding, and a clearer comprehension of the change through which the Roman state was then passing and of the causes at work. He never discerned how the new circumstances of Rome in the latter half of the third century were altering her commercial and economic condition, and were already modifying the character of the state. We owe our power of divining this to the enlarged experience of the human race.

To return to his treatment of individuals. While Thucydides leaves us to form our own impressions from their public acts and from the words which he makes them say, Polybius, in accordance with his method, analyses and discusses their qualities. But it is important to observe that he does not, like Xenophon in the *Anabasis,* and nearly all modern historians, attempt to draw complete portraits of Philip or Hannibal or Scipio, or any of the leading persons of his history, but condemns on principle such a mode of treatment. For, he says, men are inconsistent: they constantly act in a manner which belies and contradicts their real nature, sometimes under the pressure of friends, at others on account of the peculiar complexion of the circumstances. It is therefore misleading to characterize a man when he first appears on the stage, or to infer his whole character from particular acts. The right method is to criticize his actions as they occur.[32] The same man must be praised as well as blamed; he is changed by vicissitudes of affairs; his conduct, for instance, may become better or worse.[33] Characters such as that of Philip III. of Macedon, which seems to have specially attracted him as a problem, impressed him with the necessity of adopting this principle; and in the treatment both of Philip and of Hannibal we must admire the conscientious fairness of Polybius in endeavouring to understand and estimate their characters.

Psychology indeed was a subject on which Polybius seems to have reflected much. We can see his interest in it, for example, in the account which he gives of the mental process of learning to read;[34] in his observation that in fighting those have an advantage who have a stronger will to conquer, so that a battle is in a certain measure a contest of wills;[35] in his insistence on the importance of personal experience (αὐτοπάθεια); or in such a remark as that change from one kind of activity to another is a relief. His psychological ideas have furnished material for a treatise to a German scholar. One principle must specially be noticed because he applies it to his own work: the importance of connecting the unknown and remote with the known and familiar. For instance, he considers it useless to mention the names of strange places, which are mere sound conveying no meaning, unless they are brought into relation with the geographical knowledge which is familiar to the reader.[36] He does not omit to make observations on the psychology of the masses. Their chief characteristics he considers to be ignorance and cowardice; and therefore religious feeling is important for them, because they cannot endure surprises or face dangers without hope from the gods.[37] The only use of mythology is to preserve the religion of the multitude.[38] Polybius does not hold that religious belief has any value for the educated person; it would be superfluous in a state consisting exclusively of wise men. But he certainly did not underrate its importance in actual societies. He designates religion as the keystone of the Roman state.[39]

In general, it may be said that Polybius is large-minded in his judgments and aims at scrupulous fairness. While he applies ethical standards to the conduct of public men, his broad study of human nature inclines him generally to the more indulgent view of their acts. Perhaps no ancient writer was more impartial in temper than he, and the prejudices which we can detect are exceptions to the rule. These prejudices are chiefly to be discovered where he deals with the affairs of Greece. Here his patriotism has unquestionably coloured his account of Achaean politics, and he is distinctly unjust to the Aetolians. The danger of such partiality did not escape him. "A good man," he says, "should be fond of his friends and of his country, he must share in the hates and affections of his friends. But when he undertakes to write history, he must forget these attachments, he must often bestow the highest praises on enemies when facts require it, and, on the other hand, censure severely his most intimate friends when their errors demand such censure."[40] Elsewhere,[41] in censuring two Rhodian historians (Zeno and Antisthenes) for twisting facts to the credit of their country, he discusses the question whether a historian should allow himself to be influenced by patriotic feelings. "Admitting," he says, "that historians should lean to their countries, I deny that they should make assertions inconsistent with facts. We writers must unavoidably fall into many errors through ignorance, but if we write what is false, for our country's sake or to please our friends or to win favour, and measure truth by utility, we shall discredit the authority of our works and be no better than politicians." The indefeasible claim of historical truth cannot be more explicitly expressed or emphatically enforced; and the significance of these passages lies in the challenge which was thrown down to the prevailing practice of the rhetorical school of history. But Polybius has not absolutely adhered himself to his admirable doctrine. He is disposed to make their attitude to the Achaean League the measure for judging other Greek states. On the other hand, he is impartial towards Rome. The justification of Roman dominion is the *motif* of his work, and the practical lesson for his fellow-Greeks was acquiescence in that dominion. But if he fully recognised the great qualities of the Romans, his Greek sympathies secured him from being blind to their faults.

Polybius, then, stands out among the few ancient writers who understood the meaning and recognised the obligation of historical truth and impartiality. Belonging to no school, he opposed the tendencies of the current historiography of the day. But while he protests against straining after pathetic effects and such bids for popularity, he shows occasionally that he possessed the art of telling a moving tale, as in his description of Hannibal's passage of the Alps, and he can display powers of realism in describing an insurrection at Alexandria or the Mercenary war of the Carthaginians. But there is no attempt at striking word-pictures or purple passages; when he is effective, he succeeds, like Herodotus, by the simplest means. He followed the received usage of inserting speeches, and laid stress upon their importance. But he held that they should reproduce the tenor of what was actually said, and he censures Timaeus severely for having invented orations entirely out of his own imagination. Some of the speeches have a Polybian flavour, but we are bound to believe him that he had always evidence to work upon in their construction.

He was not indifferent to style; his care is shown in his scrupulous avoidance of hiatus. It is highly significant that in the Greek versions which he made of the Latin texts of the treaties of Rome with Carthage he neglected the rules of hiatus, the observance of which would have embarrassed or harmed the accuracy of the translation. He did not, so far as we know, follow literary models. To illustrate his diction and vocabulary we must look not to belles lettres but to the language of officialdom—decrees and despatches—and technical treatises on philosophy and science. Yet he had a wide acquaintance with literature and the classical poets. He quotes lyric poets, Pindar and Simonides, as well as Euripides. Like all educated Greeks, he was familiar with Homer, and the fragments of his thirty-fourth Book, which was concerned with the geography of the West, show that he was interested in Homeric criticism. The question was debated in ancient, as well as modern, times whether there was any real geographical background to the adventures of Odysseus. Do the islands of the Cyclops, of Circe, of Calypso, do Scylla and Charybdis, correspond to actual places on the Mediterranean coasts? Or are they "faery lands forlorn," and is it vain to seek their names on the traveller's chart? Eratosthenes held that Homer had here created a world of poetical imagination, and that the places are as imaginary as the people. "It is useless to look," he said,[42] "for the scenes of the wanderings of Odysseus. You will find those places when you find the man who stitched together the bag of the winds." Polybius did not agree with this view. He accepted the common opinion that the poet's geography was realistic, and did not hesitate to identify the passage of Scylla and Charybdis with the Straits of Messene. The work of M. Victor Bérard has at least shown that in principle Polybius was right.

But while rhetoric did not seduce Polybius, he could not escape from the philosophical and ethical tendencies of his age. A good deal of what I have said will have shown that he regarded the application of moral standards and the pronouncement of moral judgments as pertinent in history. His ethical preoccupation is shown very clearly in his study of political constitutions. The causes which come into play in bringing about decay and change are, according to his exposition, mainly ethical; he ignores political and economical forces. Here he is not thinking for himself; he is under the sway of the speculations of philosophical schools. Thucydides impresses us as more independent and freer from the influence of speculative theory in his criticism of facts. He was not imposed upon by constitutional forms, and never ascribed to them the significance which they possessed for Polybius. Any superiorities which Polybius seems to enjoy over Thucydides are due to the richer experience of two and a half eventful centuries of which records had been kept, to the larger stage on which Mediterranean history had come to move, and to the inspiration of the world-power of Rome pointing to a new idea of universal history.

The positive value of the historical labours of Polybius, as a trustworthy source, can hardly be appraised too highly. I may quote the judgment of Mommsen, who was not attracted towards the personality of the author. "His books are like the sun, in the field of history; where they begin, the veils of mist, which still enshroud the wars with the Samnites and with Pyrrhus, are lifted; where they end, a new and if possible more vexatious twilight begins."

Of that part of the work which was most original because he wrote as a contemporary and had not to rely entirely on other writers, only fragments have been preserved, and of the last years which saw the destruction of Greek independence very scanty fragments indeed. But much of the material has passed directly or indirectly into the books of later historians; he became, indeed, for the period which he treats the chief ultimate source of information. If another Polybius, a man of his political experience and his historical faculty, had appeared in the next generation, our knowledge of the period of the great democratic movement, a period so critical for the Roman state—from Tiberius Gracchus to the dictatorship of Sulla—would have been far clearer than it is. The task of continuing Polybius was, however, undertaken by a remarkable man of exceptional talent, Poseidonius of Apamea (*c.* 235–151 B.C.), whose wide influence as a thinker is becoming more and more recognised— recognised even to exaggeration. He was a pupil of the Stoic Panaetius; he taught in Rhodes, where Cicero heard his lectures; he was a friend of Pompey, and well known to cultivated circles in Rome. He travelled in western Europe, and embodied his geographical researches in a book *On the Ocean*, which was much used by Strabo. Besides being a philosopher and a geographer, he was a mathematician, an astronomer (he wrote a book on the size of the sun), a student of natural science, a meteorologist. He made an important contribution to the study of tides in relation to the phases of the moon. He had the encyclopaedic interest and the encyclopaedic faculty of an Aristotle or a Leibniz. History was only one, and not the chief, of his many pursuits. His historical work (in fifty-two or perhaps sixty-two Books), beginning with 144 B.C. where Polybius ended, appears to have come down to 82 B.C. We have only a few fragments of it, but it is the source of our knowledge of those times—the source from which Livy, Diodorus, Appian, Plutarch, and Josephus drew. The leanings of Poseidonius were somewhat oligarchical, and he was partial to his friend Pompey. Like Polybius he was a traveller, and like Polybius he played a part in political life; it was a smaller part, and on the tiny stage of Rhodes. He once acted as ambassador of his city to Rome. Polybius was first of all a man of action; Poseidonius was first of all a philosopher and a savant, and he had a strain of poetical imagination and enthusiasm, a certain passion, which we do not find in Polybius. It is to be feared that for the vagueness of our knowledge on some of the important facts of this period Poseidonius himself is responsible rather than those who compiled from him. His mental attitude was certainly different from that of Polybius, and the difference does not conduce to confidence in Poseidonius. For in philosophy he did not follow the sobriety of his master Panaetius; his Stoicism was of a more mystical strain; in fact, it departed so far from the earlier tenets of the sect that it may be described as a theology. He believed in the mantic art, on which he wrote a treatise,[43] and in the significance of dreams; and he was thus disposed to accept what Polybius would have rejected as fabulous. On the whole, I think we may say that while Poseidonius exercised a wide and deep influence on the intellectual life of his day, and occupies a considerable place in the history of ancient learning, and while his historical work was the chief source of the records of his time, and its loss is deplorable, he cannot be said to have advanced the study of history by new principles or methods, and in some respects he represented a retrogression from Polybius. His fragments show that general *Culturgeschichte* was a conspicuous feature of his work; and he seems to have aimed at suggesting a contrast between the rude but fresh manners of barbarians like the Gauls and Parthians, and the decadent civilisation of Egypt and Syria. We cannot form any definite idea of his general treatment, but we may say with probability that Poseidonius had qualities which entitled him to be reckoned among those historians to whose works men go, not for rhetoric or sentiment, but for the illumination of the past by reasonable thought.[44]

THE INFLUENCE OF GREEK ON ROMAN
HISTORIOGRAPHY

THE political genius of Rome might lead us to expect that the Romans would have possessed a home-grown historiography of their own, reflecting their national character. But Greek influence intervened before they had time to discover a form of historiography for themselves; and in this, as in all branches of literature, they found Greek influence irresistible. Their history was moulded by the Greeks; in its methods and principles it is Greek.

Its birth from Greek history was undisguisedly proclaimed by the fact that its founders, aristocrats contemporary with the Second Punic war, wrote their Roman annals in the Greek tongue. The chief of these writers, and the only one of whose work we can form any idea, was Q. Fabius Pictor, whose book was consulted and respected by Polybius. Greek was at that time recognised as the language of the educated world; it was the Esperanto of those parts of the universe that counted; and this fact outweighed the strong national feeling which would have suggested Latin. You may remember that Frederick the Great wrote his *Memoirs* in French, and that Gibbon at first thought of composing his *Decline and Fall* in that polite and universal idiom.

To break the tradition required an unconventional man who carried his national feelings to the length of miso-Hellenism and who was determined to go his own way, M. Porcius Cato. He wrote his history of Rome, the *Origines*, in his native tongue. It expressed his own strongly marked personality, and mirrored his prejudices. Discarding the annalistic form, he introduced freely his own observations and opinions, and in fact *liberavit animam suam*. Its significance, for our present purpose, is that it was effective in breaking the tradition: his successors wrote in Latin.

But the change was only in the vehicle. The Romans remained completely under the influence of Greek methods and models. The worst tendencies of Greek history were exemplified in the *Annals* of Valerius Antias, which came down to the time of Sulla. He outdid *Graecia mendax* in audacious falsification; all claims of truth were sacrificed to national vanity. Wachsmuth calls his work "a historical romance and of the worst kind." On the other hand we have Sallust, who was a younger contemporary. He belongs to a triumvirate of Roman historians, in which some think that his true place is second, next to Tacitus and above Livy. But unluckily of his chief book, dealing with a period of twelve years, 78–67 B.C., only some speeches and letters have survived. His monographs, the *Jugurtha* and the *Catiline,* enable us to see that his work was coloured to the core by a strong personality; it sensitively reflected the deep misgivings and gloomy outlook which the experiences of the Roman state in the days of Caesar and Pompey suggested to a pessimistic observer. It is significant that he was deeply attracted by the most original of previous Latin historians, Cato the Censor. But the writers who influenced him most were Greeks, Thucydides and Poseidonius. He came under the spell of Thucydides, but he was of too different a nature to imitate him except in superficial things.

Livy was inspired by the idea of giving to the Romans a history of the growth of their nation, which in the fulness of its treatment and the magnitude of its scale should be adequate to the theme. He rose to the majesty of his subject, and triumphantly satisfied the ideal of historiography which was popular at the time. The gentle and even flow of his style, his *clarissimus candor* and *lactea ubertas* are irresistible. But he had many of the deeply-rooted defects of the rhetorical school, though his history is incomparably superior to that of his Greek contemporary, the rhetorician Dionysius of Halicarnassus. He wished to be accurate, but his standard was not high and his methods were careless. Livy had no notion of the austere methods of historical research pursued by Thucydides and Polybius. He entirely disdained the trouble of consulting primary sources such as inscriptions or the Pontifical Acts. In one of the few cases in which he refers to an inscription, his attention was called to it by the Emperor Augustus, who displayed great interest in the progress of the work. He did not take to heart the maxim of Polybius that personal knowledge of topography is necessary for a historian in narrating military events. He did not, for instance, take the trouble to visit the scene of the Battle of Lake Trasimene, and in his story of that action he has jumbled together two inconsistent accounts. On the whole, there is a great deal of truth in the Emperor Caligula's criticism that he was "wordy and careless," *verbosus et negligens.*[1]

As the work of Sallust reflected, in its temper, the stirring age of the Civil Wars, so Livy's history mirrored the calm which settled over the Roman world after the triumph of Augustus. He was a Court historian, and his work fitted into the system of the political ideals of the Emperor. With its unimpassioned optimism, it is inevitably far less interesting than the writings of his predecessor, who so mercilessly exposed the corruption of the Roman aristocracy, and of his greater successor, who painted the dark sides of the Imperial régime. Tacitus was not only a writer of far stronger individuality than Livy, but also a far greater historian. He was more critical, and was guided by a higher standard of what historical research required. Our distrust in reading him is not of his facts or of his use of sources, but of his innuendo and his illumination. Haupt said he was born to be a tragic poet, and his pages are saturated with his personality. The dominant note of all he wrote is expressed in those words of doom, *urgent imperil fata.* The historian who exercised most influence on him was undoubtedly Sallust, whose political and ethical pessimism was akin to his own. He outdid Sallust in *brevitas Sallustiana*; he resembled him too in solemn and deadly seriousness; in his passion for psychological analysis. But here he was also affected by the tendencies of the rhetorical schools of his own time; there, too, psychological analysis and epigrammatic brevity had come into fashion. Tacitus, though an accomplished student of rhetoric, is very careful and sparing in the use of rhetorical artifices, which he always reserves for the production of some definite effect. But in his descriptions of battles he sacrifices accuracy to style; his motive for describing them at all was not military, but rhetorical, interest.

It so happens that we have a means of testing the relations of the speeches which Tacitus has introduced, to those actually delivered. A bronze tablet of Lyons preserves a considerable portion of the harangue which the Emperor Claudius addressed to the Senate when he conferred the *ius honorum* on the inhabitants of Gaul. Tacitus professes to reproduce this speech. A comparison of his version with the original shows that he took it as his basis, but remodelled it, rearranging the order, adding some new matter, cutting down tedious passages, adapting it to his own style, and eliminating the Emperor's ungainly mannerisms. For instance, Claudius in the middle of his speech suddenly addressed himself: "It is high time, O Tiberius Caesar Germanicus, to disclose yourself to the Senate and show whither your oration tends." This eccentric transition does not appear in Tacitus. But the general tenor and argument are the same. The case is highly instructive as exemplifying how the best historians like Tacitus and Thucydides constructed their speeches. When an original speech had been published, historians refrained from reproducing it. The literary canon of homogeneity of style, which the Tacitean treatment of the oration of Claudius illustrates so well, forbade them to transcribe it; and it would have been obviously out of place to challenge comparison by a paraphrase. We can prove this rule in the case of Livy, who expressly declines to give a speech of Cato for the Rhodians, which Cato had included in his own history, and in the case of Tacitus, who similarly omits the dying discourse of Seneca on the ground that it had been already published. Exceptions were only made in favour of very short pieces. For instance, Tacitus reproduces verbally a brief communication of Tiberius to the Senate, just as Xenophon reproduced the laconic message of a Lacedaemonian admiral. Otherwise, the rule which the Roman historians inherited from the Greeks was never to reproduce documents or speeches in their original form, and to avoid reproducing at all such as had been published. Suetonius and Cornelius Nepos were exceptional in not obeying this rule; they could quote the example of Polybius.

Sallust had skilfully employed the Thucydidean method of exhibiting the motives and personalities of historical actors in speeches. But he had not confined himself to this method; he also freely portrayed characters himself; for example, his two contrasted pictures of Cato and Caesar are famous; and he had freely introduced personal comments of his own. Tacitus adopted the dramatic and indirect method, but he developed that method with such elaborate skill and refinement that it became a new thing in his hands. One of the simplest examples of his art is the portrait of Augustus, which he exhibits reflected in the mirror of men's judgments about him. It is managed just as a dramatist might make two people of opposite views meet in the street and argue over somebody's character, in order to show what manner of man he was. But the *chef d'œuvre* of Tacitus is his *Tiberius*. The author had psychologically reconstructed that emperor on the assumption that the mainspring of his character was dissimulation; he never discusses it as a problem, but simply reveals the man in this light, interprets his acts and words in this sense, and uses all the devices of innuendo, of which he was so subtle a master, to bring it out. The Tacitean method is illustrated by contrasting the descriptions of Tiberius in Suetonius and Velleius Paterculus, who collect together all the traits of the Emperor and facts which attest them. It is also evident that Tacitus has produced his general effect by a limitation of his subject, by emphasizing certain sides and omitting others. The *Annals* are a history of Rome and the crimes of the Julio-Claudian dynasty. The wars of the period are indeed recorded, but it may be said with virtual truth that the book ignores the Empire. No reader of Tacitus would come away with the smallest conception of the efficiency with which the Empire as a whole was administered.

Tacitus, like Sallust, looked at history from an ethical point of view, I mean from the point of view of the morality which is valid for the individual. He judged actions by the ideals of virtue and nobility; he was not prepared to take time and circumstances into account, nor to acknowledge that the standard applied to private conduct may be inapplicable to public transactions. In this respect, he occupied the same ground as the late Lord Acton, whose first principle in reading history was the application of the strictest rules of private morality to the actions of public men. It may be thought by some that this attitude in examining the past is somewhat futile. Sociology is still in its infancy, and it may be asked, Has the time come for verdicts? Is not Thucydides more reasonable, and is not his political analysis more instructive, than the ethical criticism of Tacitus? The predominating moral interest is of course one of the features which Tacitus shares with the rhetorical school. The ethical side had been emphasized, without passion, by Greek historians since the fourth century; with Tacitus it was a question of life and death.

I have still to refer to an illustrious Latin historian who stands altogether apart from the rest, in method and style, as well as in his own relation to the facts which he records. As a clear businesslike narrative of external events, told from the inside, by one who had fuller knowledge than any other man, the *Commentaries* of Caesar are a model of excellence. In reading them, indeed, we have to remember that it was not a purely historical interest that moved the writer to assume the historian's part. He had political purposes in view. The Memoir of the Gallic War was written to show the necessity of his actions and to prove or illustrate his competence. The history of the Civil War, which he left unfinished, was designed to shift the blame from his own shoulders. Thus the works are in a certain sense political pamphlets. In the story of the conquest of Gaul we cannot control the narrative; it is possible that much has been suppressed; and

Caesar's artless simplicity may have been the instrument of most artful misrepresentation. Our present concern, however, is not the criticism of his facts, but his choice of that plain straightforward method of narration, which had been introduced by the men who had worked in the service of Alexander the Great. Of this genus of historical literature, Caesar's *Commentaries* are the only extant specimen; we can have little doubt that they are the best which antiquity produced; but they were not an original growth on Roman soil; the Memoirs of Pyrrhus and Aratus were precedents. It is, however, significant that Caesar regarded his own work as merely material for the professional, that is, the rhetorical, historian to work up.

You see then that the most eminent Roman historians moved entirely within the limits of Greek traditions, in regard to principles and methods. For them all, history was, as Cicero considered it, a branch of the art of rhetoric. We may, indeed, say that from the beginning of the Empire the distinction between Greek and Latin historians has only a subordinate significance. In studying historical literature from the time of Livy and Dionysius of Halicarnassus, Greek and Latin writers must be considered together. Rhetorical history remained in the ascendant, but antiquarian history also had some devotees. Rome has a distinguished roll of antiquarians to point to, such as Varro, Hyginus, Asconius, and it was the distinction of Suetonius to have written history which aimed simply at the industrious collection of facts, without any thought of rhetorical effects. His political attitude was very similar to that of Tacitus, but in his biographies, which (as Leo has shown) are built up on a conventional scheme, he keeps his own personal views in the background and lets the facts speak.

The development of the Graeco-Roman historiography under the early Empire, up to the time of Theodosius the Great, can now be studied in the elaborate work of Peter, the special value of which consists in treating the Greek and Latin historians together, and in showing how the writing of history was affected by the Court and by the public. He has illustrated abundantly how a writer's freedom in treating contemporary history was limited by fears and hopes; and how his scope was narrowed by the lack of interest of the public of these ages in any contemporary events except the scandals of the Court. Exceptions were few. We have been accustomed to think of Ammianus Marcellinus as the only Latin historian after Tacitus whose merits entitle him to a high place. Recently a new star has been announced, whom Kornemann, the discoverer, has named "the last great historian of Rome." This unknown writer is said to have supplied the authors of that ambiguous collection of imperial biographies known as the *Historia Augusta* with valuable material. Even if we accept the demonstrations, the place he holds among Latin historians will not be vacated by Ammianus for this anonymous author who flourished in the age of the Severi.[2]

I may say, finally, a few words about universal history, which became an established form of composition under the Roman Empire. It has often been noticed how the cosmopolitan doctrines of the Stoics, their creed of the brotherhood of men, gave a stimulus to the construction of comprehensive works embracing the annals of the known peoples of the world. The value of universal history, on the Stoic assumptions, has been stated impressively enough by Diodorus of Agyrion. "All men," he says, "living, or who once lived, belong to the common human family though divided from one another by time and space; and the universal historian who aims at bringing them all under a common view is a sort of minister of divine providence. That providence orders alike the stars and the natures of men, throughout the cycles of time, allotting to each its proper part; and those who have recorded the history of the world as if it were one town, have, in their works, supplied mankind with a sort of bourse for exchanging records of the past." Diodorus himself, however, was quite unequal to the task. There is no central idea in his work; there is no grasp of lines of development, no discernment of interconnexion between the parts of his subject, no independent thought of his own. The special histories of the various peoples rest side by side in the framework of his forty Books (was the number suggested by Polybius?). His history is a rhetorical compilation of excerpts from older writers which he has paraphrased, and its value for us lies in the circumstance that its extant portions contain so much of lost writers like Ephorus and Poseidonius.

Far superior in conception and grasp seems to have been the lost work of Pompeius Trogus, of which we know something from its Epitome by Justin. It was a universal history of the Hellenic and oriental world. Roman history was excluded up to the point at which Greek and Eastern peoples came into contact and collision with Rome. It has been plausibly conjectured that the author omitted Roman history because it had been so fully treated by his contemporary, Livy. But though its universal character was thus limited, it showed a sense of unity and continuity, like that of Polybius; and this was reflected in the title of the work, *Philippica*, which indicated that Macedonian history was, more or less, the guiding or binding thread. Older history had culminated in the Macedonian Empire, and out of it had developed the great monarchies after Alexander. The work was thus an intelligent development of Polybian ideas.

Such reconstructions helped to prepare for the new framework into which history was compressed, and the new meaning which was given to it, by the Christians. They undertook the task of synchronizing Graeco-Roman with Jewish records, and constructing a universal history in theological interests.[3] The Church could not avoid grappling with this problem. Appealing to the civilised world, Christianity was forced to take account of the past of the non-Hebrew peoples; making extraordinary and paradoxical claims for the superlative importance of Jewish history, it had to assign to the histories of the Greeks and Romans their proper place in the universal scheme. The Hebrew Scripture determined the six great ages of human history distinguished by Augustine, of which the last began with the birth of Christ, and would endure—such was the confidence of these interpreters of history—to the end of the world.[4] The Christian interpretation found the central idea of world-history in a religious and not in a political phenomenon, and it introduced into historiography a new and pernicious principle. Hitherto history had been perfectly free. Homer had indeed enjoyed an excessive authority among the Greeks, but belief in Homer was not a religious doctrine, and men like Thucydides and Eratosthenes used the Homeric poems, just as we do, like any other ancient source. It was with imperfect methods and inadequate conceptions of the conditions of the problem that the Greeks had attempted to order the traditions of their own and other races into a consistent whole; but they had worked quite freely, guided by reason alone and unfettered by dogma. Christian historiography installed the superior guidance of an indefeasible authority, the divinely inspired tradition of the Jewish records, whereby they determined the general frame and perspective of the history of the world. This was the first appearance of the principle which Cardinal Manning expressed in his famous saying that dogma must overcome history, and which guides all the historiography of the Ultramontane school.

The Christian reconstruction of history held men's minds throughout the Middle Ages, imposed as it was by the highest ecclesiastical authority. But though it marked no advancement of knowledge, though the synthesis was simply grotesque, it served to emphasize and intensify the idea of the unity of mankind which had already been preached by the Stoics. With the Stoics this idea had such a vague application that it came to little more than an abstract theory; with the Christians it acquired a real and intense meaning, inasmuch as they believed all the inhabitants of the earth to have a common and vital interest, though they might not know it, in the Christian dispensation. In so far as it accustomed men to realise the conception of a solidarity among all the races of humanity, the Christian interpretation assisted in the transition from the ancient to the modern conception of universal history. For this office a price was paid. History submitted to authority, and free inquiry was suspended for centuries.

We may also note that the conception of universal history which prevailed in the Middle Ages was connected with a general theory sometimes described as the first attempt at a philosophy of history, in so far as it professed to supply a guiding clue and a meaning to the whole development. This theory was worked out by Augustine in his *De civitate Dei,* wherein the event to which the whole world moves is defined as the victory of the *civitas Dei* (the Church) over the *civitas Diaboli* (represented by the secular kingdoms). This transcendent principle could give little help to a student desiring to comprehend the causes of the actual course of history; and the speculation of Augustine no more claims to be called a philosophy of history than the cyclical theories of the Greeks. But though *Geschichtsphilosophie* is a modern invention and Herder was its founder, the Christian construction marks an important stage: for the historical process was for the first time definitely conceived as including past and future in a totality which must have a meaning.

In these lectures I hope that I have in some measure explained how the Greeks did not suddenly create, but rather by a gradual process of criticism evolved history, disengaging it from the mythic envelope in which fact and fiction were originally blended; how this process corresponded to the development of critical thought and scientific inquiry, first in Ionia and then at Athens; how the early historians were stimulated by those political events which brought Ionia into close contact with the East and by the simultaneous beginnings of geographical exploration; and how history completed the first stage of its growth and definitely extricated itself from the mythological mists which hung about its infancy and childhood, through the brilliant inspiration which occurred to the genius of Thucydides, the idea of studying critically and recording political events as they occurred. We saw that the chief events in Greek history reacted upon Greek historiography. The Persian conquests led to the investigation of "modern" history; the defeats of Persia by Greece inspired Herodotus; the Athenian Empire stimulated Thucydides; the rise of the Macedonian power, suggesting a new possibility of Hellenic unity, suggested also the conception of a comprehensive or universal history of Hellas; the Macedonian conquest of the East enlarged the range of historical interest; and, finally, the Roman conquests created in the mind of Polybius the largest conception of history that had yet emerged. We saw too that history was intimately affected by the general intellectual movements of each successive age — by the scepticism and science of Ionia, by the great illumination of the Sophists, by the literary ideals of Isocrates, by the literary reaction of Asia against Attic convention, by the Peripatetic philosophy which created antiquarian history, and afterwards by Stoicism; we saw that it was governed in its general development by the transcendent influence of rhetoric in Greek life; and we noticed that it was affected by the fact that in some measure it supplied the demand which is now supplied by fiction. Finally, we have seen how Roman historiography followed the lines of Greek historiography from which it sprang.

It still remains to consider the ideas which the ancients entertained as to the use and purpose of studying history and recording it, in the light of modern ideas on the same subject.

LECTURE VIII

VIEWS OF THE ANCIENTS CONCERNING THE USE OF HISTORY

It was not reserved for modern historians to ask themselves why history should be studied and why it should be written. The question was considered by ancient writers; and it was first posed by Thucydides. Herodotus indeed announced that the general purpose of his work was to preserve the memory of past events and record great actions which deserve the meed of fame. This statement shows that Herodotus had not asked himself the question; he assumed, and rightly assumed, the human interest of history; but he did not examine what it meant. He was prompted to write his prose epic by the same instinct which prompted the Homeric minstrels to compose their epic poems.

μοῦσ' ἄρ' ἀοιδὸν ἀνῆκεν ἀειδέμεναι κλέα ἀνδρῶν.

The muse inspired the bard to sing of glorious deeds of men.

He esteemed the aim of the historian to be exactly the same as the aim of the epic poet—to entertain an audience. So long as it was written from this motive, it is clear that history was not likely to make truth and accuracy its first consideration.

Thucydides definitely asked himself the question why a record of human events should be kept, and his answer placed history on a new footing. He repudiated the view that its only or chief object was to provide entertainment, and he laid down a reason for its study, which, so far as we know, was discovered by himself.

154

"The accurate knowledge of what has happened," he says, "will be useful, because, according to human probability, similar things will happen again." This is the first statement of the opinion that history has another function than the satisfaction of curiosity or of patriotic pride, that it has a definite practical utility, that it contains lessons to instruct the statesman or the military commander. No historian was more profoundly convinced of the truth of this view than Polybius. He believed implicitly, as we saw, that history is a school of statesmanship as well as of the art of war; he is never weary of insisting on the practical utility of his subject; and the earnestness with which he held and preached this "pragmatical" doctrine is one of the distinctions of his work. As we have seen, the larger number of the ancient historiographers at all times laid themselves out exclusively to please the reading public. But any ancient writer, subsequent to Thucydides, if you had asked him what was the use of studying history beyond the passing entertainment which it might yield, would have replied that the study served a practical purpose, supplying examples and warnings, and enabling men to judge the present and future by the past. Moralists (and with many historians the moral interest was predominant) would have insisted further that history supplied object lessons in ethics.

Now the point I would draw your attention to is that the ancients, generally, regarded history as possessing a practical use, and found the chief justification of its study therein. Before going on to consider the assumptions on which their particular view of its utility depends, I must say a word about the general proposition that history is a subject of practical value. It seems to be opposed to a view, promulgated in the last century, which repudiates all practical ends and asserts that history must be studied purely for its own sake, as an end in itself, without any ulterior object, and that any bearings on practical life which may be assigned to it are incidental. This view, if interpreted in an absolute and literal sense, seems to me to be no more than simple nonsense. History cannot be isolated (except provisionally for methodical purposes) from the total complex of human knowledge; and human knowledge has no value out of relation to human life. But if we explain "history for its own sake" as a regulative maxim, it is important and useful. In this sense, it means that history must be studied *as if* it had no bearing on anything beyond itself; the historian, in investigating the facts of the past, must not, at least in the first instance, consider anything beyond the facts themselves. In other words, it assumes that history is a science. The study of *natural* phenomena intimately affects society in its ethics, religion, and politics; the study of *historical* phenomena must affect them too. But like physical sciences and all other branches of knowledge, history requires for its scientific development complete freedom and independence; its value is annulled and its powers are paralysed if it consents to be ancillary to politics, ethics, or theology; in order to fulfil its function, it must (like all sciences) be treated as if it were an end itself. This is the true value and, so far as I can see, the only value of the cry, "History for its own sake!" inscribed on the banner under which history has made such a striking advance in the nineteenth century. But this value, I repeat, is only that of a regulative principle; it concerns only the methods and immediate aims of historians; it does not express the final purpose of their labours.

The Greeks were the founders of antiquarianism, and in a previous lecture I spoke of this as one of their precious contributions to human progress. Once it was started, it was pursued instinctively, unreflectingly, without asking the question, why? But a general answer was given in the circumstances of its origin. It was founded, as I said, by the Aristotelian school of philosophy, and was the result of the importance which Aristotle attached to all phenomena, as things worth study and possessing significance for man's synthesis of the universe. And without being Aristotelians, or belonging to any school of philosophy, we must admit, that, as all things are interrelated, there must be a point at which every fact has a possible significance for man's view of his world, and therefore a practical value. Take historical phenomena. In the final synthesis of history, which may at least conceivably be achieved in the indefinitely distant future, all facts must have a place. And when we consider the inevitable lacunae in our records, it is clear that every fact is precious; for instance, one trivial detail may be the means of leading us to the right reconstruction, just as in a detective's investigation an apparently insignificant circumstance (such as the spelling of a word) may put the clue in his hands. You never can tell. Thus the antiquarian historian is playing the long game. He collects, sifts, and interprets facts which, if you take the short view, may seem merely curious, without relation to human life, not the business of a man whose interests are human; but at any time one of these facts may enable us to solve a problem, or prove a theory, the human interest of which is evident. We may say then that the cry of "history for its own sake," means that history has begun systematically to play the long game. Let us remember that however long be the game and however technical the rules, human interest is its ultimate justification. Let us not take the phrase "history for its own sake" to mean that it is not the proper function of history to serve any ulterior interest, and that any practical use it may have is thrown in, but not guaranteed. This idea is characteristically academic, one of those cloistral inanities which flourish, preposterous and unashamed, in the congenial air of universities.

But, further, we must not be misled into ignoring or underrating the immediate practical value which the study of history possesses; and this is the point which I would invite you especially to consider. The most important and able ancient historians, although some of them had antiquarian interests, held that the purpose of studying history must be sought in its practical value, and in immediate relations to life. But their idea of what that practical value consisted in, necessarily differs from our view of the matter at the present stage of man's development. The experience of the race and the advance of scientific thought have transformed our ideas of our own position in the universe; and now the human or practical interest in history turns out to be far more vital and deeply founded than the ancients, with their outlook on life, could have suspected.

Let us examine more closely the ancient doctrine. Both Thucydides and Polybius based their view that history possesses direct utility for men of affairs, on the assumption that similar situations recur, and that the problems of the past will come up again for solution in the future. Thucydides, according to his habit, states this doctrine in the briefest form; Polybius explains the principle with his usual elaboration, and rests it on a philosophical theory. We saw how he presented the theory of *anacyclosis,* a cyclical movement of history. At the end of each cycle a new circuit begins, and history follows, as it were, along the line of its former tracks. This view was widely current; Cicero expresses it in the phrase *miri orbes et quasi circuitus,* "certain strange orbits and revolutions." The *a priori* synthesis of universal history which was launched on the world by the early Christian fathers, in the interest of their religion, threw the cyclical theory into the background. That theory was plainly incompatible with the central dogma of Christianity. *Alter erit tum Tiphys* would have meant *alter erit tum Christus,* and this would have stultified the Christian faith. But cyclical theories reappeared at the Renaissance. Machiavelli, who agreed with the ancients, and went further than they, in his high estimation of history as an instructress in politics, similarly based his view on the principle of a cyclical movement. Guicciardini likewise believed in the doctrine.

Our longer experience has taught us that the assumptions on which the ancients grounded the claim of history to practical utility are untenable. The theory of cycles has been abandoned for the idea of indefinite "progress," and we have ascertained that history does not repeat itself; that the likenesses between historical phenomena at different times are superficial and far less important than the differences. It follows that the particular kind of use which the ancients ascribed to history cannot be upheld, and that, if it does possess value for the education of men of affairs, that value is either of a more general nature, or entirely different from what they supposed.

And, as a matter of fact, we have ceased to look on history as a storehouse of examples and warnings for the politician, though we recognise that it has an educative value by familiarising him with the variety of political phenomena and by enlarging his horizon. But the conceptions of causality and development which govern our view, but did not govern the Greek view, of the world, have shown us that any given situation, or any social or political phenomenon, cannot be understood unless we know its antecedents; or in other words, that to comprehend the significance of the present we must be acquainted with the history of the past. This, I think you would agree, is the main reason (according to our present ideas) why a study of history is desirable, if not indispensable, for the man who undertakes to share in the conduct of public affairs, and is desirable also for the private citizen who votes, and criticizes, and contributes to the shaping of public opinion.

We may therefore still make the same claim for the study of history which Polybius made for it, that it is a school for statesmen and citizens, though we base the claim on a different ground. But beyond this direct utility, it has a larger and deeper practical importance. For the last two generations historical investigation has been exercising, steadily and irresistibly, an influence on our mental attitude; it has been affecting our sense of our own position in the world and our estimate of the values of things. History, in the ordinary and narrower sense of recorded human transactions, has been advancing concurrently with that wider history, which is the business of physical science, and which embraces the evolution of life on our planet, the evolution of the planet itself, and the evolution of the cosmos. But certain results of *historical* science, though less sensational, have been in some respects not less effective, than the results of *physical* science, because they are closer to us and, at present at least, concern us more directly. These results may perhaps be summed up most concisely in the phrase used by German writers, "historical relativity." We have come to see that all events in the past, however differing in importance, were relative to their historical conditions; that they cannot be wrenched out of their chronological context and endowed with an absolute significance. They are parts of a whole, and have no meaning except in relation to that whole, just as a man's arm has no meaning apart from his body. The recognition of this truth at once affects our view of the present; for it follows that the ideas and events of to-day have no absolute value, but merely represent a particular stage of human development. Ideas and facts are thus put in their place. Some are abased, others are exalted. If they are dependent on their historical context, they may also be justified by it. For instance, from the point of view of modern conditions, we shudder at the relation which the Church held to the State in the Middle Ages; but when we study the conditions of that period, we may acknowledge that the relation was justified. It is hard to say at which of our present-day Western institutions future generations will shudder most; but we may hope that they will also discover justifications. This principle of historical relativity induces what may be called the historical attitude of mind; it changes our outlook also on the present and the future; and therefore it has a direct practical value. Perhaps it is fair to say that it is one of the most important results of the mental development of the nineteenth century.[1]

I have suggested that this change is not less effective than our new conceptions of the evolution of nature. I may illustrate this by comparing the ways in which the advance of historical science and the advance of physical science have respectively operated on theology. The discoveries of geology, the doctrine of evolution, and the Darwinian theory created loud alarm in the Churches, but they really only touched outworks; and their acceptance by ecclesiastical authorities could not have had a much greater effect on the received body of essential doctrine than the acceptance of the heliocentric system which seemed a diabolical idea to the persecutors of Galilei. Contrast the effects of the *historical* criticism which began with Strauss and Bauer. It has been operating as a steady and powerful solvent of traditional beliefs; and to-day we see that within the Churches the men who have brains and are not afraid to use them are transforming the essential doctrines, under the aegis of historical criticism, so radically that when those doctrines emerge it will be difficult to recognise them.

I may observe here, and by the way, that it is highly important for the historian to be aware that the doctrine of historical relativity applies no less to his own historical judgments than to other facts. His view is conditioned by the mentality of his own age; the focus of his vision is determined within narrow limits by the conditions of contemporary civilisation. There can therefore be nothing final about his judgments, and their permanent interest lies in the fact that they are judgments pronounced at a given epoch and are characteristic of the tendencies and ideas of that epoch. The Greeks had no notion of this. They would have said that the judgment of a wise man at any time might be final or absolutely valid. Older Christian historians thought that they were in possession of absolute criteria; and the illusion that a historical judgment may be the last word is still prevalent. It must ultimately yield to the principle of historical relativity which, as the experience of the race grows, will be more and more fully recognised.

Before I pass from this principle I may note another point. One might think *a priori* that the study of history is eminently adapted to form an antidote to chauvinism, self-satisfaction, and intolerance. It cannot, however, be said that hitherto it has actually done much to counteract these habits of mind; it has been more inclined to subserve them. But it seems probable that it may be more effective in the future. The new historical conception, which we have been considering, is evidently calculated to promote the spirit of tolerance, and cool the spirit of self-satisfaction, more efficaciously than any previous idea. The tolerance of the ordinary man who naïvely urges in excuse of the heathen that they "know no better" must be applied, on the principle of historical relativity, to ourselves; that principle bids us remember that *we* "know no better," that we stand within the strict barriers of our historical conditions, and that we shall be judged hundreds or thousands of years hence by critics who look forth from a higher specular platform of civilisation.

The thought of the judgment of a distant posterity leads us to another, though closely related, conception which has only in recent times become alive and real for us. It is remarkable how little the Greeks and Romans thought or speculated about the future of the race. The shortness of the period over which their historical records extended, their doctrine of cyclical recurrence, and the widely spread belief in a decline from a golden age, may have hindered them from taking a practical interest in the subject; though they contemplated long periods of time, for instance the *magnus annus,* equivalent in duration to 12,954 ordinary years. Tacitus, in a very interesting passage, asks: What do we mean by using the terms ancient and modern? "The four hundred years, which separate us from Demosthenes, seem long in comparison with the brevity of human life; but they are almost a vanishing quantity if you compare them with the duration of the ages (*ad naturam saeculorum*); why, if you consider even the *magnus annus,* Demosthenes, whom we call an ancient, seems to belong to the same year, nay the same month, as ourselves." This passage stands almost alone, I think, in its appreciation of historical perspective. But such flashes of consciousness of our position in time did not awaken any serious or persistent curiosity about the future fortunes of the race. The Greeks were imbued with what may justly be called a progressive spirit; but they did not associate their labours for the improvement of civilisation with any notion of an indefinite advance of the human race in knowledge, in mastery of nature, and in the structure of society. I think we may safely say that the general conditions of their own life and thought seemed to the Greeks final, capable only of modification and improvement in details; they never dreamed that more complex forms of civilisation, and entirely different from theirs, might be reached by a gradual development in the course of time. They dreamed of a golden age, but they generally placed it behind them. They sought it in simpler, not in more complex, conditions. And their eagerness to improve the lot of man did not take the form of a conscientious or passionate sense of obligation to posterity. The idea of duty towards posterity which often appears in Greek patriotic orations has mainly a rhetorical value, and does not imply any serious concern about future generations. Afterwards, the fancy of the Christians that the life of the human race on earth would be very brief, and that men would then pass into monotonous states in which there would be no history, excluded any thoughts of future terrestrial progress; and the psychological effects of this error, promulgated by the Church, are a distinct factor in human development. It is only since this fiction has been exploded that the vista of progress in an indefinitely long future has become part of our mental outlook, and has introduced, as all ideas of such a range must introduce, a new ethical principle, namely, duty towards the future heirs of the ages. Progress was a feature in the philosophy of Leibniz. In 1750 Turgot stated a theory of historical progress very clearly. But though the doctrine was not new at the time of the French Revolution, the full significance of the idea was first impressed on the world in the famous book of Turgot's friend, Condorcet, *Esquisse d'un tableau historique des progrès de l'esprit humain* (1795). Here the meaning of the historical process was declared to be social and political progress. It is easy to see that this view, which was diffused by the writings of Comte and Buckle, as well as by the speculations of Saint-Simon and Fourier, was calculated to stimulate interest in the past more powerfully than any previous conception. It imparts to history an intenser meaning. We are led to conceive the short development which is behind us and the long development which is before us as coherent parts of a whole; our "pragmatic" interest in the destinies of our race necessarily communicates a "pragmatic" interest to its past fortunes.

"Progress" of course implies a judgment of value, and is not scientific. It assumes a standard,—some end or ends, by relation to which we judge historical movements and declare that they mean progress. We have no proof that absolute progress has been made, for we have no knowledge of an absolute end; and, therefore, scientifically we are not justified in speaking of the history of civilised man as progress; we can only be sure that it is a causal sequence of transformations.

It may, then, be objected that the indefinite progress of the race is only an assumption, which time may disprove. It may be asked too, what guarantee have we that our Western civilisation, granting that it is on an upward gradient, and that no bounds or bars to its ascent are yet in sight, may not some day reach a definite limit, through the operation of some cause which is now obscure to our vision? Fully admitting that such theoretical scepticism is justifiable, and that persistent progress is an assumption, I submit that it does not affect my point. The idea of progress is, in the present age, an actual, living force; and what I have said as to its bearing on the study of history remains valid. May we not even say that the uncertainty which hangs about the question, with the possibility of man's progress on the one hand, and of his decadence on the other, communicates an appealing interest to the study of the past, as a field in which we may discover, if we can penetrate deep enough, some clue to the destinies of civilisation?

The absence of the idea of an indefinite progress in Greek and Roman speculation is one of the gulfs which separate us from the ancients. Its emergence has had the consequence of making history far more alive. With the Greeks, who applied the inadequate conception of Tyche or Fortune, the reconstruction of the past was an instinct which they justified by reasons which were superficial. For us, because we have a deeper insight into the causal connexion of past and future, because we have grasped the idea of development and dreamed the dream of progress, the reconstruction of history has become a necessity.

It has also become a science. The promotion of history to the rank of a science or *Wissenschaft* is due to the conception of development. We conceive every historical event or phenomenon as a moment in a continuous process of change, and the historian's problem is to determine as completely as possible its connexions with what went before and with what came after, to define its causal relations and its significance in the development to which it belongs. The unattainable ideal of historical research is to explain fully the whole development of human civilisation. This is as much a scientific problem as to trace the history of the solar system or of animal life on the earth, though natural and historical science deal with very different kinds of data, and employ different methods. If the Greeks had possessed records extending over the history of two or three thousand years, the conception of causal development would probably have emerged, and they might have founded scientific history. The limitation of their knowledge of the past to a few centuries disabled them from evolving this idea; and history therefore always remained subordinate to immediate practical ends. But we must not underrate the importance of the new view which Thucydides announced to the world, that history is not merely a story book, but an education for statesmen. That view marked a great advance. It meant a new conception of the historian's responsibility and the inauguration of a higher standard of accuracy. Its proclamation by Thucydides may be placed beside the announcement of scientific history in 1824[2] by Ranke, who suggested that the historian's task is not to teach lessons or pass judgments, but simply to investigate how things happened. And as the view of Thucydides was combined with the requirement of accuracy, so the appearance of the modern doctrine was contemporaneous with the introduction of scientific methods.

As a science, history is disinterested. Yet the very idea of development, which led to the conception of history as a science, has enhanced its interest for mankind. So far, indeed, is the Greek view that history has a value for life from being exploded, that the bearing of the past on our mental outlook, on our ideas and judgments, on the actualities of the present and the eventualities of the future, is increasing more and more, and is becoming charged with deeper significance. The Hellenic conception of history as humanistic is truer than ever.

APPENDIX

THE RE-HANDLING OF HIS HISTORY
BY THUCYDIDES

THE natural probability that Thucydides occupied the years of his exile after the Fifty Years' Peace in finishing and revising the history of the war which was apparently over, is borne out by a number of passages which evidently contemplate only the Ten Years' War, and must have been differently phrased if they had been composed after 404 B.C. But, on the other hand, there are also a number of passages which refer to later events, and imply the Sicilian expedition and the fall of Athens. The obvious explanation is that the author read over the first portion of his work, and made a number of additions and alterations, but allowed some inconsistent phrases to escape his eye.[1]

The most unmistakable of these additions is the passage[2] in which the author escorts Pericles from the scene and characterizes his statesmanship in the light of the subsequent events which approved its wisdom, showing that if his policy had been pursued, and if he had had a successor like himself, the issue would have been different. Here Thucydides comments on the Sicilian expedition and refers to the later events of the war.[3]

But there is a far longer and more important section in the first Book which must be judged a subsequent insertion: the historical sketch of the growth of Athens from the year 478 to 435 B.C. The purpose of this sketch is to exhibit the growth of the Athenian hegemony, and its justification is that the true cause of the war, so far as the Spartans were concerned, was to prevent Athens from increasing that hegemony still more. Now if Thucydides had grasped this idea from the first, the appropriate place for his historical sketch, both logically and chronologically, was at the beginning of his work, in the Introduction. It would have formed a natural continuation of the still earlier history which he had sketched there. Instead, it comes in after the account of the First Assembly of allies at Sparta, strangely interrupting the narrative. It serves perhaps an artistic purpose; for it affords a not unwelcome pause after the strain of the four speeches in the First Assembly, before we pass to the immediately following speech of the Corinthians in the Second Assembly. But while this consideration may have determined the place chosen for its insertion, it was, I believe, an afterthought. There is internal evidence that it was not originally part of the work.[4] For the Introduction, where, as I said, we might have expected to find such a sketch, actually contains a brief summary of the relevant features of the period.[5] Further, Thucydides had before him, as he tells us, the Attic chronicle of Hellanicus; the defects of that work supplied him with a special motive for writing a more adequate and accurate narrative; and this work of Hellanicus was not published in its earlier form till 411 B.C., in its later till 404 B.C. And may we not fairly say that these prolegomena had a fuller justification in a history of a war ending in the catastrophe of the Athenian empire than in the narrative of a war ending with the indecisive Peace of 421 B.C., which left things pretty much as they were?

Again, we may reasonably suspect that the speech of Hermocrates at Gela in 424 B.C. was composed and inserted after the Sicilian expedition. While it contains remarks which seem to imply that the later events were before the author's mind,[6] the decisive consideration is that the significance of the transactions of 424 B.C. was not apparent till the events beginning in 415 B.C., and it seems most improbable that but for those events Thucydides would have emphasized the Congress of Gela by introducing the speech of Hermocrates.

It is a delicate question whether some of the other speeches in the early section have been retouched, and reflect light impinging from what at the time lay in the obscurity of the future. For instance, in the appeal for peace which Spartan envoys addressed to the Athenian assembly,[7] at the time of the Sphacterian episode, they hold up an ideal of conduct which sounds like an ironical reflexion on Sparta's own treatment of Athens twenty years later. To Eduard Meyer, the funeral oration pronounced by Pericles on those who had fallen in the first year of the war seems designed by the author to be in truth a funeral oration on Athens herself. This is a pretty idea, but I cannot find anything in the speech necessarily implying that it was written after the catastrophe. On the other hand, in the later speech of Pericles, delivered to encourage the Athenians in their despondency, there is a passage which seems to accuse him of second sight. There is a vein of pessimism or melancholy, a note which Pericles would not have struck on such an occasion, and which the author would hardly have introduced before the worst had befallen. The speaker observes that decline and fall (ἐλασσοῦσθαι) is a law of nature, and that if Athens should fall, she will leave a great memory of her empire, her military successes, and her wealth. This is the consolation one might proffer after 404 B.C.; it is not what would have been said to comfort the citizens in 429 B.C.; it is hardly what would have been written in the interval.

The narrative of the last years of the first war may have demanded revision for another reason. The author was absent from Athens ever since he assumed the command of a fleet in Thrace, and there were documents and information which *perhaps* he had no opportunity to procure until he returned to his country after his exile. It has been suggested by Kirchhoff that the text of the armistice between Athens and Sparta in 423 B.C.[8] was a subsequent insertion. It might, of course, have been procured at Sparta. The text too of the Peace of 421 B.C.[9] is inserted in a narrative which reads rather as if it had been composed without accurate knowledge of the precise stipulations;

but this can hardly be pressed. In general it seems probable that all the verbal copies of documents which appear in the text would, in the final revision, have been reproduced in the author's own words.

Although Thucydides re-handled his early work, which was now to be only part of a much greater work, he never prepared it finally for publication or gave it the last touches of revision. Passages remain which exhibit the earlier view that the war was over in 421; and there are difficulties here and there which are probably due to want of final correction.

In the transition from the first to the second part of his history (v. 20–26) there are clear signs of imperfect joining, due to the successive views which Thucydides entertained of the war, namely:

(1) Before 414 B.C.: one war of ten years (*τοῦ πολέμου τοῦδε*, 20. 1);

(2) After 414 B.C.: two wars, of which the second began in this year and was in progress;

(3) After 404 B.C.: one war of twenty-seven years.

In the first place we can see, I think, how Thucydides originally concluded his history of the first war, before he thought of a continuation (414 B.C.). We have two conclusions, c. 20 and c. 24. C. 20 is the natural conclusion; it immediately follows the Fifty Years' Peace which terminated the war. But then cc. 21–24 relate the alliance between the Athenians and Lacedaemonians which followed a little later; and a phrase in c. 24 betrays the fact that this was inserted after 404 B.C.: *καὶ τὸ θέρος ἦρχε τοῦ ἐνδεκάτου ἔτους*. The eleventh year, of what? Of the war of twenty-seven years. After these words there follows: *ταῦτα δὲ τὰ δέκα ἔτη ὁ πρῶτος πόλεμος ξυνεχῶς γενόμενος γέγραπται*. Obviously this is (1) out of place here; it ought to come in c. 20 after the Peace; and (2) in point of grammar, *ταῦτα* is not intelligible, for no ten years have been mentioned in the context. But if it came originally in c. 20 (whether after the last sentence or after the first; in both positions *ταῦτα* would be equally in place), it was considerably altered, for the point of *ξυνεχῶς* is the contrast between the Ten Years' War and the Twenty-seven Years' War. But the alteration was made hastily and provisionally; and ταῦτα, which betrays it, shows the lack of a careful final revision.

Cc. 25, 26 form the introduction to the second part of the history. C. 26 declares itself to have been written after 404 B.C. C. 25 *may* have been written while Thucydides still considered the second part to be the history of a second war; but there is no proof of this hypothesis.[10] On the other hand, the introduction of πρώτῳ, πρῶτος at the end of the first part (20 *ad fin.*, 24 *ad fin.*) might naturally have been made when he began his continuation after 414 B.C.

It is an interesting philological problem to penetrate into the secrets of the historian's workshop, but here I have been only concerned to illustrate the important facts that the first part of the work was re-handled and that in some parts it needed further revision.

ENDNOTES

LECTURE I

[1] Hesiod's *Theogony* contains a first crude idea of a history of civilisation in the legend of the Five Ages of man, which evidently brings up to date an older version in which the ages were Four. The fanciful notion of marking the degeneration of the race by four ages named after four metals is improved upon by interpolating the age of Homeric heroes before the last or iron age.

[2] In this connexion Mahaffy notes an "anxiety to show hereditary rights in all the usurpers of power throughout early Greek history" (*Prose Writers*, i. 10).

[3] Cp. Murray, *Rise of the Greek Epic*, p. 162.

[4] The main authority for Aristeas is Herodotus iv. 13–16 (cp. Macan's notes). The date here (15) assigned, "240 years ago," is obviously that of the foundation of Cyzicus (*c.* 680 B.C.) and may be used to fix the composition of Book IV. to *c.* 440 B.C. For the guess that Aristeas lived in the sixth century, it may be said that Dionysius, *De Thuc.* 23, brackets him with Cadmus; but this is hardly enough to establish even a presumption.

[5] It is believed that much about the same time a western Greek, Theagenes of Rhegium, was attempting to interpret Homer allegorically. According to Tatian, *adv. Graecos* 31, he flourished in the time of Cambyses; schol. Ven. to *Il.* 67 (533 ed. Bekker) he was the first to write on Homer, and he introduced allegorical interpretation; the schol. on Dionysius Thrax (Bekker, *Anecd. Gr.* 729) suggests that he dealt with grammar.

[6] It is remarkable that Xenophanes wrote two epic poems on quasi-historical subjects —the Origin of his native home Colophon, and the colonisation of his adoptive home Elea; but no traces of these works have survived. It would be interesting to know how he handled definite traditions.

[7] It seems probable it was from his geographical work that Herodotus derived the explanation of the legend of the nursing of Cyrus by a female dog, as meaning that he was suckled by a woman named Spako, which signified dog in the Medic language (Prášek).

[8] Chief sources for Cadmus: Dionys. Hal. *De Thuc.* 23; Strabo i. 2. 6; Pliny, *N.H.* v. 31, vii. 56; Josephus, *c. Ap.* i. 2; Suidas, *sub nomine.* The passages of Strabo and Pliny show that the creation of prose was variously ascribed to Cadmus and Pherecydes (of Syros). This was, of course, the result of Alexandrine investigation. From Dionysius we learn that an extant work which bore the name of Cadmus was strongly suspected of being a fabrication. We may take it for granted that it was spurious, but it seems highly probable that its subject was that of the genuine work which had long since perished. Hence, I think, we may pretty securely accept the information of Suidas (whether derived from the pseudo-Cadmus or from Alexandrine sources) that Cadmus composed κτίσιν Μιλήτου καὶ τῆς ὅλης Ἰωνίας. From Dionysius we also infer that Cadmus belonged to a distinctly older generation than Hecataeus. The posthumous rivalry between him and Pherecydes for the origination of literary prose points to the first half of the sixth century; for Anaximander's prose treatise on Nature cannot have been much later than 550 B.C. Cp. Gomperz, *Griechische Denker,* i. p. 41.

[9] The fragments do not enable us to appreciate his style. According to Hermogenes (*De gen. dic.* ii. 12) his prose had a charm, but he was less careful in composition than Herodotus.

[10] Wilamowitz-Möllendorff, *Isyllos,* 65. For the story of Cephalus and Procris as told in the epics, Pherecydes substituted what seems to have been the family tradition of the Cephalidae. Bertsch, *Pherek. Studien,* p. 2.

[11] Murray has an interesting section on Herodorus in his *History of Greek Literature,* pp. 127 sq.

[12] His *Hôroi* (see below, p. 18) seems to have been published after 465–4 B.C. Compare Schwartz's article in Pauly-Wissowa. I cannot see any proof that the *Persica* was merely an excerpt from the *Hôroi.*

[13] This is the most natural inference from Dionysius, *Letter to Pompey,* 3. 7 Ἑλλανίκου τε καὶ Χάρωνος τὴν αὐτὴν ὑπόθεσιν (as Herodotus) προεκδεδωκότων. (The *Persica* of Hellanicus cannot have been prior to the composition of Herodotus vii.–ix.)

[14] One fragment of Dionysius (*Persica*) has been preserved, in the scholia on Herodotus (cod. B) iii. 61 (ὁ μάγος Πατιζεσίθης): Διονύσιος ὁ Μιλήσιος Πανξούθην ὀνομάζεσθαι τοῦτων λέγει. See Stein's *Herodotus* (ed. 1869–71), vol. ii. p. 438. I mention this solitary fragment, because it does not appear in Müller's *F.H.G.*

[15] Edited, interpreted, and discussed by Wilcken, *Hermes,* xli. pp. 103 sqq., 1906.

[16] On this work see Gutschmid, *Kleine Schriften,* iv. p. 144, who thought it must be part of a large work, and Wilcken, *op. cit.* pp. 125–6.

[17] *De Thucydide* 5. Dionysius distinguishes three chronological groups of historians: (1) Cadmus, whom he associates with Aristeas; (2) Eugeon, Deiochus, Eudemus, Democles, Hecataeus, Acusilaus, Charon, Melesagoras (perhaps

Διονύσιος ὁ Μιλήσιος has fallen out after has fallen out after Ἑκαταῖος ὁ M.); (3) Hellanicus, Damastes, Xenomedes, Xanthus, καὶ ἄλλοι σύχνοι. 450 B.C. would roughly mark the division between 2 and 3. The work of Eugeon (Euagon) of Samos was appealed to c. 200 B.C. in a dispute between Samos and Priene which was decided by Rhodes (see *Greek Inscriptions in the British Museum*, ccciii. 109, 120). Deiochus wrote a chronicle of Cyzicus. For Democles see Strabo i. 58 and xii. 551; for Damastes, *F.H.G.* ii. 64–7. The work which passed under the name of (A)melesagoras (*F.H.G.* ii. 21) was a fraud: see Wilamowitz-Möllendorff, *Antigonos von Karystos*, p. 24.

[18] Gutschmid, *Kleine Schriften*, iv. pp. 307 sqq.

[19] See Herodotus i. 7: 22 generations = 505 years.

[20] Of Seeck; see *Klio* iv. pp. 289–90. We have no data to conjecture the scope of Eugeon's *Hôroi* of Samos.

[21] Kullmer refers p. 33 to the Ambracian-Acarnanian war of 429 B.C.

[22] See Lehmann-Haupt in *Klio* vi. pp. 127 sqq. Apollodorus used the earlier edition.

[23] We can be virtually certain that the chronology of Ephorus and Diodorus for the period of the Fifty Years depended on Hellanicus, so far as Ephorus may not have modified it by the indications of Thucydides. For Thucydides and Hellanicus seem to have been the only fifth-century historians who recorded that period. Diodorus distributes over the years 460–59, 459–8, 458–7 events in Egypt, at Halieis, and Aegina, and Megara, which, the well-known Erechtheid stone (*C.I.A.* i. 433) instructs us, occurred in the same civil year (459–8).

[24] The subject of the early list of Olympian victors, constructed by Hippias of Elis without trustworthy data, has recently been discussed by A. Körte (*Hermes* xxxix. pp. 224 sqq., 1904), who confirms in essential points the conclusions of Mahaffy.

[25] Herodotus ii. 145 *ad fin.*

LECTURE II

[1] There are passages which cannot have been written before 431–0 B.C. vii. 233 (cp. Thucydides ii. 2) and ix. 73 (cp. Thuc. ii. 23) imply 431 B.C.; vii. 137 (cp. Thuc. ii. 67) implies 430 B.C. Cp. also iii. 160; and v. 77. The reference to Artaxerxes in vi. 98 does not imply that the words were written after his death (425 B.C.); cp. Macan's note *ad loc.*

[2] Compare the pertinent remarks of Wachsmuth, *Rheinisches Museum*, lvi. 215–8 (1901).

[3] This has been well brought out by Macan.

[4] In the last part the unity is much more marked than the triplicity; in fact, the division of Book VII. from Book VIII. is somewhat arbitrary.

[5] The most complete appreciation of the evidence will be found in the Introduction to Macan's ed. of *Herodotus*, vii.-ix. (§ 7 and § 8).

[6] Some few additions were made subsequently: thus in vii. 93 and 108 there are references to passages in the books which are earlier in order but were later in composition. It is probable that the whole work never received a final revision, and this would be sufficient to explain the unfulfilled promise of vii. 213, which is the insufficient but only real argument for the hypothesis that the ninth Book is not complete. [How gratuitous this hypothesis is, Macan shows at length, *ib.* § 6.] On the other hand it seems not improbable that Herodotus intended to include in the early portion of his work a summary of Babylonian history (Ἀσσύριοι λόγοι): this seems to me more likely than that in i. 106 and 184 he is referring to another work.

[7] He says expressly that προσθῆκαι are a feature of his work, iv. 30.

[8] *Letter to Pompeius*, 3. Longinus calls Herodotus ὁμηρικώτατος, *De subl.* 13. 4.

[9] Fr. 353 (Longinus, *De subl.* 27). Cp. Mahaffy, *Prose Writers*, i. p. 33. The statement in Marcellinus, *Vita Thuc.* 38, has not much weight.

[10] Thucydides i. 23 (λογογράφοι) is not conclusive; he was thinking chiefly, perhaps only, of Herodotus.

[11] Similarly Pan son of Penelope, Dionysus son of Semele, are to be distinguished from the synonymous gods.

[12] Cp. viii. 77.

[13] ii. 143.

[14] When Herodotus cites what οἱ Ἕλληνες say, it is sometimes assumed that he means Hecataeus (or some other Ionian writer). In that case he would have said Ἴωνες. He is really quoting criticisms of Hecataeus on οἱ Ἕλληνες, that is, on the current mythology of epic tradition.

[15] Plutarch, Περὶ τῆς Ἡροδότου κακοηθείας, 2, takes this quite seriously.

[16] *Pyth.* ii. 87–8.

[17] The clear allusion of Otanes, in his defence of democracy, to the Athenian constitution under the lot-system does not necessitate by any means an Athenian origin. — It may be conjectured that the peculiar privileged position which Otanes and his descendants were said to have held in the Persian realm suggested the idea of transferring this singularly Hellenic discussion to Susa. Otanes, it is said, was exempted from subjection to the kings because, though he was the leading organizer of the conspiracy, he resigned all claims to the throne which Darius secured. He was thus neither ruler nor subject, an anomalous position which in Greece had a sort of parallel in the membership of a democracy. Hence the suggestion that Otanes believed in democracy, and, when he did not convince his fellow-conspirators, obtained for himself personally and his family the freedom which a democracy bestows.

[18] I have been here expressing dissent from the view of some critics that the passages enumerated indicate sophistic influence.

[19] It may be held, however, that this is still an open question. A fragment of an anonymous Dialogue, discovered by Grenfell and Hunt (*Oxyrhynchus Papyri*, iv. No. 664), represents Solon as in Ionia when Peisistratus became tyrant (560 B.C.). If this were so, the meeting with Croesus would become chronologically possible.

[20] S. Reinach, "Xerxès et l'Hellespont," in the *Revue archéologique*, sér. 4, vol. vi. pp. 1 sqq., 1905. The symbolic marriage of the Doges of Venice with the Hadriatic is the same story, and Reinach also finds the same *motif* underlying the story of Xerxes and the Hellespont (Herod. vii. 35) and the rite practised by the Phocaeans, *ib*. i. 165, and by the Ionians, Aristotle, Ἀθ. π. 23.

[21] v. 86.

[22] viii. 8.

[23] viii. 36–39.

[24] I do not add the fall of the rocks; for this might have been engineered. The rocks were shown to Herodotus in the temple of Athena Pronaïa (ch. 39); this was just the sort of evidence which would impress him.

[25] vii. 152.

[26] iv. 96.

[27] iv. 142.

[28] By E. Meyer.

[29] vii. 161; ix. 27.

[30] vii. 162.

[31] vi. 121.

[32] v. 71 rests on the Alcmaeonid tradition. It has been suggested that this sympathy of Herodotus may explain his curious treatment of Themistocles. To this statesman Athens chiefly owed the decisive rôle she played in the war, and though his good counsels are recognised, he is also treated in an unfriendly spirit of detraction, and represented as an intriguer rather than as a statesman. This looks as if the memory of Themistocles were under a cloud, and this partial obscuration were reflected in Herodotus. Afterwards, Thucydides made a point of doing him justice.

[33] vii. 139.

[34] μακρῷ πρῶτοι v. 78.

[35] Plutarch, Περὶ τῆς Ἡροδότου κακοηθείας, 26. There is nothing incredible in the story that he recited part of his work at Athens c. 445 B.C. His work then consisted of the last three Books.

[36] So Lehmann-Haupt. There is little evidence for a source of this kind in the history of the years 500–490 B.C. = Books V. VI. Chronology is conspicuously absent, but the few dates we get suggest a Persian history as their source (Charon or Dionysius?). See vi. 18, 42 *ad init.*, 43 *ad init.*, 46 *ad init.*

[37] *Persae* 827. In *Agam.* 749, Aeschylus rejects the vulgar doctrine (παλαίφατος ἐν βροτοῖς γέρων λόγος) that wealth, inordinately increased, necessarily leads to unappeasable woe.

[38] A complete library of Greek prose works on history would have been very small in 450 B.C., and it would not have been very much larger in 430 B.C. It is difficult to suppose that Herodotus would not have been acquainted with all the historical literature that had been published, or that the works of Dionysius and Charon could have escaped him. Besides Hecataeus the only historian to whom he refers is Scylax (iv. 44), but he mentions him as an explorer and not as an author, though obviously his brief account of the exploration is taken from the report of Scylax. Could he have failed to know the book of this Carian writer on Heracleides of Mylasa? It is remarkable that he ignores the part played by Heracleides of Artemisium (see Sosylus fragment, mentioned above, p. 15). Heracleides is mentioned v. 121. The geographical works of the Ionians are referred to in iv. 36.

[39] Compare, *e.g.,* ii. 99. I have little doubt that Herodotus visited and examined the battlefield of Plataea. Our difficulties in reconstructing the battle (elucidated by Grundy, Woodhouse, and Macan) from his description are not an objection. We may remember that the account of the battle of Trasimene by Polybius, who had visited the place and was a master of military science, lends itself to different interpretations. The features of the Pass of Thermopylae as described by Herodotus can be recognised by any traveller to-day; but he can hardly have been there, for he orients it N.S. instead of E.W.

[40] See Wiedemann, *ad* Her. ii. 125.

[41] This has been shown by Lehmann-Haupt in his paper on Semiramis. Herodotus is similarly unlucky about Mithra. He makes him a goddess, i. 131.

[42] He signalises the years 490–481 by reference to the year of Marathon, but he does not mention the eponymous archon of that year. Even if he had done so a reader would have required a list of Attic archons, in order to follow his dates intelligently. Herodotus does not assist his readers by reckoning back from a fixed point which they could realise. Thucydides saw that without such a point dates were entirely in the air, and he dated backward from the first year of the Peloponnesian war.

LECTURE III

[1] That he knew Sparta is a legitimate inference from i. 10. 2, and 134. 4.

[2] There were conflicting stories as to the manner and the place of his death. His tomb, which may have been a cenotaph, was shown at Athens, in the burying-place of the family of his kinsman Cimon, near the Melitid gate.

[3] v. 26.

[4] Perhaps before his return.

[5] See Appendix.

[6] Instructive. I revert to this important point in Lecture VIII.

[7] For instance: of the answer of the oracle to the Spartans (ὡς λέγεται), i. 118. 3; of the motives of Archidamus, ii. 18. 5; of the end of Nicias, vii. 86.

[8] viii. 18, 37, 58.

[9] By Wilamowitz-Möllendorff.

[10] Cp. ii. 24; iv. 16. Wilamowitz-Möllendorff, *Die Thukydides-legende.*

[11] Some errors are due not to the author but to very early scribes. For instance, Andocides in i. 51, Methone for Methana in iv. 45 (cp. Wilamowitz-Möllendorff, *op. cit.*). It is unquestionable that he makes grave topographical mistakes in his account of the episode of Pylos-Sphacteria. He has completely misconceived the size of the entrances to the bay, and he gives the length of Sphacteria as 15 stades, whereas it is really 24. These errors have led Grundy to deny that Thucydides had ever visited the spot; while R. M. Burrows (who has shown that the whole narrative is otherwise in accordance with the topography) thinks that his measurements were wrong. My view is that he first wrote the story from information supplied by eye-witnesses who gave him a general, though partly inaccurate, idea of the place, and that he afterwards tested it on the spot and probably added local touches, but omitted to revise the errors of distance. We have a somewhat similar case in the description of New Carthage by Polybius (see below, p. 123). It is indeed possible that the blunder in the length of the island may have been exaggerated by a scribe's pen. For κ was exposed to confusion with (ις or) ιε. — The topography of the siege of Plataea has been elucidated by Grundy.

[12] Thus no modern historian, probably, would have omitted to note the psephisma of Charinus, which followed up the decrees excluding Megara from the markets of Athens and her empire, by excluding Megarians on penalty of death from the very soil of Attica. Thucydides would have said that it did not affect the outbreak of the war.

[13] A part of it would naturally have appeared in a footnote, had footnotes been then in use.

[14] ii. 96–7; cp. ii. 29.

[15] H. Nissen and F. M. Cornford.

[16] But cp. iv. 87. 4.

[17] i. 42. 2.

[18] We do not know whether the Megarian business figured in the *Dionysalexandros* of Cratinus (430–29 B.C.), which satirised Pericles as being the cause of the war. See the Argument of the play, recovered by Grenfell and Hunt, *Oxyrhynchus Papyri,* iv. No. 663.

[19] F. M. Cornford has ably explained the geographical importance of the Megarid as a commercial route between East and West, taking as his text what he calls Bérard's "law of isthmuses"; and those who do not accept his inferences as a criticism of Thucydides must recognise the value of his investigation.

[20] He takes a matter-of-fact account of the establishment of the Pelopid dynasty in Argolis from some previous writer, i. 9. 2 λέγουσι δὲ καὶ οἱ τὰ σαφέστατα Πελοποννησίων μνήμη παρὰ τῶν πρότερον δεδεγμένοι (where Πελοποννησίων depends on οἱ). A Peloponnesian on ancient Argive history suggests Acusilaus. We should expect a man interested in history like Thucydides to have read all or most of the historical works which then existed. The only particular works he mentions (besides Homer) are the συγγραφὴ Ἀττική of Hellanicus and the *Apology* of Antiphon; but he refers generally to the works of poets and prose writers (λογογράφοι, i. 21) on early Greece, and of prose writers he was here thinking chiefly of Herodotus, whom he admittedly criticizes elsewhere. It has been conjectured with much probability that in writing the early chapters of Book VI. on the colonisation of Sicily he used the history of Antiochus of Syracuse (Wölfflin). He cannot have failed to know the books of Ion of Chios and Stesimbrotus, which must have been read with avidity at Athens.

[21] In the Pentekontaëteris. He is careful to mark the beginning of the Peloponnesian war (ii. 2) by the archon, the Spartan ephor, and the Argive priestess of Hera (this last dating, which he puts first, shows the influence of Hellanicus, which has also been conjectured in iv. 133). Similarly, when he starts afresh after the Ten Years' War, the date is marked by archon and ephor, v. 25. But we may legitimately criticize him for not having indicated formally the chronology of the four years (435–2) which are treated in Book I. A date is obviously wanted in c. 24.

LECTURE IV

[1] vi. 18 οὐκ ἔστιν ἡμῖν ταμιεύεσθαι ἐς ὅσον βουλόμεθα ἄρχειν, and στορέσωμεν τὸ φρόνημα,— noted by the scholiast as κατ᾽ Ἀλκιβιάδην.

[2] It has been rightly pointed out by Mahaffy that it is a misapprehension to explain the obscurities of Thucydides as due to condensation of thought. He is "condensed in expression but not in thought" (*Greek Literature*, ii. 1. 112).

[3] ii. 44.

[4] I point out in the Appendix that it was composed or wrought over after the end of the war.

[5] The epigram of the Thucydidean Pericles on the virtue of women (ii. 45) may have been suggested by a saying of Gorgias. Wilamowitz-Möllendorff, *Hermes*, ii. p. 294.

[6] This was observed by Dionysius.

[7] ii. 38. 7.

[8] In the second speech of the Corinthians and the first of Pericles.

[9] Bruns was the first to study systematically the methods of the ancient historians in depicting character. I am much indebted to his well-known book.

[10] v. 16. 1.

[11] v. 16. 2 (Jowett's translation).

[12] νενομισμένη. This interpretation is favoured by F. Cauer.

[13] *Knights*, 1304.

[14] F. M. Cornford touches on this point in his *Thucydides Mythistoricus*. I think he is right. The hypothesis of personal spite is superfluous.

[15] vi. 15.

[16] vi. 12; 16.

[17] He speaks indeed strangely of the frequency of solar eclipses during the war (i. 23. 3), as if they had some significance for the human race; we may wonder what comment Anaxagoras would have made.

[18] Cp. Gomperz, *Griechische Denker*, i. p. 61 (on Heracleitus).

[19] Democritus, in Mullach, *Frag. Phil.* 167. Thucydides observes *sub persona Hermocratis* (iv. 62. 4) that in war the incalculable element has its uses; it is the same for both and conduces to caution and prudence.

[20] *Letter to Pompeius*, 3. 9.

[21] But he also blames Thucydides, 3. 4, 5, for the choice of his subject. The war was οὔτε καλὸς οὔτε εὐτυχής, and therefore should be forgotten and ignored by posterity.

[22] ii. 37.

[23] viii. 97 καὶ οὐχ ἥκιστα δὴ τὸν πρῶτον χρόνον ἐπί γ᾽ ἐμοῦ Ἀθηναῖοι φαίνονται εὖ πολιτεύσαντες. Is the reserve ἐπί γ᾽ ἐμοῦ simply cautiousness, or is it an allusion to the πάτριος πολιτία of early times?

[24] Since writing this paragraph, I observe that Murray had already compared this ἀρετή to *virtù* (in his chapter on Thucydides, *History of Greek Literature*).

[25] ἀρχαϊκόν τε καὶ αὔθαδες κάλλος, Dionysius περί συνθ. ὀν. 165.

[26] Dexippus and Procopius are instances.

[27] The servile imitation of Thucydides is ridiculed in Lucian's πῶς δεῖ ἱστορίαν συγγράφειν;

LECTURE V

[1] This is an observation of von Wilamowitz-Möllendorff.

[2] The preservation of his works is due to the overestimate which was formed of him under the Atticistic revival; he was canonized by literary judges, with Thucydides and Herodotus. Cp. Lucian, πῶς δεῖ 4, "Everybody wants to be a Thucydides, a Herodotus or a Xenophon" (Θουκυδίδαι καὶ Ἡρόδοτοι καὶ Ξενοφῶντες).

[3] B. i. and B. ii. to iii. 10.

[4] They remind us of the character-portraits of the dead Argive leaders in the *Suppliants* of Euripides (861 sqq.).

[5] For these remarks on the rise of biography I have used F. Leo's admirable work *Die griechisch-romische Biographie* (1901).

[6] *De Glor. Athen.* ad init. (ed. Bernardakis, ii. p. 455).

[7] The only other; for the claim put forward for Androtion by G. de Sanctis is obviously out of court. It is enough to say here that the narrative of the campaigns of Agesilaus could not possibly have appeared in Androtion's Attic history. — The case against Theopompus, who is considered to be the author by Wilamowitz-Möllendorff and E. Meyer, has been stated impartially by Grenfell and Hunt, who, however, incline to this theory, and has been forcibly presented by De Sanctis. I will not go over the arguments which they have put so well. But I would emphasize that the few positive indications of contact between the papyrus and fragments of Theopompus may be otherwise accounted for (as Theopompus would naturally have used Cratippus); that what we know about the life of Theopompus, unsatisfactory as it is, renders it highly unlikely that he wrote his *Hellenica* before 350 B.C.; and that the hypothesis — to which the advocates of his authorship are forced to resort — that the *Hellenica* was entirely different in the style of treatment from the *Philippica,* is contradicted by a passage of Porphyrius (Eusebius, *Praep. evang.* x. 3, cited by De Sanctis in his tract, p. 9) and by the way in which Dionysius (in his appreciation in the *Letter to Pompeius,* 6) associates both works closely together and describes the character of his "historiography" without the faintest suggestion that the earlier work presented a radical contrast to the later. [Since the above was written, papers have appeared by W. A. Goligher, in the *English Historical Review,* April 1908, and W. Rhys Roberts, in the *Classical Review,* June 1908, arguing against the Theopompus theory.]

[8] E. M. Walker thinks it was written before the end of the Phocian war.

[9] Dionysius, *De Thucydide,* 16.

[10] *Ib.*

[11] The passage, on which nothing persuasive has been suggested, is in col. x., where οὐ γὰρ ὥσπερ ο[ί(?)πλεῖστοι τῶν δν]ναστευόντων and δη[μο]τικωτ are the slight clues. Could it possibly be Dionysius of Syracuse? That Sparta was interested in some of his proceedings described by Diodorus, xiv. 7. 8, might conceivably have led to a mention of him here and a digression on his policy.

[12] *History of Sicily,* iii. 63.

[13] Dionysius, περὶ μιμήσεως, 426 (Usener and Radermacher, p. 208); Cicero, *De Orat.* ii. 13. The differences in style between Thucydides and Philistus are explained by Dionysius, *Letter to Pompey,* 5. The style of Philistus was tediously uniform.

[14] "Capitalis creber acutus brevis paene pusillus Thucydides": *ad Q. fr.* ii. 11. I give the renderings of Tyrrell and Purser, vol. ii. ed. 2, p. 136.

[15] Cicero, *Div.* 1. 33 = fr. 48. Cp. fr. 57.

[16] His work came down to Philip's death.

[17] Cp. Schwartz, art. "Ephoros," in Pauly-Wissowa.

[18] A thirtieth Book was added by the author's son, coming down to the siege of Perinthus, 310–339 B.C. The treatment must have been considerably more summary than in the work of Ephorus himself, whose last ten Books seem to have covered not more than thirty-four years (since 390 B.C. was treated in Book XIX.). See Schwartz, *op. cit.* pp. 5, 6.

[19] This work (which was not published before 324 B.C., cp. frags. 108, 334) consisted of fifty-eight Books.

[20] See Wachsmuth, *Einleitung,* 537 sqq.

[21] He said expressly that in myths he would outdo Herodotus, Ctesias, and οἱ τὰ Ἰνδικὰ συγγράψαντες. Strabo, i. 2. 35.

[22] *Letter to Pompey,* 6, 7. "I suppose," adds Dionysius, "that the mythical judges in Hades conduct their trials of the dead with the punctual severity of Theopompus."

[23] 340–256 B.C.; exiled 317 B.C.

[24] Fr. 2 (ed. Müller, *Scr. rer. Alexandri Magni,* p. 140):

> ὅμοιον πεποίηκας Ἀλέξανδρε
> Θήβας κατασκάψας,
> ὡς ἂν εἰ ὁ Ζεὺς
> ἐκ τῆς κατ᾽ οὐρανὸν μερίδος
> ἐκβάλοι τὴν σελήνην.
> τὸν γὰρ ἥλιον ὑπολείπομαι ταῖς Ἀθήναις.
> δύο γὰρ αὗται πόλεις
> τῆς Ἑλλάδος ἦσαν ὄψεις.
> δοὸ καὶ περὶ τῆς ἑτέρας ἀγωνιῶ νῦν.
> ὁ μὲν γὰρ εἷς αὐτῶν ὀφθαλμὸς ἡ Θηβαίων
> ἐκκέκοπται πόλις.

See the rhythmical analysis in Norden, *Griechische Kunstprosa,* i. 136.

[25] We must remember that Polybius was disposed to be unfavourable to Phylarchus as a partisan of Cleomenes.

[26] Especially the work of Nearchus on his voyage in the Indian Ocean.

[27] He wrote about the end of the fourth century. From the criticisms of Longinus and Demetrius, it appears that his style was marked by features which heralded the Asianic school.

[28] We may indeed compare parts of Xenophon's *Anabasis.* And the work of Nearchus may remind us of the report which Scylax made for Darius.

[29] Compare J. Kaerst, *Die antike Idee der Oekumene in ihrer politischen and kullurellen Bedeutung,* 1903.

[30] *L'Apologie d'Antiphon, ou λόγος περί μεταστάσεως,* 1907 (Geneva-Bâle).

[31] The same scholar has made it probable that one portion of the *Panegyrie* of Isocrates was aimed against the pamphlet of an Ionian who (*c.* 404 B.C.) wrote against the Athenian supremacy and in favour of Sparta.

[32] To the literature on this subject belong the συμβουλευτικός of Thrasymachus (411 B.C.); the pamphlet from which Aristotle derived much material for his Ἀθ. π.; then, later (403 B.C.), Lysias, περὶ τοῦ μὴ καταλῦσαι τὴν πάτριον πολιτείαν Ἀθήνησι. [The puzzle of the περὶ πολιτείας, vulgarly ascribed to Herodes Atticus, has been discussed in a minute and careful study by E. Drerup, 1908 (*Studien zur Geschichte und Kultur des Altertums*, ii. 1, Paderborn). His solution is very interesting. From a variety of indications he concludes that it was written in the summer of 404 B.C. by an Athenian belonging to the party of Theramenes, and is a political pamphlet concerning the Athenian politics of the hour, Thessaly, the nominal subject, being merely a disguise. So an Irish patriot might put a plea for Home Rule in the mouth of a Bohemian. If Drerup is right, his further inference that the "speech" of Thrasymachus ὑπὲρ Λαρισαίων was a brochure of the same sort seems probable.]

[33] As Nissen has done.

[34] Compare Bauer, p. 274.

[35] One of the important results of the discovery of the Ἀθηναίων Πολιτεία is the light gained for the lost historians of Athens who stood on the shoulders of Hellanicus, and who formed a principal source of Aristotle. It is notable that some at least of these chroniclers were religious *exêgêtai τῶν πατρίων*, who are the nearest analogy at Athens to the pontifices of Rome. Cp. Wilamowitz, *Aristoteles und Athen*, i. 280 sqq. We know the names of Cleidemus, Melanthius, Phanodemus (? Anticleides); Androtion is more than a name. The series was continued by Demon and closed by Philochorus, an *exêgêtês*, the last and greatest, whose work eclipsed its predecessors. The recovery of Philochorus would mean a greater addition to our historical knowledge than the Ἀθηναίων Πολιτεία. Some new fragments are contained in the Commentary of Didymus on the Philippics of Demosthenes.

[36] See Wilamowitz, *op. cit.* i. c. 7.

[37] *Laws*, 678–9, transl. Jowett. The cycle of degenerate states in *Republic* viii. is a sequence in thought, not in time.

[38] Susemihl, i. 6.

[39] Strabo, vii. 3. 6; cp. also 1. 23–25.

[40] Tacitus, *Dial.* 37.

LECTURE VI

[1] i. 3. 4. This unity does not become clear till after the defeat of Carthage; but the Eastern events during the Second Punic war went to determine the subsequent intervention of Rome.

[2] i. 5. 1.

[3] i. 4. 1.

[4] Old plan i. 1–5 and iii. 1–3; new plan iii. 4–6.

[5] It has been shown that in his description of New Carthage Polybius was in error as to the orientation. After he had seen the place he inserted (x. 11. 4) a correction of current statements as to the circumference, but left the other errors uncorrected. See Cunz, *Polybius,* 8 sqq., and Strachan Davidson, *Selections,* Appendix.

[6] The beginning of the Polybian year, however, did not coincide with that of the Olympiad (July), but fell some three months later (*c.* Oct. 1). This division seems to have been determined by the fact that the autumn equinox and the beginnings of the official years of the Achaean and Aetolian *stratêgoi* fell about the same time. See Nissen, *Rheinisches Museum,* 26. 241 sqq. He calls attention to a passage, xii. 11. 1, which suggests that Timaeus may have been partly responsible for this system.

[7] i. *op. cit.* The theory is favourably entertained by Susemihl, ii. 125.

[8] In Book VI. The intervening Books IV. and V. deal with synchronous events in Greece. See iii. 118.

[9] iii. 9.

[10] There is indeed, in xvi. 16. 5, a curious statement as to the position of Mycenae relative to Corinth.

[11] v. 33.

[12] ix. 2. 5. This is one of the rare passages in which an ancient writer betrays a sense of "progress."

[13] ii. 37. 3; cp. iii. 1. 3.

[14] iii. 6.

[15] It is not preserved, but its general argument and contents were transferred by Plutarch into his *Consolation to Apollonius.* Consult the work of von Scala.

[16] i. 4. 5.

[17] xxix. 21. 5–6.

[18] xxxvi. 17. 1–4.

[19] ii. 38. 5.

[20] i. 63. 9.

[21] i. 21. 34.

[22] In Book VI.

[23] vi. 5. 5.

[24] Cp. Gompera, *Griechische Denker,* i. 46, 54, 113 sqq.

[25] It is interesting to observe that Dionysius (Περὶ τῶν ἀρχαίων ῥητόρων, 2) suggests periodicity as an explanation of the Attic renaissance: εἴτε θεοῦ τινος ἄρξαντος εἴτε φυσικῆ ς περιόδου τὴν ἀρχαίαν τάξιν ἀνακυκλούσης.

[26] ii. 21. 8.

[27] ix. 1.

[28] ii. 56.

[29] iii. 20. 5 κουρεακῆς καὶ πανδήμου λαλιᾶς. Compare his criticism on the insinuations of Timaeus against Aristotle, xii. 8. 5–6.

[30] The change was made after Book v. See beginning of Book xi.

[31] viii. 5. 3; i. 35. 3.

[32] On this principle he only draws general portraits of subordinate persons who appear but once or twice. The preliminary account of Scipio in x. 2 is concerned only with his youth.

[33] xvi. 28.

[34] x. 47.

[35] Fr. 58.

[36] v. 21; iii. 36.

[37] x. 2. 10.

[38] xi. 12. 9.

[39] vi. 56. 6 sqq.

[40] i. 40. 4.

[41] xvi. 40.

[42] xxxiv. 2. 11.

[43] Used by Cicero in *De Divinatione*, Book I.

[44] Some interesting aspects of the work of Polybius, on which I have not been able to touch in this lecture, are brought out in Mahaffy's valuable chapter on the historian in *Greek Life and Thought.*

LECTURE VII

[1] It is to be noted that Professor Howard has successfully defended Livy against the charge that he was at first deceived by the extravagant statements of Valerius Antias, and, having afterwards become convinced of that writer's untrustworthiness, avenged his own credulity by holding him up to obloquy. Howard shows that the evidence is not there, and that Livy always used Valerius with caution. See his paper on the question, in *Harvard Studies in Classical Philology*, xvii., 1906.

[2] E. Kornemann, *Kaiser Hadrian und der letzte grosse Historiker von Rom*, 1905; O. Th. Schulz, *Das Kaiserhaus der Antonine und der letzte Historiker Roms*, 1907.

[3] The Christian world-chronicle was constructed by Sextus Julius Africanus, and then, on the basis of his work, by Eusebius.

[4] The succession of the four great monarchies (Assyrian, Persian, Macedonian, and Roman), in which Greek writers had already seen a principle of chronological division, was brought into connexion with the prophecies of Daniel by Jerome; and Jerome had no doubt that the Roman was the last.

LECTURE VIII

[1] Although the principle of historical relativity, with its implication that there are no absolute values in history, that values vary according to time and place, is a modern idea; nevertheless the Greeks made virtual application of it, occasionally and in very simple cases. Thucydides furnishes an instance. He suggests that, if the Greeks of his day regard piracy as an offence against morals, they must not apply their standard to a different stage of civilisation, when piracy was esteemed an honourable profession. This is one of the few examples to be found in ancient writers of what we call an historical sense. Another example is furnished by Eratosthenes, who pointed out that in studying Homer the historical conditions of his age must be taken into account, and that his geographical ideas corresponded to the ignorance which then prevailed; his authority therefore has no value transcending the conditions of his own time.

[2] Preface to *Geschichten der romanischen und germanischen Völker von* 1494 *bis* 1535.

APPENDIX

[1] As iv. 48. 5; ii. 94. 1 (which was not revised in the light of viii. 96. 1).

[2] ii. 65. 5 to end.

[3] The last sentences of ii. 81 were posterior to the Sicilian expedition. The notice of Archelaus (413–399 B.C.), ii. 100. 2, is a late insertion; likewise iv. 74. 4. E. Meyer has noted that κρῆναι γὰρ οὔπω ἦσαν αὐτόθι, ii. 48. 2, points to a date after 414 B.C. (schol. Arist. *Av.* 997).

[4] The allusion to the destruction of the long walls (c. 93. 5) cannot be pressed, as it might have been introduced alone. But it is to be noted that the Pentekontaëteris is ignored in i. 146; while i. 23. 6 seems to be a later insertion.

[5] Cc. 18, 19. The Introduction (i. 1–23) was evidently written before 414 B.C. as a Preface to the history of the Ten Years' War. A few phrases may have been changed or added, but not so much as an allusion to the fall of Athens was introduced.

[6] iv. 60: allusions to the Athenian expedition and to Melos.

[7] iv. 17–20.

[8] iv. 118–119.

[9] v. 18–19.

[10] It involves the corollary that the words καὶ τὴν ξυμμαχίαν—Ἀθηναίων (25. 1) were subsequently added, concurrently with the insertion of 21–24.

INDEX

Achaeans, Polybius on, 128, 136, 137

Acton, Lord, 147

Acusilaus of Argos, mythographer, 11, 12–13, 16, 65

Aegina, miracle of statues in, 36

Aeschines, *Dialogues* of, 114

Aeschylus, 41, 43, 69

Africanus, Sextus Julius, 186n[3]

Agathocles, books on, 106, 107, 109

Agesilaus, 96, 97

αἰτία in Thucydides, 58, 59, in Polybius, 126

Alcibiades, conjectural relations with Thucydides (Kirchhoff), 53; treatment of, by Thucydides, 55, 75, 80 *sq.;* forcible style, 68

Alcidamas, 107

Alcmaeonids, Herodotus on, 38, 40

Alexander the Great, 100, 102; Hegesias on, 108; influence of his conquests on historiography, 111 *sqq.,* 112

Alexandria, libraries, 118; antiquarianism at, 118 *sqq.*

Ammianus Marcellinus, 149

Anacyclosis. See under Cyclical

Anaxagoras, 82

Anaximander, 7, 9, 130

Anaximenes, historian, 102

Androtion, 113, 182n[7], 184n[35]

Annus, magnus, 162

Anticleides, 184n[35]

Antiochus of Commagene, 108

Antiochus of Syracuse, 16 *sq.,* 180n[21]

Antiphon, 75 *sq.,* 91, 113, 180n[21]

Antiquarianism, 119 *sqq.*

Antisthenes, 114

Antisthenes of Rhodes, 137

Apollodorus, his use of Hellanicus, 175n[22]

Apollonius of Rhodes, 106

Appian, 140

Aratus, Memoirs of, 111, 148

Archidamus, 57, 71

ἀρετή 91, 181n[12]

Aristeas of Proconnesus, 4, 174n[17]

Aristobulus, Memoirs of, 111

Aristophanes, 62, 77

Aristotle, 113; 115 *sqq.,* 156

Arrian, 111

Artaxerxes I., reference to, in Herodotus, 175n[1]

Artemisium, battle of; incident not recorded by Herodotus, 16

Asconius, 148

Asianic style, 107 *sqq.,* two kinds of, 107 *sq.;* example, 108 *sq.*

Assur-bani-pal, his history of his own reign, 2

Astyochus, Spartan general, 53

Ἀθηναίων πολιτεία, anonymous, 113

Athens, partiality of Herodotus to, 39 *sqq.;* Herodotus at, 23, 40, 106; Athenian tradition of Persian war, 41; Lectures III. and IV. *passim,* 98; educational and literary centre, 101, 105

Atthidographers, 115

Atticism, 94, 107, 185n[25]

Augustine, St., 150, 152

Augustus, Emperor, 144, 146

Bérard, V., 5, 139, 179n[19] Bertsch, H., 174n[10], Biography, 93, 97 *sq.,* 148

βίος, pregnant meaning of, 97, cp. 118

Bismarck, 90

Blass, F., 99

Brasidas, 89

Bruns, I., 180n[9]

Buckle, H. T., 163

Burrows, R. M., 179n[11]

Cadmus of Miletus, evidence for, 9–10; 174n[17]

Caesar, Julius, Commentaries of, 111, 147 *sq.*

Caligula, Emperor, 144

Callimachus, poet, 106

Cannae, battle of, 124

Carian population in Aegean islands, 65

Carthage, 132, 138

Carthage, New, 179n[11], 185n[5]

Cato, M. Porcius, the Censor, 142, 143, 145

Cauer, F., 181n[12]

Cavour, 90

Charinus, decree of, 179n[12]

Charon of Lampsacus, 13 *sq.,* 14, , 18, 42, 174n[17]

Cheirocracy, 130

Christian construction of world-history, 150 *sqq.*

Chronology, of early historians, 17 *sqq.;* uncertainty of early, 20; want of a fixed era, *ib.;* of Herodotus, 45 *sq.;* of Thucydides, 66 *sq.;* Olympiads, 105, 185n[6]

Chrysippus, a determinist, 129

Cicero, 101, 140, 148, 158

Cimmerians, invasion of, 4

Cimon, 47, 178n[2]

Civilisation. *See* under History

Claudius, Emperor, 145

Cleidemus, 184n[35]

Cleitarchus of Colophon, 111

Cleon, his speech on Mytilene, 72 *sq.,* 87; treatment by Thucydides, 74, 77

Comte, Auguste, 163

Condorcet, 163

Conon, 99

Corbulo, Memoirs of, 111

Corinth, her instigation of Peloponnesian war, 60 *sq.*

Cornelius Nepos, 146

Cornford, F. M., 78, 179n[15], 179n[19], 181n[14]

Craterus, 120

Cratinus, 179n[18]

Cratippus, 98 *sqq.,* 104

Crete, thalassocracy of, 65

Critias, 113

Critobulus, 94

Croesus, interview with Solon, 28, 36; pyre of, 36

Ctesias, 183n[21]

Cunz, O., 185n[5]

Curiositas, antiquarianism, 119

Cyclical theory of history, 130 *sq.,* 158

Cyclôpes, legend of their death, treated by Pherecydes, 12

Damastes, 174n[17]

Davidson, J. Strachan, 185n[5]

Deiochus, historian, 174n[17], 175n[17]

Delbrück, H., 125

Delos, digression of Thucydides on, 56 *sq.*

Delphi, legends emanating from, 6; miraculous deliverance from Persians, 37 *sq.*

Demetrius Phalereus, 118; his Περί τύχης, 127 *sq.*

Democles, 174n[17], 175n[17]

Democritus, 82

Demon, 184n[35]

Dexippus, 181n[26]

Dicaearchus, 118

Didymus, Commentary on Demosthenes, 184n[35]

Diodorus, use of Hellanicus by, 175n[23] note; used Timaeus, 106, used Poseidonius, 140; Universal History of, 149 *sq.*

Diodotus, 72, 87

Dionysius of Halicarnassus, on Charon, 174n[13], on the stylo of the early historians, 15; list of early historians, 174n[17]; on Herodotus, 26; on Thucydides, 56, 64, 66; on the style of Thucydides, 69 *sq.*, 71 *sq.*, 94; charges Thucydides with want of patriotism, 83 *sq.*; on exaggerated admiration of Thucydides, 93; on Cratippus, 99, 100; on Philistus, 100; on Theopompus, 105; on Atticism, 130; his History, 1433

Dionysius of Miletus, 14; sole fragment of, 42, 174n[14]

Dionysius I. of Syracuse, 100, 101

Dionysus, god distinguished from man, 175n[23]

Disraeli (Lord Beaconsfield), 90

Dorian institutions, Plato on, 117

Drerup, E., 184n[32]

Duris, 109 *sqq.*, 132

Eclipses (solar) in Thucydides, 181n[17]

Egypt: mythical traditions compared with those of Greece, 9, 30; Athenian expedition to, 26; Hecataeus and Herodotus on, 31 *sq.*

Ephorus, 102 *sqq.*; his history rather quasi-national than universal, 103; rhetorical features, 103; 105; 134

Epics, the Greek: regarded as history by early Greeks, 1 *sqq.*; corpus of Trojan epics (poets of the epic cycle), 3; genealogical epics, *ib.*; local, 4; geographical, 173n[4]; influence of, 10

Epidaurus, 54

Eratosthenes, 106, 119, 187n[1]

Eucrates, 77

Eudemus, historian, 174n[17]

Eudemus, philosopher, 130

Euemerus, 13

Eugammon ("cyclic" poet), 10

Eugeon (Euagon), 174n[17], 175n[20]

Eumelus, *Corinthiaca*, 4, 10

Euripides, 97, 134, 138

Europa, legend of, rationalised, 12

Eusebius, 186n[3]

Exêgêtai, 184n[35]

Fabius Pictor, Q., 127, 142 Fiction, history as supplying place of, 110 *sq.*, 153

Flaminius, agrarian law of, 132

Fortune. *See* Tyche Fourier, Charles, 163

Frederick the Great, 142

Freeman, E. A., 33, 79, 100

Galilei, Galileo dei, 160

Geffcken, J., 106

Generations, reckoning by, 17

Gibbon, E., 30, 66; on Herodotus, 36; 142

Goligher, W. A., 182n[7]

Gomperz, Th., 174n[8], 181n[18], 185n[24]

Gorgias, style, 69, 78, 107; 105

Gracchi, revolutionary movement of the, 131

Greek language in the Roman empire, 142

Grenfell, B. P., and Hunt, W. S., 98, 100, 177n[19], 179n[18]

Grundy, G. B., 178n[39], 179n[11]

Guicciardini, 158

Gutschmid, A. von, 174n[16], 175n[18]

Hannibal, 135, 137

Hecataeus of Miletus, founder of history, 7, 10, 11, 22; his works and travels, 7–11; rationalism, 8–9; influence on mythography, 11–13: chronology, 17; source of Herodotus, 31 *sq.*, 41, 43; on Egypt, 31 *sq.*, genealogy of, 32

Hegesias of Magnesia, 107 *sq.*, 108 *sq.*

Helen, Herodotus on, 29, 33

Hellanicus of Lesbos, 17 *sqq.*, 55, 115, 168

Heracleides, prince of Mylasae, 15, 16, 178n[38]

Heracleitus, 130

Heracles, Herodotus on, 29 *sq.*, 30

Herder, 152

Hermocrates, 76, 86

Herodes Atticus, Περὶ πολιτείας, wrongly ascribed to, 184n[32]

Herodorus of Heraclea, 13

Herodotus:

life, 23 *sq.;* travels, 25; visit to Euxine regions, 26; at Plataea, 43; rewarded by Athenians, 40

work, artistic plan of, 24 *sq.;* genesis of, 25 *sq.;* geographical excursus, 25 *sq.;* epic features, 26 *sq.*, 54; speeches, 26 *sq.;* his theme, 28;

largeness of his conception, 28; historical anecdotes, 35 *sqq.;* chronology, 17, 45 *sq.;* unfulfilled promise, 25; Assyrian *logoi, ib.*

debts to Hecataeus, 7, 8, 30, 31 *sqq.;* criticism on Hecataeus, 31 *sq.;* sources for history of Persian invasion, 41 *sqq.;* influenced by Athenian drama, 42; no traces of sophistic influence on, 34, 35; Ionian stories about Persia, 34 *sqq.;* on Aristeas, 4; omits incident at Artemisium recorded by Sosylus, 16

maxims of historical criticism, 43 *sq.;* errors about Egypt and Babylon, 44 *sq.;* misorients Thermopylae, 44; incompetence in accounts of warfare, 45

anti-Ionian spirit, 38 *sqq.;* phil-Athenian sentiments, 39 *sqq.;* on Pericles and Alcmaeonids, 40; treatment of Themistocles, *ib.*

scepticism and rationalism, 29 *sqq.;* credulity and incredulity, 36 *sqq.;* irony, 30; distinction between age of gods and heroic age, 30; belief in superhuman control of events, 42, 78 *sq.;* on oracles, 81

on antagonism of Asia and Europe, 33 *sqq.;* on Egypt, 32 *sq.*, 44

alluded to by Thucydides, 65; canonized, 181n[2]

Hesiod, scheme of successive ages, 4, 118

Hieronymus of Cardia, 112, 120

Himerius, 107

Hippias of Elis, 175n[23]

Historia Augusta, 149

History and historiography:

origin of word (Ionic ἱστορίη), 10

accuracy, 51, 124, 132

"ancient" and "modern" Greek history, 11, 103, 120; ancient (mythography), 11 *sqq.*, 21, 29

antiquarian history, 118 *sqq.*, 157 *sq.*

causes, historical, 58 *sq.*, 126 *sqq.*

civilisation, history of, 28, 65, 116 *sqq.*, 122, 126

constitutional history, 115 *sqq.*, 131 *sq.*

contemporary history, 7, 11, 14 *sq.*, 49, 51 *sq.*

critical history; principles of criticism in Herodotus, 43 *sqq.;* Thucydides first really critical historian, 46

cyclical theory of history, 130 *sq.*, 158

dogma and history, 151

epics regarded as history, 1

fiction, history serving as, 111

Graeco-Roman historiography, 148 *sq.*

individuals, their role in history, 135

influence on historiography of: Ionian science, 6 *sqq.*, 21; Persia, 7, 21; Sophists, 47, 48; rhetoric, 101 *sqq.*, 132 *sq.*, 145; Alexander's conquests, 111 *sq.*, 112 *sq.;* political speculation, 113 *sqq.;* Peripatetics, 118 *sqq.;* Stoics, 129 *sqq.*, 149 *sq.*, 151

Ionian school of history, 13 *sqq.*

national history, 143

origin of history in Ionia (at Miletus), 7 *sqq.*

perspective of history, 162

philosophy of history, 151 *sq.*

political history (founded by Thucydides), 49, 95

pragmatical history, 126, 155 *sqq.*

progress in history, 158, 163 *sqq.*

psychology, in historiography, 67 *sq.*, 93, 97, 135 *sq.*, 148

realistic history, 109

relativity, historical, 159 *sqq.*

Roman historiography, 142 *sqq.*

scientific, Greek historians not, 93, 165

speeches: historiographical conventions as to, 145 *sq.;* in Herodotus, 26 *sq.;* in Thucydides, 68 *sqq.;* in Xenophon, 96; in Ephorus, 103; in Polybius, 137 *sq.;* Cratippus on, 99

summary of development of Greek historiography, 152 *sq.*

universal history: (Herodotus), 28; (Ephorus), 102 *sq.*, 126; (Polybius), 122, 126; under Roman empire, 149 *sqq.;* Christian construction of, 150 *sqq.*

Holzapfel, L., 179

Homer, prestige of, 1; authority of, 151; historical background, 3; archaism, 4; geographical interest in *Odyssey,* 5; sceptical spirit in late parts of *Iliad* and *Odyssey,* 6; influence on Herodotus, 26 *sqq.*, 28; treatment by Thucydides, 66; Eratosthenes on, 119, 138 *sq.;* geography of, 138 *sq.*

Howard, Albert, 186n[1]

Hunt, W. S. *See* Grenfell

Hyginus, 148

Hyperbolus, 76 *sqq.*

Intaphernes, story of wife of, 34

Ion, memoir writer, 55, 64, 133

Ionia, sceptical spirit in, 6; science and philosophy of, 6; history of, 15 *sq.;* Herodotus on, 39; works of Ionian geographers, 43

Isocrates, *Evagoras,* and influence on biography, 97; influence on history, 101 *sqq.; Panegyric,* 183n[31]

ἵστωρ, 10

Jerome, 186n[4]

Josephus, 140

Justin, epitomizer of Trogus, 150

Kaerst, J., 183n[29]

Kirchhoff, A., 169

Kornemann, E., 149

Körte, A., 175n[24]

Kromayer, 125

Kullmer, H., 175n[21]

Laomedon, legend of, rationalised, 13

Lehmann-Haupt, C., 175n[22], 177n[36], 178n[41]

Leibniz, 163

Leo, F., 148, 181n[5]

Libanius, 107

Livy, 140, 143 *sqq.*, 145

Logographoi or *logopoioi* = prose writers, 10; list of early historical, 174n[17]; use of term by Thucydides, 27

Longinus, on Herodotus, 176n[8]

Lucian, 181n[27], 181n[2]

Lycophron, poet, 106

Lygdamis, 23

Lyons, bronze tablet of (speech of Claudius), 145

Lysicles, 77

Macan, R. W., on Herodotus, 173n[4], 175n[1], 175n[3], 175n[5], 176n[6], 178n[39]

Macedonian conquests, Demetrius on, 127; fall of Macedonia, 121, 127

Macedonian hegemony, 102, 104

Machiavelli, 90 *sqq.*, 158

Mahaffy, J. P., 4, 20, 176n[9], 180n[2], 186n[44]

Manning, Cardinal, 151

Megara, Athenian decrees concerning, 179n[12]; embroilment with Athens, its connexion with Peloponnesian war, 59 *sqq.;* geographical importance, 63

Melanthius, 184n[35]

Melesagoras, 174n[17]

Melos, conquest by Athens, 87 *sqq.*

Memoirs, historical; earliest, 111; 112; 147 *sq.*

Merope, land of, 104

Meyer, E., 40, 169, 177n[28], 182n[7], 187n[3]

Miletus, centre of Ionian culture, 112

μίμησις, 109

Minos, 65

Mithra, in Herodotus, 178n[41]

Mommsen, Th., 139

Mucianus, 120

Murray, Gilbert, 3, 6, 13, 181n[24]
  Myths, later type of (7th, 6th centuries), 6, 36 *sq.*
  comparative mythology, 30

Mytilene, revolt against Athens, 72, 88

Naupactia, 4

Nearchus, 111

Nicias, Thucydidean portrait of, 74

Nicole, J., 113

Nissen, H., 123, 179n[15], 185n[6]

Nitocris (Nebuchadnezzar), 44

Norden, E., 107, 108

Oecumene, idea of, 112

Oenobius, decree of, 48

Olympiads, reckoning by, 106, 123

Orbis terrarum, 113

Orpheus, treatment of, by Pherecydes, 11

Otanes, conspiracy of, 35

Palaephatus, 13

Pan, son of Penelope, 176n[11]

Panaetius, 129, 140, 141

Panyassis, poet, 16, 23

Pausanias, digression of Thucydides on, 55

Peisistratids, digression of Thucydides on, 55

Pentekontaëteris, the, 180n[22], 187n[4]

Pergamon, 118

Pericles, expedition to the Pontus, 26; funeral oration in 439 B.C., 40; Herodotus on, 40; private life ignored by Thucydides, 54; detached attitude of Thucydides towards, 60, 84 *sqq.*; speeches of, in Thucydides, 71 *sqq.*, 71 *sqq.*; idealism, 72 *sq.*; characterized by Thucydides, 75, 80; not λαμπρός, 81; his personality not revealed in Thucydides, 93

Peripatetic school, influence on history, 118 *sqq.*; on Polybius, 126 *sqq.*, 158

Perseus, Herodotus on, 29

Persia: influence of Persian conquest of Ionia on the rise of history, 7, 15, 21, 152; Ionian stories about, 34 *sqq.*; Persian war, treatment of, by early historians, 139 *sqq.*; by Herodotus, 41 *sqq.*; conquest of Persia by Alexander, 111

Peter, H., 148

Phanodemus, 184n[35]

Pherecydes (of Leros), mythographer, 11–12, 13

Pherecydes (of Syros), 9

Philip II. of Macedon, 104

Philip III. of Macedon, 135

Philistus, 100 *sq.*, 105

Philochorus, 184n[35]

Philosophy, influence on history, 113 *sqq.*, 138. *See* under Peripatetic school, and Stoicism

Philosophy of History, 153 *sq.*

Phoronis, 4

Phylarchus, 109, 132

Pindar, on custom, 35; on forms of constitution, 35; 138

Plataea, Herodotus at, 43; siege of, 53, 54

Plato, 113; *Gorgias*, 114; on origins of civilisation, 116 *sqq.*; on cycle of constitutions, 116, 129

Plutarch, on Herodotus, 34, 40; biographies, 97; on Cratippus, 98; his *Consolation to Apollonius*, 185n[15]

Polemon of Ilion, 120 ποιτεία, in Athens, *c.* 411 B.C., 85; πάτριος, 114

Political literature, in last part of fifth century B.C., 113 *sqq.*

πολυπραγμοσύνη (antiquarianism), 118

Polybius:

life, 121 *sqq.*; travels, 122, 125; at New Carthage, 123

work, first design of, 121; second plan, 122; additional insertions, 122 *sq.*; supposed symmetry of, 123 *sq.*; chronology, 123; speeches, 138 *sq.*; narrative power, 138; style, 138; Mommsen on, 139

on requisites of historian, 124 *sq.*; on accuracy, 124; denounces rhetoric, 132, and gossip, 133; didactic, 134; on patriotism, 136; fair-mindedness of, 136, *sq.*; on Fabius, 125; on Aratus, 125; on Ephorus, 126; on Phylarchus, 109, 132; on Homer, 138 *sq.*

topography, 125; on Lake Trasimene, 144; on New Carthage, 179n[11], 185n[5]

pragmatism, 126, 155, 163; on causes, 126 *sqq.*; on *Tyche*, 127 *sqq.*; cyclical theory of history, 130 *sq.*, 158; theory of constitutions, 130 *sq.*; views on religion, 136; on national character, 134; treatment of individuals, 135 *sq.*; interest in psychology, 135 *sq.*; Peripatetic influence on, 126 *sqq.*; Stoic influence on, 129 *sqq.*

on Roman institutions, 124, 131 *sq.;* on Gracchan movement, 131 comparison with Thucydides, 132 *sqq.*

Polycrates, story of ring of, 36

Pompeius Trogus, 150 *sqq.*

Pompey, 140

Poseidonius, 140 *sqq.*, 144

Potidaea, 61 *sq.*

Pragmatical, meaning of term in Polybius, 126. *See* under History

Präöek, J. V., 173n[7]

Procopius, 181n[26]

Progress, idea of, 126, 162 *sqq.*

πρόφασις , in Thucydides, 58, 59

Ptolemy I., Sotêr, Memoirs of, 111, 118

Ptolemy II., Philadelphus, 118

Publicists: early poetical (*e.g.* Solon), 2

Purser, L. C., 182n[14]

Pylos and Sphacteria, episode of, in Thucydides, 53, 54, 80

Pyrrhus, 106; Memoirs of, 111, 148

Pythagoreans, cyclical theory of, 130 *sq.*

Ranke, L. von, 165

Reinach, S., 177n[20]

Rhetoric, influence on history, 101, 105; Isocratean, 104, 106; Asianic, 107 *sqq.*; Greek love of, 110 *sq.*; at Rome, 146, 148

Rhodes, 140, 141

Roberts, W. Rhys, 182n[7]

Rome: Roman constitution, 131 *sq.*; decline of Rome, 132; historiography of, Lect. VII.

Saint-Simon, Claude H. de, 163

Sallust, 143 *sq.*, 144, 146, 147

Samos, Herodotus at, 23; Duris on, 109

Sanctis, G. de, 182n[7]

Scala, R. von, 127

Schulz, O. Th., 186n[2]

Schwartz, E., 174n[12], 182n[17], 183n[18]

Scione, 88

Scipio Aemilianus, 125, 129, 131

Scipio Africanus, 135, 135

Scylax of Caryanda, 15 *sq.*, 183n[28]

Seeck, O., 175n[20]

Sellasia, battle of, 125

Semiramis, 44

Sicily, Antiochus on, 16; Thucydides on early history of, 55; Athenian expedition to, 79 *sq.;* Timaeus on, 106

Simonides, 138

Sitalces, digression of Thucydides on, 56

Socrates, pupils of, 97

Solon, date of his visit to Ionia, 36; his elegies, 2, 114, 115

Sophistic movement, 34, 35, 47, 48, 97

Sophocles, 69

Sosylus, historian, 15

Sparta, Thucydides at, 47; reason for entering on Peloponnesian war, 59 *sqq.*; war party at, 61; constitution of, 131

Stahl, Th., 176

Stesichorus, 5

Stesimbrotus, 55, 114, 133, 180n[21]

Stoicism, influence on Polybius, 129; on Universal History, 149

Strabo, 140

Suetonius, 146, 148

Susemihl, H., 185n[7]

Syracuse, 48

Tacitus, 144 *sqq.*, 162

Theagenes of Rhegium, 173n[5]

Thebes, 108

Themistocles, treatment of, by Herodotus, 55; by Thucydides, *ib.*, 56, 81

Theognis, 2, 114

Theophrastus, 109, 120

Theopompus, 104 *sqq.;* Oxyrhynchus, fragment ascribed to, by some, 99; condemned by Duns, 109; 113

Theramenes, 76, 114

Thirty Years' Peace (445 B.C.), instrument of, 54

Thrace, Thucydides in, 47, 48; 56

Thrasymachus, 113, 114

Thucydides:

life, 47 *sqq.;* stages and changes in composition of his work, 49 *sqq.* (cp. Appendix); initiates true contemporary history, 49; founder of political history, *ib.;* his work a great step in historiography, 93

influence of Sophists on, 47, of Athenian empire on, 48 *sq.*

principle of accuracy, 51 *sq.;* principle of relevance, 54 *sq.,* 63; omissions, 54 *sq.*

digressions, 55 *sqq.;* limitations of, 93 *sq.*

view of the purpose of historiography, 51, 154 *sq.,* 164 *sq.;* renounced popularity, 106

collection of information, 52 *sqq.;* use of documents, 53 *sq.;* reference to an inscription as written ἀμυδροῖς, 19; references to Herodotus, 51, 56, 65; references to older works, 65; on Hellanicus, *ib.,* 65 *sq.;* on ancient piracy, 160

artistic method, 57 *sq.;* dramatic method, 68, 73 *sqq.;* differences in his style, obscurity, etc., 69 *sqq.;* style influenced by drama, 78

speeches, 62 *sq.,* 68 *sqq.;* of Pericles, 71, 84 *sqq.* (*Epitaphios*), 71 *sq.,* 84, 86, 92 *sq.;* of Cleon, 69, 72 *sq.;* of Diodotus, 72, 87; of Corcyrean envoy, 59; of Corinthians, 60 *sq.,* 73; of Alcibiades, 68; dialogue of

Archidamus and Plataeans, 71; Melian dialogue, 70, 71, 87 *sqq.* Cp. Appendix

reflexions on civil sedition (in connexion with Corcyra), 71, 92

treatment of chronology, 45, 66 *sq.;* of economic facts, 57 *sq.;* sketch of early history of Greece, 64 *sqq.;* of the *Pentekontaëteris,* 187n[4] *sq.;* on the heroic age, 65

on the causes of the Peloponnesian war, 58 *sqq.;* use of αἰτία and πρόφασις, 58; on general course of the war and causes of collapse of Athens, 78 *sqq.;* on the Athenian empire, 85 *sqq.;* on *Tyche,* 78; on oracles, 81; charged with want of patriotism, 83 *sqq.* on the logic of policy, 87, 88 *sq.,* 147; comparison with Machiavelli, 90 *sqq.*

topographical mistakes, 54; errors in text of, *ib.*

Book V., 53, 169 *sq.;* Book VIII., 53, on Themistocles, 55, 75, 76, 81; view of Pericles, 72, 73, 76, 80 *sq.,* 83 *sqq.;* on Cleon, 74, 77; on Nicias, 74 *sq.;* on Alcibiades, 75, 80 *sq.;* on Antiphon, 75 *sq.;* on Hermocrates, 76; on Theramenes, *ib.;* ou Hyperbolus, 76 *sqq.;* comparison of Athens and Sparta, 73

influence of, on historiography, 94 *sq.,* 95; on Philistus, 100 *sq.;* imitators of, 95; canonized, 95; continuations of his work, 96, 97; compared with Cratippus, 99; compared with Polybius, 132 *sqq.*

Tiberius, Emperor, 146

Timaeus, 105 *sqq.;* popularity of, 109; antiquarianism, 119; studies by Polybius, 122, 123, 124, 132, 133, 137; influence on Sallust, 143

Trajan, history of Dacian war, 111

Trasimene, battle of, 144

Trogus. *See* Pompeius Trogus

Trojan war, origin of, according to Acusilaus, 12: used as an era, 20; origin of, in Herodotus, 33 *sqq.;* treatment by Thucydides, 64 *sq.*

Troy, building of walls, according to Herodorus, 13

Turgot, A. R. J., 163

Tyche, in Thucydides, 79; in Polybius, 133 *sqq.*

Tyrrell, R. Y., 182n[14]

Valerius Antias, 143, 186n[1]

Varro, 148

Velleius Paterculus, 146

Virgil, 130

Virtu, 92

Wachsmuth, C., 24, 104, 143

Walker, E. M., 99

Wiedemann, A., 44

Wilamowitz-Möllendorff, U. von, on Pherecydes, 12; on Melesagoras, 16; on Thucydides, 53, 54, 55, 57, 71, 95; on Theopompus, 98; on political literature, 113; on Atthidographers, 115

Wilcken, U., 15

Wölfflin, J., 108n[21]

Woodhouse, J., 178n[39]

Wunderer, C., 135

Xanthus, historian, 16

Xenomedes, historian, 174n[17]

Xenophanes, his rationalism, 7; epic poems, 7, 11

Xenophon, 96 *sqq.; Anabasis,* 96, 135; *Hellenica, ib.; Agesilaus,* 97; *Memorabilia,* 97; as a biographer. 97 *sq.;* 135; 146

Zalmoxis, 38

Zeno of Rhodes, 125, 137

Zoilus, 102

SUGGESTED READING

BAYNES, NORMAN H. *A Bibliography of the Works of J. B. Bury, Compiled with a Memoir.* Cambridge: Cambridge University Press, 1929.

BROWN, T. S. *The Greek Historians.* Lexington, MA: Heath, 1973.

DOVER, SIR KENNETH J. *Thucydides.* Oxford: Clarendon Press, 1973.

FORNARA, CHARLES W. *The Nature of History in Ancient Greece and Rome.* Berkeley: University of California Press, 1983.

GOULD, JOHN. *Herodotus.* London: Weidenfeld and Nicolson, 1989.

HUNTER, VIRGINIA J. *Past and Process in Herodotus and Thucydides.* Princeton: Princeton University Press, 1982.

LUCE, T. J. *The Greek Historians.* New York: Routledge, 1997.

MARINCOLA, JOHN. *Greek Historians.* Oxford: Oxford University Press, 2001.

MOMIGLIANO, ARNALDO. *The Classical Foundations of Modern Historiography.* Berkeley: University of California Press, 1990.

STARR, CHESTER G. *The Awakening of the Greek Historical Spirit.* New York: Knopf, 1968.

TEMPERLEY, H., ED. *Selected Essays of J. B. Bury.* Amsterdam: Adolf M. Hakkert, 1964.

WALBANK, F. W. *Polybius.* Berkeley: University of California Press, 1972.

Look for the following titles, available now from
The Barnes & Noble Library of Essential Reading.

Visit your Barnes & Noble bookstore,
or shop online at www.bn.com/loer

BEST SELLERS

Age of Revolution	Winston Churchill	0-7607-6859-5	$9.95
Autobiography of Benjamin Franklin	Benjamin Franklin	0-7607-6199-X	$6.95
Autobiography of Charles Darwin	Charles Darwin	0-7607-6908-7	$7.95
Birth of Britain	Winston Churchill	0-7607-6857-9	$9.95
Common Law	Oliver Wendell Holmes, Jr.	0-7607-5498-5	$9.95
Critique of Judgment	Immanuel Kant	0-7607-6202-3	$7.95
Critique of Pure Reason	Immanuel Kant	0-7607-5594-9	$12.95
Democracy in America	Alexis de Tocqueville	0-7607-5230-3	$14.95
Democracy and Education	John Dewey	0-7607-6586-3	$9.95
Discourse on Method	Rene Descartes	0-7607-5602-3	$4.95
Fall of Troy	Quintus of Smyrna	0-7607-6836-6	$6.95
Flatland	Edwin A. Abbott	0-7607-5587-6	$5.95
Great Democracies	Winston Churchill	0-7607-6860-9	$9.95
Guide for the Perplexed	Moses Maimonides	0-7607-5757-7	$12.95
Introduction to Mathematics	Alfred North Whitehead	0-7607-6588-X	$7.95
Island of Dr. Moreau	H. G. Wells	0-7607-5584-1	$4.95
Leviathan	Thomas Hobbes	0-7607-5593-0	$9.95
Lives of the Caesars	Suetonius	0-7607-5758-5	$9.95
Love and Freindship and Other Early Works	Jane Austen	0-7607-6856-0	$6.95

Man Who Was Thursday	G. K. Chesterton	0-7607-6310-0	$5.95
Martian Tales Trilogy	Edgar Rice Burroughs	0-7607-5585-X	$9.95
Meditations	Marcus Aurelius	0-7607-5229-X	$5.95
Montcalm and Wolfe	Francis Parkman	0-7607-6835-8	$12.95
Montessori Method	Maria Montessori	0-7607-4995-7	$7.95
Mysteries of Udolpho	Ann Radcliffe	0-7607-6315-1	$12.95
New World	Winston Churchill	0-7607-6858-7	$9.95
Nicomachean Ethics	Aristotle	0-7607-5236-2	$7.95
Notes on Nursing	Florence Nightingale	0-7607-4994-9	$4.95
On War	Carl von Clausewitz	0-7607-5597-3	$14.95
Outline of History: Volume 1	H. G. Wells	0-7607-5866-2	$12.95
Outline of History: Volume 2	H. G. Wells	0-7607-5867-0	$12.95
Passing of the Armies	Joshua Lawrence Chamberlain	0-7607-6052-7	$7.95
Personal Memoirs	Ulysses S. Grant	0-7607-4990-6	$14.95
Problems of Philosophy	Bertrand Russell	0-7607-5604-X	$5.95
Recollections and Letters	Robert E. Lee	0-7607-5919-7	$9.95
Relativity	Albert Einstein	0-7607-5921-9	$6.95
Tractatus Logico-Philosophicus	Ludwig Wittgenstein	0-7607-5235-4	$5.95
Trial and Death of Socrates	Plato	0-7607-6200-7	$4.95
Up From Slavery	Booker T. Washington	0-7607-5234-6	$6.95
Voyage of the Beagle	Charles Darwin	0-7607-5496-9	$9.95
Wealth of Nations	Adam Smith	0-7607-5761-5	$9.95
What Is Art?	Leo Tolstoy	0-7607-6581-2	$6.95

THE BARNES & NOBLE
LIBRARY OF ESSENTIAL READING

This newly developed series has been established to provide affordable access to books of literary, academic, and historic value—works of both well-known writers and those who deserve to be rediscovered. Selected and introduced by scholars and specialists with an intimate knowledge of the works, these volumes present complete, original texts in a modern, readable typeface—welcoming a new generation of readers to influential and important books of the past. With more than 100 titles already in print and more than 100 forthcoming, the *Library of Essential Reading* offers an unrivaled variety of thought, scholarship, and entertainment. Best of all, these handsome and durable paperbacks are priced to be exceptionally affordable. For a full list of titles, visit www.bn.com/loer.